Doing Visual Research with Children and Young People

'This is a timely, very important contribution to the growing fields of pupil participation and visual research with and on young people. It explores and extends an increasingly vibrant and significant field of enquiry in ways which engage our imagination and excite us to action. Theoretically sophisticated and accessibly written, it will quickly establish itself as a key text for professionals and academics alike.'
Professor Michael Fielding, Institute of Education, University of London, UK

'... filled with useful techniques for researchers in any discipline studying children.'
Eric Margolis, Arizona State University, USA, and President of the International Visual Sociology Association

Visual media offer powerful communication opportunities. *Doing Visual Research with Children and Young People* explores the methodological, ethical, representational and theoretical issues surrounding image-based research with children and young people. It provides well-argued and illustrated resources to guide novice and experienced researchers through the challenges and benefits of visual research.

Because new digital technologies have made it easier and cheaper to work with visual media, Pat Thomson brings together an international body of leading researchers who use a range of media to produce research data and communicate findings. Situating their discussions of visual research approaches within the context of actual research projects in communities and schools, and discussing a range of media from drawings, painting, collage and montages to film, video, photographs and new media, the book offers practical pointers for conducting research. These include:

- why visual research is used
- how to involve children and young people as co-researchers
- complexities in analysis of images and the ethics of working visually
- institutional difficulties that can arise when working with a 'visual voice'
- how to manage resources in research projects.

Doing Visual Research with Children and Young People will be an ideal guide for researchers both at undergraduate and postgraduate level across disciplines, including education, youth and social work, health and nursing, criminology and community studies. It will also act as an up-to-date resource on this rapidly changing approach for practitioners working in the field.

Pat Thomson is Professor of Education and Director of Research in the School of Education, University of Nottingham, UK. She is a former school principal of disadvantaged schools in Australia.

Doing Visual Research with Children and Young People

Edited by Pat Thomson

Routledge
Taylor & Francis Group

LONDON AND NEW YORK

First published 2008
by Routledge
2 Park Square, Milton Park, Abingdon, Oxon OX14 4RN

Simultaneously published in the USA and Canada
by Routledge
270 Madison Ave, New York, NY10016

Routledge is an imprint of the Taylor & Francis Group, an informa business

© 2008 Selection and editorial matter, Pat Thomson, individual
chapters, the contributors

Typeset in Times by Wearset Ltd, Boldon, Tyne and Wear
Printed and bound in Great Britain by CPI Antony Rowe,
Chippenham, Wilts

British Library Cataloguing in Publication Data
A catalogue record for this book is available from the British
Library

Library of Congress Cataloging in Publication Data
Doing visual research with children and young people / edited by
Pat Thomson.
p. cm.
1. Visual learning. 2. Learning, Psychology of. I. Thomson, Pat,
1948–
LB1067.5.D65 2008
300.7'2–dc22   2007047924

ISBN 10: 0-415-43109-3 (hbk)
ISBN 10: 0-415-43110-7 (pbk)

ISBN 13: 978-0-415-43109-5 (hbk)
ISBN 13: 978-0-415-43110-1 (pbk)

With thanks to Steven Sasson, inventor of the digital camera

Contents

Illustrations

Figures

Tables

Notes on contributors

Sara Bragg PhD, is Academic Fellow in Child and Youth Studies at the Open University, UK. She has worked at the University of Sussex and at the Centre for the Study of Children, Youth and Media at the Institute of Education, London, and before that as a media studies teacher. Her research interests include young people and 'violent' media such as horror films, media education, creative research methods, and young people's participation rights in schools. Recent publications include *Consulting young people. A review of the literature. A report for creative partnerships* (Arts Council UK, 2007); *Young people, sex and the media: the facts of life?* with David Buckingham (2004) and *Students as researchers: making a difference* with Michael Fielding (Pearson 2003).

David Buckingham PhD, is Professor of Education at the Institute of Education, London University. He is the Founder and Director of the Centre for the Study of Children, Youth and Media. Buckingham pioneered the development of research in media education in the UK, and has played a major role in the application of cultural studies approaches to analysing children's and young people's interactions with television and electronic media. He has directed more than twenty externally-funded research projects on these issues, funded by bodies such as the ESRC, the AHRC, the Broadcasting Standards Commission, the Arts Council of England, the European Commission and the Gulbenkian, Spencer and Nuffield Foundations, and he has been a consultant for bodies such as UNESCO, the United Nations, Ofcom and the Institute for Public Policy Research. He is the author, co-author or editor of twenty-two books, and over 180 articles and book chapters. His work has been translated into fifteen languages. His key publications include: *Children talking television* (Falmer, 1993), *Moving images* (Manchester University Press 1996), *The making of citizens* (Routledge, 2000), *After the death of childhood* (Polity, 2000) and *Media education* (Polity, 2003). Forthcoming books include *Beyond technology: learning in the age of digital media* (Polity) and *Global children, global media: media,* *migration and childhood* (with Liesbeth de Block, Palgrave). In 2005, he was awarded the Jesse McCanse Award by the US National Telemedia Council for his work on media education.

Catherine Burke PhD, is Senior Lecturer in Education at the School of Education, the University of Leeds, UK where she developed, managed and now teaches on the undergraduate BA (Hons) programme, Childhood, Education and Culture. Her doctorate was in labour history, which led her to research and teach in the area of women's history and gender. After many years teaching and working in adult and community education, she moved to the higher-education sector and has since taught, researched and published in the area of children's perspectives on education, community and culture. A regular contributor to the European Conference on Educational Research (ECER), she is lead convenor of the Histories of Education Network. Her recent publications include *The school I'd like. Children and young people's reflections on an education for the 21st Century* (Routledge, 2003) with Ian Grosvenor, and, forthcoming, *School* (Reaktion Press). Catherine's research interests and activities are in the following areas: the history of childhood and education; material cultures of childhood and education; the historical and contemporary relationship between pedagogy and architecture and design in learning environments; and visual methods in incorporating a child's view or perspective in research. In 2005, she acted as co-investigator, with Dr Jon Prosser (University of Leeds) and Judy Torrington (University of Sheffield), for 'The View of the Child: explorations of the visual culture of the made environment'. This was a funded (EPSRC/AHRB) Research Cluster, part of the Designing for the 21st Century Programme.

Marisol Clark-Ibáñez PhD, is an assistant professor in the Department of Sociology at California State University San Marcos. Dr Clark-Ibáñez has published on the topics of photo-elicitation interviews (PEI), ethnography, and the sociology of childhood. She has just completed a book manuscript called *Learning inequality: an ethnography of charter school reform and inner-city classrooms*. Her current book project is a PEI study of urban childhoods. She conducted a workshop on PEI for the Researching Children Conference 2006 in England and has presented her research on photo-elicitation at 'Childhoods 2005' in Olso, Norway, the International Visual Sociology Association Conference, and the American Sociological Association Conference. Additionally, Dr Clark-Ibáñez has published in the areas of social relationships, urban schooling and classroom micro-interactions. Please see her website for more resources and citations about visual research: www.csusm.edu/Sociology/Faculty/m_ clarkibanez.html

Peter Egg PhD, did his dissertation on the topic of participation; this was awarded the first prize of the Development Programme for Child and Youth Research in Salzburg in 1997, and published as a book by Kid-Publishers, Bonn. He has been a lecturer at the University of Innsbruck since 1994, teaching Educational Science, Research Practice and Methods/Participatory Pedagogy – Participatory Practice and Methods with Children and Young People. Since 1999, he has conducted projects on participatory pedagogies and participatory practice. Since 1989, he has been involved in participatory work with children and young people in the fields of village revival/development with young people, living surroundings, school development, youth forums, youth platforms, youth in communal politics, development plans drawn up with the cooperation of children, development of playgrounds and play space, development of town centres suitable for children, future workshops, social fiction with young people, town festivals with participation of children and young people, planning and participatory development of youth work in towns and rural areas, media projects and creating participatory milieus. He works as a consultant adviser on the topic of Co-determination of Children and Young People (participation)/Every-Day Democracy in Europe, and since 2006 has been responsible for the Tyrolean governmental strategy to implement child and youth participation. He is currently working on a book with Rob Walker and Barbara Schratz on researching children.

Christine Hall PhD, is Professor of Education in the School of Education at the University of Nottingham. She worked as an English teacher in schools and is now very involved in teacher education as Director of Initial Teacher Education. She has written on issues concerning English teaching, literacy, children's literature and children's reading choices. Currently, her research is into the teaching of the arts, and the pedagogies and policies that promote inclusion and creativity.

Kaye Haw PhD, is a principal research fellow in the School of Education at the University of Nottingham. Her work with different Muslim communities in inner-city areas has led her to work in the UK, Europe and Pakistan. Her more recent research experience is in working cross-culturally with a range of 'hard to reach' and vulnerable groups, and with a collective of individuals from a range of backgrounds, not just academics, who are committed to effecting change using a very different view of research as a basis. The past five years have seen major methodological advances in two areas of her work; first in the area of 'voice' and young people, and secondly in the use of multi-media case studies in working with silenced groups. More recently, this work has been developed in two ways: in a project that used on-line discussion and the establishment of web pages to maintain confidentiality and anonymity for Muslim women across Europe to discuss issues of domestic violence, and in a piece of research on the perceptions of strip-searching amongst prisoners and staff. Her most recent projects use a diversity of new technologies to product multimedia case studies aimed at bridging the gaps between 'hard to reach' and vulnerable groups of young people, researchers and practitioners so that the materials produced will meaningfully impact on practitioners and policy-makers alike. She has published in the areas of social action research, community development and methodological issues, as well as a book, *Educating Muslim girls: shifting discourses* (1998, Open University Press). She is currently working on a book on voice and video for Routledge.

Kaye Johnson Ed D, is an experienced primary-school principal in Adelaide, South Australia. From 2001 to 2007 she was principal of Woodville Primary School which has a student population of more than 500. Kaye is now a curriculum project officer in the Department for Education and Children's Services. Kaye has been involved in practitioner research programmes for many years, and has published in both professional and academic journals on school change, student-negotiated curricula, and student involvement in whole-school decision-making. She has developed with students in her school a set of research ethics which guide action research and other forms of change-linked inquiry. Her Ed D involved working in partnership with students in her school to discover children's perspectives on their place(s) in the primary school. It describes how they both shape and are shaped by these places. In 2003, as an associate researcher with the NCSL, Kaye explored ways of enabling primary-school children to become co-researchers and co-participants in transforming schools. Her report, *Children's voices: pupil leadership in primary schools* can be found at www.ncsl.org.uk

Ian Kaplan MSc, is a research associate at the School of Education, University of Manchester, UK. He has previously worked as a teacher and as an educational researcher for the UK National Society for Prevention of Cruelty to Children (NSPCC). His recent research has focused on issues of social and educational marginalisation and inclusion, partnership research, learning disability, and development education. He has worked as an educational consultant for a variety of UK Local Authorities, schools and international development organisations. Alongside his research he lectures on image-based research and research with children, and has piloted courses and programmes in using photography as a form of action research. He publishes on issues of image-based research and school culture, and has given presentations in the UK and abroad. He has also worked with the Enabling Education Network (EENET), based at the University of Manchester, on projects with children and teachers in schools in Zambia, Indonesia and Burma, to consider their perspectives on education. He has recently given invited presentations on the use of participatory photography with children in schools at an international symposium on child-friendly schools in Indonesia, and at the World Bank.

Ruth Leitch PhD, is a senior lecturer at the School of Education, Queen's University, Northern Ireland, where for the past five years she has been Head of School. A clinical psychologist before becoming a teacher educator, she is now lecturing and researching in the areas of the impact of trauma on children and young people, student voice and teacher identity. Her main area of research interest is the use of arts-based educational inquiry (particularly visual methods) and transformational methodologies within qualitative research. She attended Lesley College MA as a post-doctoral fellow studying Expressive Therapy under Professor Shaun McNiff. She is a winner of the AERA, Mary Catherine Ellwein Qualitative SIG Outstanding Dissertation Award for her doctoral work, entitled *Journey into paradox: re-searching unconscious in teacher identity using creative narrative*, and was responsible for the initiation of the first Arts-Based Educational Research conference in the UK in Queen's in June 2005, which over 100 national and international delegates attended. Research which has been or is based on arts-based inquiry includes: ESRC/TLRP 2005–2007, *Consulting pupils on the assessment of their learning* (www.cpal. qub.ac.uk); and Department of Education (NI) and Office of the First Minister and Deputy First Minister (OFMDFM) 2004–2006, *Enabling young voices: pupil support post-conflict* (www.enablingyoungvoices.org).

Julianne Moss PhD, is a senior lecturer in Curriculum, Teaching and Learning – Artistic and Creative Education – in the Faculty of Education, University of Melbourne. She is deeply interested and engaged in the practices of curriculum reform, curriculum theory, teacher professional learning, and the impact of how education systems cater for students who are margin-alised and oppressed. Her international contribution is recognised through the volume and video published by UNESCO (1999), *Welcoming schools: case studies of inclusive practice around the world*. These materials have been used extensively in support of the UNESCO Salamanca Statement (1994), the international policy framework for furthering the development of inclusive communities. Her current consultancy and research and development activities extend to the Ministry of Education, Singapore; the Centre for Research in Pedagogy and Practice, National Institute of Education, Singapore; and the delivery of the Principles of Learning and Teaching (PoLT) for the Department of Education and Training (DE&T), Victoria. She is an active faculty member and supervises many research higher-degree students at all levels – Masters, Doctorate of Education and PhD – studying issues of curriculum change, practitioner inquiry, teacher education and qualitative research methodology.

Andrew Noyes PhD, is Associate Professor in the University of Nottingham's School of Education, and a member of the Centre for Research in Equity and Diversity in Education. He has just completed duties as PGCE Course Leader, and is the programme leader for the MA in Learning and Teaching. Andy's doctoral thesis was in the sociology of mathematics education and the nature of educational transitions. He has written in this area, and also has research interests in initial teacher education, the sociology of education, social justice, metaphor, pupil voice and video diary research methodology. He recently completed a TDA-funded project examining the use of video diaries as a tool for understanding teachers' pre-service development. He has co-edited *Research in mathematics education 7* and *8*, and has published a book entitled *Rethinking school mathematics* (Sage, 2007). Andy is now directing two substantial projects on mathematics curriculum, assessment, participation and attainment in the 14–19 age range.

Barbara Schratz PhD, works as research manager and researcher at the headquarters of the international organisation SOS Children's Villages, at the Hermann Gmeiner Academy in Innsbruck, Austria. A sociologist and educator by background, she has experience in adult education, organisation development and process facilitation, and is currently focusing on participatory research, evaluation and knowledge-sharing in multicultural and cross-cultural settings. Her work repeatedly leads her into countries in Asia, Africa and Latin America.

Pat Thomson PhD, is Professor of Education, Director of Research in the School of Education, and Director of the Centre for Research in Equity and Diversity in Education (CREDE) at the University of Nottingham. She is also an Adjunct Professor at the University of South Australia, and Visiting Professor in education at Deakin University, Victoria, Australia. A former school principal, her current work is underpinned by a commitment to social justice and an interest in questions of identity, place, pedagogy and power. Her current research focuses on the arts, pedagogies and inclusion, students excluded from school, students and teachers as researchers, school redesign, and the changing work of school principals. Her publications include *Schooling the rust belt kids: making the difference in changing times* (2002, Allen and Unwin, Australia; Trentham, UK); and, with Barbara Kamler, *Helping doctoral students write: pedagogies for supervision* (2006, Routledge). She is currently working on two further Routledge books, *School leadership – heads on the block?* and, with Jill Blackmore, *Changing schools through systematic inquiry: why and how school leaders do research*.

Rob Walker PhD, is Director of the Centre for Applied Research in Education at the University of East Anglia, and was previously a professor of

Education at Deakin University, Australia. Although initially trained as a survey researcher, most of Rob's work has been in the use of case studies in education, particularly in the context of evaluation and action research, and wherever possible involving photographs, video or film. His publications include an early paper (with Clem Adelman in 1974) on filming classrooms in the *Journal of Motion Picture and Television Engineers*, and a recent paper (with Babis Bakopoulos in 2005) in *First Monday* on chatroom relationships. His current projects include CAMOT, an EU project collecting multimedia case studies on education and technology; UNITE, which is developing a cross-Europe learning environment; and emerging projects in architecture and pedagogy.

Preface

This book grew out of an ESRC seminar series entitled *Engaging critically with pupil voice*. Over an eighteen-month period, a core group of about forty people from schools, universities, non-government organisations and local authority offices met to debate the various ways in which 'pupil voice' was being taken up in the UK and beyond in policy, in school and network development, and in research. Early on, we realised that a number of us were using visual methods as a means of exploring and representing the perspectives of children and young people. We decided to bring this work together in one volume which would explicitly make the connections between 'the visual' and 'pupil voice'.

After the seminar series had finished, and faced with the task of acting on the decision, I decided that, rather than a book which explored the history of visual methodologies, or one which simply gave examples of their use, I would ask colleagues to write a set of 'stories from the field' which addressed the reasons for image work, explained how this work was conducted, and discussed some of the dilemmas and challenges that the researchers faced. This collection therefore contains some chapters that address issues that research methods books often gloss over, some that tell 'warts and all' stories, and others that raise questions for which there are no easy answers.

The research in this volume comes from Europe, Australia and the United States. I do not spend time explaining the different contexts, although something of the flavour of the different places leaks into the writing. This very often happens through the actual images reproduced in the text, or through the descriptions of the image work that was undertaken. Local distinctiveness is a constant companion in visual research. I have left these particularities open to readers' interpretations.

Many of the projects described in this volume involved children and young people as co-researchers. This is perhaps not so surprising, since the contributions are all written by researchers active in fields where there is a great deal of interest in young people's perspectives. The work represented here is not only based in schools, but also in the wider everyday lives of children and young people in their communities and networks. However, the educational expertise of the contributors means that they bring specific intellectual resources to discussions of how young people were actually involved in their research. There is thus, in some of the chapters, a strong focus on what adult researchers did in order to produce children and/or young people as skilled visual co-researchers. This pedagogical 'show and tell' is one of the distinctive features of this book.

Signposts to the book

I do not propose to trawl through each of the chapters in this book one by one, as is sometimes the case in edited collections. Rather, I want to explain the approach taken to the selection of material and its organisation.

The book intends to make some of the processes involved in visual research more visible. Its goal is to complement existing research methods texts, not duplicate them. It also hopes to provide something 'dirtier' than is often found in the somewhat sanitised reports of research findings. In some chapters the writers have also provided their own take on visual research, while others rely on the discussion in the introduction. All of the contributions are intended to stimulate discussion and debate, rather than to act as how-to-do-it blueprints.

The introductory chapter places the contributions in context. It begins with a discussion of 'voice' and moves to the 'visual turn' in social science research before addressing the scope of activities which bring both students' voices and the visual together. The reasons for undertaking visual research are canvassed further through three reflections by researchers on projects they have conducted with children: each brings a different theoretical lens to their reflections. The following eleven chapters focus on practical aspects of visual research, together with reflexive accounts of the dilemmas that inevitably arise. And because this book is written with the understanding that it may be used in research methods courses, there is a short introduction to each chapter noting the specific issues discussed. A brief concluding section provides guidance to additional material of interest for those wishing to pursue visual research further. It also lists additional resources for research with children.

Acknowledgements

Before beginning the book proper, there are some people to acknowledge and thank. I want to put on record that this book owes a great deal to the pioneering collection *Image-based research. A sourcebook for qualitative researchers*, edited by Jon Prosser (Falmer Press 1998). This has become a standard text for those interested in visual research and for those undertaking research methods courses. One of the contributors to that collection, Rob Walker, another accomplished visual researcher, was a participant in our ESRC seminar series and is also represented in this volume.

The book also owes a considerable debt to the late Jean Rudduck, whose name is synonymous with pupil consultation, and to key international youth participation researchers and activists – Michael Fielding, Roger Holdsworth and

Alison Cook Sather – all of whom were part of the ESRC seminar series. The contributions of colleagues from the Universities of Nottingham, Sussex and Manchester Metropolitan, as well as those from the now defunct Networked Learning Communities programme of the National College for School Leadership, were important in the development of this collection. I hope that they can see in this text the traces of the many debates that we had.

No book comes into being without technical and editorial support. I am indebted to Darren Ellis for his work in bringing the manuscript to a publishable state, and Christine Hall for her editorial attention to the niceties of English expression. Without this backing, the editor's lot would indeed have been an unhappy one. The enthusiasm and encouragement from Philip Mudd at Routledge has also been important: he is not simply a knowledgeable editor but also a very entertaining friend.

In conclusion, I want to note the importance of the ESRC seminar series funding programme, which supports the intellectual work of developing knowledge and practice. While hardly lavish, it provided enough funds for our travel and sandwiches and, perhaps more importantly, acknowledged our premise that pupil voice was not to be taken at face value and needed critical interrogation. Not all of the contributions here were part of the series, but the seminar's collective discussions spawned the ideas for and informed the shape of this collection. Without the ESRC this could not have happened.

Pat Thomson
July 2007

Chapter 1

Children and young people
Voices in visual research

Pat Thomson

There is no biological 'truth' to suggest that being young equates with nothing to say. As scholars involved in the 'new' childhood studies argue, it is a product of our place and times to judge the nature and capabilities of people on the basis of their age. Not very long ago children in Western countries were paid workers, and many still work as carers and doing home duties, while the exploitation of child labour remains a dreadful reality in some parts of the world. However, despite the evidence that connections between age and the capacity to take responsibility are culturally constructed, we more often than not see children and young people as persons whose views are completely 'immature' and not to be taken seriously (Ariès, 1962; James & Prout, 1997; Mason & Fattore, 2005; Qvortrup, Bardy, Sigritta, & Wintersberger, 1994).

Researchers who contributed to this book share the view that children and young people are *capable* of providing expert testimony about their experiences, associations and lifestyles. Instead of seeing children and young people simply as family members or students or as 'becomings', that is, people not yet mature enough to have an opinion or act responsibly, contributors to this volume see them as competent 'beings' whose views, actions and choices are of value (see Alanen & Mayall, 2001 for further discussion). Indeed, the perspectives of children and young people are of interest to contemporary social scientists precisely because they offer specific and unique insights – about their everyday lives at home and school and their view and hopes for their futures – which can easily slip below the horizons of older inquirers. The omission of these perspectives can easily lead to researchers making interpretations and representations that are very short-sighted and which miss the point.

The writers represented here also share the view that it is the *right* of children and young people to have a say about things that concern them. This view is evidenced in the United Nations Convention on the Human Rights of the Child (United Nations (UN), 1990), which goes beyond arguing for the protection of children from abuse and exploitation to spell out an entitlement to education, health and well being, and to set out the case for children and young people having civil and political rights. Article 12 of the Convention states that governments and nations shall assure to the child who is capable of forming his or her own views the right to express those views freely in all matters affecting the child, the views of the child being given due weight in accordance with the age and maturity of the child.

This article ascribes to children and young people an entitlement to participate in discussion and decisions, and an obligation on institutions to ensure that this happens. Many social scientists, and all of those in this book, now take this also to mean a right to a view about, and in, research which concerns them.

The notion of the right of children and young people to speak has also been enacted in public policy. For example, in many English speaking and European nations, children and young people have emerged not simply as objects of school change, but also as participants in its production. In Australia student participation (Holdsworth, 2000a, 2000b; Thomson & Holdsworth, 2003; Thomson, McQuade, & Rochford, 2005), and in the UK 'pupil consultation' and 'pupil voice' (Flutter & Rudduck, 2004; McBeath, 1999; Macbeath, Demetriou, Rudduck, & Myers, 2003; Rudduck & Flutter, 2000, 2004a, 2004b), have had official policy endorsement, whereas in the US interest in the active role of students in change has largely emerged from reform movements and through opposition to top-down reforms (Cook-Sather, 2002; Mitra, 2003; Nieto, 1994; Rubin & Silva, 2003; Shultz & Cook-Sather, 2001; Soohoo, 1993; Wasley, Hampel, & Clark, 1997; Wilson & Corbett, 2001). These trends are of particular interest to social science researchers because they offer the opportunity to consider the rhetoric and reality of children's rights and citizenship.

The two beliefs in and about children and young people – their capacity to speak, and their right to do so – come together in the notion of 'voice'.

Social science research finds voice(s)

Many social scientists and social activists became interested in the idea of voice through critical analyses of the knowledges that were produced and valued in the academy, policy and in professional contexts. Feminist scholars, for example, argued that the perspectives of women were largely invisible across the disciplines (e.g. Alcoff & Potter, 1993; Haraway, 1990; Lather, 1991), and postcolonial scholars argued for their subjugated knowledges to be respected but not incorporated (e.g. Bhabha, 1984; Spivak, 1988); both suggested that dominant forms of knowledge (and their advocates) needed to move from centre stage and make room for more diverse meanings, and ways of making meaning (e.g. Weiler, 2001). The move to 'voice' resulted in a range of new courses in schools and universities, such as women's, queer, dis/ability and postcolonial studies. It also heralded radical changes in existing disciplines such as history, politics, medicine, sociology, law and education. The subsequent shift from the idea of a singular (oppressed) voice to diverse and multiple voices was not without heated debate, but it is now more generally accepted by researchers (if not policymakers), that it is not possible to write about any particular social group as if they spoke as one. Thus, while the idea of 'voice' is still used in social science, it is now most often very specifically situated and its internal modulations and variations carefully represented.

The idea of voice was also taken up through research methodology/ies where there were ongoing efforts made to find ways to bring previously unheard voices into scholarly and associated professional conversations – 'giving voice to the voiceless' (e.g. Visweswaren, 1994). Researchers became interested in a range of qualitative methodologies and the potential they offered to allow marginalized groups to (apparently) speak for themselves (Reinharz, 1992). Discussions – about the power relationships inherent in research and the ways in which these worked against voices being heard and truthfully represented – were foregrounded (Ribbens & Edwards, 1998). Debates – such as whether there could ever be situations where researcher and researched were on an equal footing and how those being researched might become co-researchers – began and are still not settled. Lather (2007, p. 136) argues that qualitative researchers became too obsessed with voices, romanticizing what research informants say, and indulging in 'confessional tales, authorial self-revelation ... the reinscription of some unproblematic real'. She argues instead for 'complexity, partial truths, and multiple subjectivities'.

Together with voice, the notion of rights also permeated social science and was primarily folded into new approaches to research ethics. Practices such as the right to informed consent, and the right to withdraw from participation in research, can also be seen as expressions of the voices of research participants. These are perhaps a somewhat minimalist version of voice, but it is certainly a case of research 'voice or exit' (Hirschman, 1970). 'Ethics' is an area, however, where there are still mixed views: it is common practice to ask parental permission to conduct research with children, for example, but researchers often pay only lip-service to explaining the purposes, uses and practices of their research to children and young people. Getting their permission for involvement is often bypassed.

As part of these more general shifts in research practice, those social scientists whose research concerned children and young people widened their search for ways to solicit their views and voices and to represent them in publications. They asked – what methods can most adequately elicit the voices of youthful participants? What are the advantages and limitations of interviews and focus groups? How might less popular approaches such as life histories and narrative more adequately 'give voice'? These re-searching questions led to an interest in visual research. It seemed to offer different ways to elicit the experiences, opinions and perspectives of children and young people, as well as a new means of involving them as producers of knowledge. This is discussed further later in the chapter.

Researching voices is complex

Voice is generally taken to mean 'having a say', but as Britzman (1989, p. 146) notes, the word carries three sets of meanings:

> The concept of voice spans literal, metaphorical and political terrains: in its literal sense, voice represents the speech and perspective of the speaker; metaphorically, voice spans inflection, tone, accent, style and the qualities and feelings conveyed by the speaker's words; and politically, a construct of voice attests to the right of speaking and being represented.

So, voice can mean not only having a say, but also refers to the language, emotional components and non-verbal means used to express opinions. Undertaking research which attends to voice may thus mean listening to things that are unsaid and/or not what we expect. Researchers can be challenged by the words that come from the mouths of children and young people, but a commitment to hearing marginalized voices requires not censoring particular views and modes of expression. It may be hard to hear confrontative stories and terms, but listening does not equate with condoning (see the last chapter in Fine & Weis, 1998 for a discussion about violent voices).

As noted earlier, the notion of voice suggests both a particular point of view, and also one which is not universal. Children and young people do not speak as one – just like adults, they have different experiences, opinions and modes of expression. However, the situation is more complex than this, with diversity not being the only complicating factor to work with voice. According to Hadfield and Haw (2001) there are not just differences between people, but each individual also uses more than one voice. They nominate three:

1   *Authoritative.* This is a representative voice intended to speak on behalf of a group – children say, adolescents believe.... It is exercised politically in consultations, and through elected bodies such as councils and working parties. Researchers also elicit an authoritative voice: through surveys, where majority opinions are taken to be representative of a larger group; through the use of quotations either from interviews which have been coded and thematized or selected from a discourse analysis; or through narratives which 'ring true'.

2   *Critical.* This voice is intended to challenge the status quo. It may be directed towards policies and practices, or towards stereotypical portrayals. It may also mean putting into the public arena perspectives that are rarely, if ever, heard. As already noted, this is the voice which social scientists concerned with equity and inclusion work to bring into research practices and knowledge-producing communities.

3   *Therapeutic.* This voice occurs in safe spaces where people are able to discuss painful and/or difficult experiences and are then supported to find

ways of dealing with them. Speaking with the therapeutic voice is not simply a matter of personally coping, but also of seeing the social production of seemingly individual problems. The therapeutic voice may be deliberately elicited in qualitative research with vulnerable populations. Ethical guidelines draw attention to situations where the therapeutic voice is likely to be evoked, require researchers to make clear to participants the likelihood of distress, and demand that researchers ensure that no harm comes to research subjects. In the case of children and young people, working with the therapeutic voice always requires specialist training and support.

Bragg (2007) adds a fourth to this list:

4 *Consumer*. This voice expresses preferences about lifestyle and culture or leisure-related activities and experiences. The consumer voice is also embedded in (delimited) choices about identity/ies and affiliations. The consumer voice of children and young people is much sought after by commercial interests who do not have the same kinds of ethical safeguards as social scientists. The task of market research is to draw out the consumer voice, while social science researchers are concerned to understand it.

Arnot and Reay (2007) focus on a fifth kind of voice:

5 *Pedagogic*. They suggest that children and young people speak with a voice that is literally schooled, that is, it is created by the experiences of being educated within particular kinds of pedagogic, curriculum and assessment regimes. They suggest that talk can be focused on classrooms, subjects, identities and/or codes (the tacit and explicit rules which govern ways of being in school). They argue that researchers need to carefully differentiate between the kinds of talk on which they focus, and should look past the surface of what children and young people say to the tacit categories and rules which govern expression. They caution against seeing voice as authentic and pure.

The former three kinds of voice imply some kind of political change. Through speaking, the person may feel differently, or make new alliances. Those in power are confronted. The person who speaks has exercised some agency and control of circumstances which previously felt beyond reach. However, this is not the case in the fourth kind of voice. In market research people rarely have the opportunity to have any involvement in how their voice is used or exploited (see Kenway & Bullen, 2001), whereas with other kinds of voice this is the very point of speaking up and speaking out. Pedagogic voice, on the other hand, can be complicit, resistant or mediating, and it is up to those wanting to engage with pedagogic voices to sort out which kind of talk they are interested in, and how they might work with it.

To complicate matters even further, voice is very dependent on the social context in which it is located. Being able to say what you think, in the ways that you want, is highly dependent on what you are asked, by whom, about what, and what is expected of you. What is said in one setting to one person may not be the same as what is said on a different day to a different person. Power relations of class, gender, race, ethnicity, dis-ability, sexuality and age all constrain social relations and may profoundly limit what can be said (Kramer-Dahl, 1996; Orner, 1992) – as well as how it is heard (Ellsworth, 1989). Speaking therapeutically or critically, for example, always entails a judgment about the possible responses of the listeners. As Fielding (2001) suggests, it all depends on who is listening, what they choose to do as a result, and in whose interests they act. Understanding that social context makes a difference to voice is of importance to researchers, who must work in the knowledge that what is said to them does not come from an 'authentic', fixed and stable voice. Rather, it is always produced in a particular time, place and situation, and in response to specific questions and anticipated responses.

These issues around voice(s) are writ large in research with children and young people, who may be particularly reluctant to say anything which they judge may displease the interviewer or may feel that they need to speak with a particular kind of voice since that is what is expected of them. They may easily be intimidated by meeting by themselves with adult researchers, and feel more at ease in a pair or a group. Even the seating arrangements can make important differences to what can be said. Working with the voices of children and young people is thus not a simple matter.

These methodological issues play out in visual research in specific ways, as will be explained.

Researching about – or researching *with* – children and young people

As explained already, a research focus on voice/s emanates from concerns about equity and social justice. There are therefore debates about the power relations involved in research and the benefits that accrue from it. Those who are the subjects of research often share these concerns. Many adult research participants wonder 'what's in it' for them, since they are not the ones who are published, or gain degrees or career recognition. Children and young people are no exception: they too worry about this.

This does not mean that all research has to have rewards for those directly involved in it. Like adults, children and young people may participate in projects whose findings will inform policy, or will help improve the training of those who work with them, or just help others understand them better. These kinds of projects can be said to work in the long-term interests of children in general, even if the specific participants do not immediately benefit. However, not all projects do bring benefits to their participants. In Australia, New Zealand and

Canada, where there has been a history of research which served to perpetuate colonial power relations (Smith, 1999), indigenous peoples now have the right to refuse permission for projects which do not work in their interests. And those who live in poverty are probably the most researched group, and there is arguably less payoff for their involvement than there might be. The existence of research which is not in their interests might also be true of some research with children and young people – an unsettling possibility.

One response to the problems arising from doing research on marginalized and vulnerable groups has been for researchers to consider how they can work *with* research participants, rather than *on* them. In working *with*, researchers aim to transform not only the power relations embedded in their research, but also those in the context in which the research is being conducted. This difference can be seen in Thiessen's (2007) typology of educational research in classrooms, where the first two – 'how students participate and make sense of life in classrooms and schools' and 'who students are and how they develop in classrooms and schools' – are research *on* students, while the third – 'how students are actively involved in shaping their own learning opportunities and in the improvement of what happens in classrooms and schools' – is research *with* them. All three kinds of research are of course equally valid and important, but the third has an immediate change agenda at its heart.

There is in some states in Australia and in England a growing tradition of research *with* children and young people at school, simply called students-as-researchers: this is a subset of the range of activities which come under the general label of student participation/voice. Those who advocate a students-as-researchers approach argue that school change does not occur simply by discussing a problem in order to arrive at an answer, as is assumed when there are consultations with a student council or the whole student body about priorities for change. Nor is it simply about the use of existing data, as might be the case, for example, if a student council decided to use pupil attendance data to provide an evidence base for a discussion about student engagement. Rather, a students-as-researchers approach means that children and young people conduct a specifically designed inquiry, about a topic they have decided on, to provide data to inform recommendations for change (Atweh & Burton, 1995; Edwards, 2000; Fielding & Bragg, 2003) or simply to pursue a matter that is of interest to them (Kellett, 2005). Students might survey their peers, or conduct a range of focus groups across year levels or interview a representative sample of the school. Such an investigation takes them beyond a role as representatives, and allows them to speak about the views of all students, rather than simply giving their own opinions.

Helen Gunter and I have argued that in schools, research with children and young people can be seen as student 'standpoint research' which:

- addresses issues of importance to students and is thus in their collective interests

- works with students' subjugated knowledges about the way in which the school works
- allows marginalized perspectives and voices to come centre stage
- uses students' subjectivities and experiences to develop approaches, tools, representations and validities
- interrupts the power relations in schools including, but not confined to, those which are age related, and
- is geared to making a difference.

(Thomson & Gunter, 2007, p. 331)

These criteria can be extended to all situations where children and young people are engaged as researchers in their own right or as co-researchers with adult social scientists.

This book is focused on research *with*, not research about or on. As the title states, it is 'doing visual research *with* children and young people'. Most of the chapters in the book therefore involve children and young people as active co-producers of data. Some engage children and young people in dialogue about the data, and some extend that involvement to analysis. In all cases, the data that are produced are visual, or both visual and verbal.

Visual research

This is not a book about visual research per se, a compendium of approaches, a straightforward methods text. Reference to such texts can be found in the concluding chapter. Nevertheless, it not only grows out of the emerging field of participatory research, but also from 'the visual turn' in the social sciences. This move occurred in response to, and as part of, the increased production and flows of images in conditions of high or late modernity (Burgin, 1996; Crimp, 1993; Gitlin, 2001; Jenks, 1995; Mirzoeff, 2003). It is appropriate therefore to make some comments about visual research – or, as it is sometimes called, image-based research.

There are two ways in which social scientists approach the visual: the first is to take visual artefacts and to investigate their production, uses and interpretations (Barthes, 1977; de Lauretis, 1987; Emmison & Smith, 2001; Heywood & Sandywell, 1999; Kress & Van Leeuwen, 2006; Margolis, 2000; Schirato & Webb, 2004); the second is to manufacture visual artefacts as part of the process of doing research (Betlin, 2005; Collier & Collier, 1986; El Guindi, 2004; Harper, 2002; Pink, 2001, 2006; Pink, Kurti, & Afonso, 2004; Russell, 2007). Elizabeth Chaplin (1994) calls the former 'the sociology of the visual' as opposed to the latter, 'visual sociology'. Both of these approaches can be combined, and often are. This book is primarily, but not exclusively, concerned with visual sociology – that is, situations where children and young people are involved in making images as part of a research project.

It is important to spell out some understandings about the visual which underpin the assumptions made by many of the contributors to this book.

The image and its capacities for deception

The production of images as part of the research process is not new, despite the use of the term 'the visual turn'. For example, anthropologists have used film and photography as an integral part of their practice for quite some time, whereas other social science disciplines took longer to pick up their cameras and sketch books (Chaplin, 1994). Current interest in the visual stems from the simultaneous proliferation of the means of making images (the development of affordable cameras and film processing, followed by the digitization of still and moving-image production), and the proliferation of image-based systems of communication in everyday life (film and television, graphic novels, multimedia and advertising).

However, contrary to popular sayings such as 'a picture never lies', 'every picture tells a story', and 'it was there in black and white', the social science community understands that an image is not a simple window on the world. Rather, just like a word, an image is a human construction and culturally specific. As scholars pursued semiotics, the study of the practices of making meaning through language systems (words, numbers, images, movement), the studies of visual social phenomena and the use of visual means to study social phenomena, were folded into what is often called 'the crisis of representation' (see Hall, 1997). This term is generally taken to mean the acceptance by scholars of the premise that life is lived through 'language games' (Derrida, 1976, 1978; Wittgenstein, 1976), where language is an approximation of the material world rather than an exact equivalent. Such language is culturally determined, and meanings change over time and from place to place. Thus, if concepts and ideas vary between cultural groups and historically, it follows that notions foundational to scientific endeavour, such as 'objectivity', 'truth' and 'fact', are undermined (Burbules & Philips, 2000; Game & Metcalfe, 1996; Scheurich, 1997; Silverman, 1997). The consequences are that new ways of thinking about, and doing, research are required. These understandings mean that questions of reliability, validity, and truthfulness are less than straightforward, and they have been and remain the stuff of the collective work of the research community (Harding, 1998).

Social scientists are also now conscious of the ways in which they and their social position/production are implicated in their research. As Donna Haraway (2003, p. 110) puts it, it is

> simply impossible to engage in authoritative writing as if the subject who did such a thing weren't implicated in the practice, and as if the history of writing weren't the history of the differentiation of the world for us with all of the sticky threads to power and to whose way of life is at stake in marking up the world that way rather than some other way.

The two arguments, that knowledge is not absolute but is culturally constructed and that the researcher and her milieu are always implicated in the research, play out across the social sciences. They have two important implications for both visual sociology and the sociology of the visual.

First, an image is not neutral. It is literally and socially constructed by a person or team of people through processes of:

- selection – where the image-maker literally stands, what is the foreground and background, what is in focus and out of focus, where the borders are constructed, what is out of the frame and what is excluded altogether.
- processing – aesthetic judgments are made about whether the image is manipulated, airbrushed, in black and white or colour, or digitally treated. If trimming occurs, then issues of borders, inclusions and exclusions also come into play.
- editing – how the image is mounted, what comes before or after it, what is next to it, what other images accompany it as montage or collage.

There are a myriad of such decisions and choices that are made by the image producer, and these decisions are themselves in part determined by virtue of who the person or team is, where they are, what they think is important, their intentions and values, and their historical position and social membership. The capacities of new digital technologies to manipulate images merely enhance the deceptiveness of the visual – it appears to 'capture' social reality, but it is in reality a profoundly manufactured object.

Researchers using visual media to produce data therefore need to approach the practices of selection, processing and editing with a very self-critical and reflexive disposition. And if it is children and young people who are engaged in making images, then they need to discuss their selection, processing and editing choices so that their assumptions are also made explicit and available for discussion.

Second, an image can be read in multiple ways. Despite the intention of the maker, an image, like any other text, is presented to people who bring their own social and cultural understandings as well as their unique life trajectories to the act of interpretation. Researchers using visual research thus take on board the understandings that *their* intentions about what images mean will not necessarily be how they are translated, and thus the ways in which their images will be read may not be what they anticipate.

This slipperiness also means that any analysis of images must be a highly conscious activity. Visual analysis requires the use of specific and explicit approaches which must be systematic, thorough and open to scrutiny. A reader must be able to track what has been done in order to understand the subsequent interpretation. This is particularly important in the case of visual research conducted by children and young people, whose images may not be amenable to straightforward adult readings. They may be very surprised by the ways in which their images are interpreted by (older) others.

These methodological considerations must be borne in mind when thinking about the ways in which image-based research can be conducted with children and young people. But it is important to recognize that these issues are not confined to visual research. *Exactly* the same set of concerns about selection, processing, editing and representation apply equally to the use of words and numbers; it is just that we are more used to working with them. Their very familiarity actually means that we may forget their coyote-like nature: all language systems are equally tricksters. There is therefore no reason to relegate visual research to a lesser status than any other.

Approaches to visual research

Researchers who are interested in the lives and experiences of children and young people have been drawn to visual research in part because many children and young people themselves are interested in images. They like working with visual tools and media: photography, drawing, cartooning, multimedia production and film-making are already part of their image-saturated everyday lives (Bach, 1998; Bloustien, 2003; Goldman-Segall, 1998; Wagner, 1999). But this is not the only reason for social scientists to consider visual research.

Images communicate in different ways than words. They quickly elicit aesthetic and emotional responses as well as intellectual ones (Freedman, 2003). For this reason researchers hope that the use of images for data generation may well elicit different responses than research methods which are primarily speech and written word-based (see, for example, Burke & Grosvenor, 2004; Burnard, 2002; Clark-Ibáñez, 2004; Egg, Schratz-Hadwich, Trubwasser, & Walker, 2004; Kaplan & Howes, 2004; Karlsson, 2001; Kendrick & Mackay, 2002; Schratz & Sterner-Loffler, 1998; Veale, 2005). Some researchers argue that image-based research will particularly allow those children and young people who have difficulty with words an alternative means of expression (Moss, Deppeler, Astley, & Pattison, 2007). Other researchers suggest that through the creation of images young people are more ready to express their beliefs and emotions (Leitch & Mitchell, 2007), although such images are always of course discursive (Mitchell, 2006; see Weber & Mitchell, 1995 for a case where children drew stereotypical views of teachers and classrooms despite this not being their material circumstances). Furthermore, when children and young people are themselves engaged in visual research, they also seem to take pleasure in the process, suggest that they are 'getting something' out of their participation and, if they are students, compare the word-laden nature of schooling and the enjoyment gained from doing something different.

Visual research is used in projects where children and young people are the subjects of inquiry, what I have called research *on* or *about*. Table 1.1 presents some examples of this kind of research.

Researchers working *with* children and young people also use visual research approaches. There is less published research to date in this area, and little discussion of the kinds of approaches that support children to use visual equipment

Table 1.1 Research where young people are the subjects of inquiry

Process	Example
Adult making images of children as part of a research project	Photographs or video of everyday life in school Video of children working in classroom, playing in yard, or in conversation with each other
Adult using images to elicit views of young people	Trigger photographs or videos used to stimulate conversations Websites where young people are invited to add their opinions Story-telling cards to elicit details of events Toys and puppets used to stimulate projected narratives of experience or opinion
Adult analysing found images: 1 made by young people or 2 of interest to young people	1 Analysis of children's drawings 2 Analysis of children's magazines, websites, television programmes
Adult making images to represent findings about young people	Photojournalism in a research report DVD Website

and approaches (Ewald & Lightfoot, 2001), and this book aims to contribute to filling this space.

Table 1.2 lists some of the ways in which visual research with children and young people might occur. (Some projects, of course, might combine research both on and with children and young people).

These tables are not intended to be definitive but indicative of the kinds of approaches that can be adopted.

Indeed, one of the interesting things about visual research is that it is a field where there is ongoing change – the growth of interdisciplinary groups with common interests in visual research provides arenas where image-based methods cross over conventional disciplinary borders. In addition, new technologies afford new opportunities and thus new approaches continue to be developed. Mobile phones with cameras, SMS and MP3 players, accessible multimedia capacity websites such as Flickr, Myspace, Bebo, Facebook and YouTube open up new possibilities not only for the production of visual research but also for the interrogation of hybrid multimedia genres. These require the development of new forms of analysis (e.g. Kress & Van Leeuwen, 2006; Leander, 2003; Mavers, Somekh, & Restorick, 2002). At the same time, it cannot be assumed that children and young people are technically competent with any given visual medium just because it is readily available. If researchers involve children and young people in visual research, they must now consider

Table 1.2 Young people as partners in research and students-as-researchers' projects

Process	Example
Young people making images for adult researchers to analyse	'Draw and write' Cartoons Videos Scrapbooks Mindmaps
Young people making images which they help to analyse	Mapping the school or neighbourhood Photographs or drawings of places I like and dislike Photographs of drawings of typical interactions with peers or teachers Life-lines and story boards
Young people making images as part of a student research project	Photographs or video of everyday life in school Video of working in classroom, playing in yard, or in peer conversation Evaluative photographs Video diaries Scrapbooks Photo-surveys
Young people making images to elicit the views of young people as part of a student research project	Photo-elicitation Trigger videos Posters
Young people analysing found images: • made by peers • of interest to them • of interest to peers	Graffiti around the school or neighbourhood Popular magazines, television programmes, games, SMS Art work School photos, family portraits Editing events
Young people making images as a representation of their views	Powerpoint displays Animation Annotated photographs Films Posters Exhibitions
Young people using images to document their research	Images used to stimulate reflection on process

what they have to do in order to teach them about the equipment and its capacities and limitations.

But the ubiquity of new technologies also raises new ethical issues. Researchers working with children must always ask who owns the image – the child or the adult researcher? An individual or a team? But because new technologies offer the capacity for serial workings on images, the issue becomes even more complex – who owns the multiply manufactured image, and how is permission to be given for its reproduction? These questions are addressed by some of the contributors to this book.

A further caveat: the visual as aesthetic

The image is seductive. It is everywhere in modern life. It is relatively easy to produce and, at first glance, seems relatively simple to interpret. But this is not all there is to the visual.

As Eisner (2002) points out in his analysis of the creation of children's paintings and drawings, visual work can be a sensual experience. Paint and clay bring tactile pleasures; experimenting with line, shape, angle, perspective and colour are interesting experiences in their own right. In other words, the actual processes involved in producing images and the final products are an aesthetic practice and experience. Thus, children given a camera may become interested in exploring and representing light, or in trying to capture the intricate patterns made by clouds, or the patterns made by buildings, or they may wish to experiment with ways of representing the symbolic importance of a particular place. They may wish simply to produce a beautiful image.

Experimentation with form and finding enjoyment in working with a specific medium are quite likely to happen when children are invited to work visually. When faced with images constructed in this mode, visual researchers may struggle to understand what has happened and what they are looking at. They may also feel that the data are not useful.

It is important to remember that the production of visual material not only requires specific skills but also particular sensibilities and knowledges. Perhaps because we are accustomed to photographs and video produced for domestic purposes, we are less aware of their aesthetic dimensions. We take a family photo, for example, as being 'simply that' – a record of an event, a document of something that occurred, a memory made material (for discussion of the family photo as more than this, see Rose, 2003). And as adult researchers we are not primarily interested in the aesthetic, unless this is the very question we are investigating. We use the visual as a means to an end. But very often we also work with what we think 'looks good' without having the language or knowledge to explain why we are doing what we do and what we hope it means. Nevertheless, we do understand the complexity of images and their production in other circumstances. If we visit a contemporary art gallery, it rapidly becomes clear that the art that is 'on show' is communicating ideas, speaking back to other works of art, and commenting on social events and everyday life.

There are ongoing conversations conducted through the visual arts – and indeed other art forms – which can require specific learning/teaching. Just as we do not expect to understand complicated machinery without the requisite knowledge, it is also the case that our understanding of work with the visual is enhanced if we understand more about it. However, many visual researchers are poorly educated in such matters. Because of the general marginalization of the arts in schooling, and the skewing of visual art school curricula to particular kinds of modernist traditions in which chronology and techniques are favoured over other approaches (Atkinson & Dash, 2005; Grumet, 1995), many of us have to teach ourselves about aesthetic traditions. While we do not have to become artists or art teachers to undertake visual research, it certainly helps if we can see the visual as something beyond technique, and as a social practice which has traditions, genres, debates, grammars and hierarchies of distinction.

Even if we are using the visual as a medium of inquiry about something else, some understanding about the pleasures of its aesthetic dimensions is helpful. We cannot gloss over the reality that working with images can be important and enjoyable in its own right, and that the process of producing visual data may mean more to children than just the research and its outcomes.

References

Alanen, L., & Mayall, B. (Eds.). (2001). *Conceptualising child–adult relations*. London: Routledge Falmer.

Alcoff, L., & Potter, E. (1993). *Feminist epistemologies*. New York, NY: Routledge.

Ariès, P. (1962). *Centuries of childhood*. New York, NY: Vintage Books.

Arnot, M., & Reay, D. (2007). A sociology of pedagogic voice. *Discourse, 28*(3), 327–342.

Atkinson, D., & Dash, P. (Eds.). (2005). *Social and critical practices in art education*. Stoke on Trent: Trentham.

Atweh, B., & Burton, L. (1995). Students as researchers: rationale and critique. *British Educational Research Journal, 21*(5), 561–575.

Bach, H. (1998). *A visual narrative concerning curriculum, girls, photography etc.* Edmonton, Alberta: Qual Institute Press.

Barthes, R. (1977). Rhetoric of the image. In A. Trachtenberg (Ed.), *Classic essays on photography* (1980 ed., pp. 269–285). New Haven, CN: Leete's Island Books.

Betlin, R. (2005). Photo-elicitation and the agricultural landscape: 'seeing' and 'telling' about farming, community and place. *Visual Studies, 20*(1), 56–68.

Bhabha, H. (1984). Of mimicry and man: the ambivalence of colonial discourse. *October, 28*, 125–133.

Bloustien, G. (2003). *Girlmaking. A cross-cultural ethnography of the processes of growing up female*. Oxford: Berghahn Books.

Bragg, S. (2007). *Consulting young people: a review of the literature. A report for Creative Partnerships*. London: Arts Council England.

Britzman, D. (1989). Who has the floor? Curriculum teaching and the English student teacher's struggle for voice. *Curriculum Inquiry, 19*(2), 143–162.

Burbules, N., & Philips, D. (2000). *Postpositivism and educational research*. Lanham CO: Rowman & Littlefield.

Burgin, V. (1996). *In/different spaces. Place and memory in visual culture*. Berkeley, CA: University of California Press.

Burke, C., & Grosvenor, I. (2004). *The school I'd like*. London: RoutledgeFalmer.

Burnard, P. (2002). Using image-based techniques in researching pupil perspectives. *Communicating, 5*, 2–3.

Chaplin, E. (1994). *Sociology and visual representation.* London: Routledge.

Clark-Ibáñez, M. (2004). Framing the social world and photo-elicitation interviews. *American Behavioural Scientist, 477*(12), 1507–1527.

Collier, J., & Collier, M. (1986). *Visual anthropology: photography as a research method.* New Mexico: New Mexico University Press.

Cook-Sather, A. (2002). Authorising students' perspectives: toward trust, dialogue, and change in education. *Educational Researcher, 31*(4), 3–14.

Crimp, D. (1993). The photographic activity of postmodernism. In T. Docherty (Ed.), *Postmodernism. A Reader* (pp. 172–179). New York, NY: Harvester Wheatsheaf.

de Lauretis, T. (1987). *Technologies of gender. Essays on theory, film and fiction.* Bloomington, IN: Indiana University Press.

Derrida, J. (1976). *Of grammatology.* Baltimore, MA: Johns Hopkins University Press.

Derrida, J. (1978). *Writing and difference* (A. Bass, trans. 1995 ed.). London: Routledge.

Edwards, J. (2000). *Students-as-researchers.* Adelaide: South Australian Department for Children's Services.

Egg, P., Schratz-Hadwich, B., Trubwasser, G., & Walker, R. (2004). *Seeing beyond violence: children as researchers.* Centre for Action Research in Education, University of Norwich: http://www.uea.ac.uk/care/people/RW_recent_writing/SEEING_BEYOND_VIOLENCE.html (accessed 6 February 2005).

Eisner, E. (2002). *The arts and the creation of mind.* New Haven, CT: Yale University Press.

El Guindi, F. (2004). *Visual anthropology.* Thousand Oaks, CA: Sage Publications.

Ellsworth, E. (1989). Why doesn't this feel empowering? Working through the repressive myths of critical pedagogy. *Harvard Education Review, 59*(3), 297–324.

Emmison, M., & Smith, P. (2001). *Researching the visual.* Thousand Oaks, CA: Sage Publications.

Ewald, W., & Lightfoot, A. (2001). *I wanna take me a picture: teaching photography and writing to children.* Boston, MA: Beacon Press.

Fielding, M. (2001). Students as radical agents of change. *Journal of Educational Change, 2*(2), 123–141.

Fielding, M., & Bragg, S. (2003). *Students as researchers: making a difference.* Cambridge: Pearson.

Fine, M., & Weis, L. (1998). *The unknown city. The lives of poor and working class young adults.* Boston, MA: Beacon Press.

Flutter, J., & Rudduck, J. (2004). *Consulting pupils. What's in it for schools?* London: Routledge Falmer.

Freedman, K. (2003). *Teaching visual culture. Curriculum, aesthetics, and the social life of art.* New York, NY: Teachers College Press.

Game, A., & Metcalfe, A. (1996). *Passionate sociology.* London: Sage Publications.

Gitlin, T. (2001). *Media unlimited. How the torrent of images and sounds overwhelms our lives.* New York, NY: Metropolitan Books.

Goldman-Segall, R. (1998). *Points of viewing children's thinking. A digital ethnographer's journey.* Mahwah, NJ: Lawrence Erlbaum.

Grumet, M. (1995). Somewhere under the rainbow: the postmodern politics of art education. *Educational Theory, 45*(1), 35–42.

Hadfield, M., & Haw, K. (2001). 'Voice', young people and action research: hearing, listening, responding. *Educational Action Research, 9*(3), 485–499.

Hall, S. (Ed.). (1997). *Representation. Cultural representations and signifying practices.* London: Sage Publications.

Haraway, D. (1990). A manifesto for cyborgs. Science, technology, and socialist feminism in the 1980s. In L. Nicholson (Ed.), *Feminism/Postmodernism* (pp. 190–233). London: Routledge.

Haraway, D. (2003). Interview. In G. Olsen & L. Worsham (Eds.), *Critical intellectuals on writing* (pp. 109–114). New York, NY: State University of New York Press.

Harding, S. (1998). *Is science multicultural? Postcolonialisms, feminisms, and epistemologies.* Bloomington, IN: Indiana University Press.

Harper, D. (2002). Talking about pictures: a case for photoelicitation. *Visual Studies, 17*(1), 14–26.

Heywood, I., & Sandywell, B. (Eds.). (1999). *Interpreting visual culture. Explorations in the hermeneutics of the visual.* London: Routledge.

Hirschman, E. (1970). *Exit, voice and loyalty. Responses to decline in firms, organizations and states.* Boston, MA: Harvard University Press.

Holdsworth, R. (2000a). Schools that create real roles of value for young people. *Prospects, 115*(3), 349–362.

Holdsworth, R. (2000b). What is this about a 'whole-school approach'? In R. Holdsworth (Ed.), *Discovering democracy in action. Learning from school practice.* Melbourne: Australian Youth Research Centre & Commonwealth of Australia.

James, A., & Prout, A. (1997). *Constructing and reconstructing childhood* (2nd ed.). London: Falmer.

Jenks, C. (Ed.). (1995). *Visual culture.* New York, NY: Routledge.

Kaplan, I., & Howes, A. (2004). 'Seeing with difference eyes': exploring the value of participative research using images in schools. *Cambridge Journal of Education, 34*(2), 143–155.

Karlsson, J. (2001). Doing visual research with school learners in South Africa. *Visual Sociology, 16*(2), 23–38.

Kellett, M. (2005). *How to develop children as researchers. A step by step guide to teaching the research process.* London: Paul Chapman.

Kendrick, M., & Mackay, R. (2002). Uncovering literacy narratives through children's drawings. *Canadian Journal of Education, 27*(1), 45–60.

Kenway, J., & Bullen, E. (2001). *Consuming children. Entertainment, advertising and education.* Buckingham: Open University Press.

Kramer-Dahl, A. (1996). Reconsidering the notions of voice and experience in critical pedagogy. In C. Luke (Ed.), *Feminisms and pedagogies of everyday life.* New York, NY: State University of New York Press.

Kress, G., & Van Leeuwen, T. (2006). *Reading images. The grammar of visual design* (2nd ed.). London: Routledge.

Lather, P. (1991). *Feminist research: with/against.* Geelong: Deakin University Press.

Lather, P. (2007). *Getting lost. Feminist efforts toward a double(d) science.* New York, NY: State University of New York Press.

Leander, K. (2003). Writing traveler's tales on new literacyscapes. *Reading Research Quarterly, 38*(3), 392–397.

Leitch, R., & Mitchell, S. (2007). Caged birds and cloning machines: how student imagery 'speaks' to us about cultures of schooling. *Improving Schools, 10*(1), 53–71.

MacBeath, J. (1999). *Schools must speak for themselves. The case for school self evaluation*. London: Routledge.

MacBeath, J., Demetriou, H., Rudduck, J., & Myers, K. (2003). *Consulting pupils: a toolkit*. Cambridge: Pearson Publishing.

Margolis, E. (2000). Class pictures: representations of race, gender and ability in a century of school photography. *Education Policy Analysis Archives, 8*(31).

Mason, J., & Fattore, T. (Eds.). (2005). *Children taken seriously: in theory, policy and practice*. London: Jessica Kingsley Publishers.

Mavers, D., Somekh, B., & Restorick, J. (2002). Interpreting the externalised images of pupil's conception of ICT: methods for the analysis of concept maps. *Computers in Education, 38*(1–3), 187–207.

Mirzoeff, N. (Ed.). (2003). *The visual culture reader* (2nd ed.). London: Sage Publications.

Mitchell, L. M. (2006). Child-centred? Thinking critically about children's drawings as a research method. *Visual Anthropology Review, 22*(1), 60–73.

Mitra, D. (2003). Student voice in school reform: reframing student–teacher relationships. *McGill Journal of Education, 38*(2), 289–304.

Moss, J., Deppeler, J., Astley, L., & Pattison, K. (2007). Student researchers in the middle: using visual images to make sense of inclusive education. *Journal of Research in Special Educational Needs, 7*(1), 46–54.

Nieto, S. (1994). Lessons from students on creating a chance to dream. *Harvard Educational Review, 64*(4), 392–427.

Orner, M. (1992). Interrupting the call for students' voice in liberatory education: a feminist postructuralist perspective. In C. Luke & J. Gore (Eds.), *Feminisms and critical pedagogy* (pp. 74–89). London: Routledge.

Pink, S. (2001). *Doing visual ethnography. Images, media, representation*. London: Sage Publications.

Pink, S. (2006). *The future of visual anthropology. Engaging the senses*. London: Routledge.

Pink, S., Kurti, L., & Afonso, A. I. (Eds.). (2004). *Working images. Visual representation in ethnography*. London: Routledge.

Qvortrup, J., Bardy, M., Sigritta, G., & Wintersberger, E. (Eds.). (1994). *Childhood matters. Social theory, practice and policy*. Aldershot: Avebury.

Reinharz, S. (1992). *Feminist methods in social research*. New York, NY: Oxford University Press.

Ribbens, J., & Edwards, R. (Eds.). (1998). *Feminist dilemmas in qualitative research. Public knowledge and private lives*. London: Sage Publications.

Rose, G. (2003). Domestic spacings and family photography: a case study. *Transactions of the Institute of British Geographers, 28*, 5–18.

Rubin, B., & Silva, E. (Eds.). (2003). *Critical voices in school reform*. New York, NY: Routledge.

Rudduck, J., & Flutter, J. (2000). Pupil participation and pupil perspective: 'carving' a new order of experience. *Cambridge Journal of Education, 30*(1), 75–89.

Rudduck, J., & Flutter, J. (2004a). *The challenge of Year 8*. London: Pearson Publishing.

Rudduck, J., & Flutter, J. (2004b). *How to improve your school*. London: Continuum.

Russell, L. (2007). Visual methods in researching the arts and inclusion: possibilities and dilemmas. *Ethnography and Education, 2*(1), 39–55.

Scheurich, J. J. (1997). *Research method in the postmodern*. London: Falmer.

Schirato, T., & Webb, J. (2004). *Reading the visual*. Crow's Nest, Sydney: Allen & Unwin.

Schratz, M., & Sterner-Loffler, U. (1998). Pupils using photographs in school self-evaluation. In J. Prosser (Ed.), *Image based research* (pp. 235–251). London: Routledge Falmer.

Shultz, J., & Cook-Sather, A. (2001). *In our own words. Students' perspectives on school*. Lanham: Rowman & Littlefield.

Silverman, D. (Ed.). (1997). *Qualitative research. Theory, method and practice*. London: Sage Publications.

Smith, L. T. (1999). *Decolonising methodologies. Research and indigenous peoples*. London: Zed Books.

Soohoo, S. (1993). Student as partners in research and restructuring schools. *The Educational Forum, 57*, 386–393.

Spivak, G. C. (1988). *In other worlds: essays in cultural politics*. New York, NY: Methuen.

Thiessen, D. (2007). Researching student experiences in elementary and secondary school: an evolving field of study. In D. Thiessen & A. Cook-Sather (Eds.), *The international handbook of student experience in elementary and secondary school* (pp. 1–76). Dordrecht: Springer.

Thomson, P., & Gunter, H. (2007). The methodology of students-as-researchers: valuing and using experience and expertise to develop methods. *Discourse, 28*(3), 327–342.

Thomson, P., & Holdsworth, R. (2003). Democratising schools through 'student participation': an emerging analysis of the educational field informed by Bourdieu. *International Journal of Leadership in Education, 6*(4), 371–391.

Thomson, P., McQuade, V., & Rochford, K. (2005). 'My little special house': re-forming the risky geographies of middle school girls at Clifftop College. In G. Lloyd (Ed.), *Problem girls. Understanding and supporting troubled and troublesome girls and young women* (pp. 172–189). London: Routledge Falmer.

United Nations (UN). (1990). *Convention on the rights of the child. UN document A/44/25*. Geneva: UN.

Veale, A. (2005). Creative methodologies in participatory research with children. In S. Greene & D. Hogan (Eds.), *Researching children's experiences: approaches and methods* (pp. 253–272). London: Sage Publications.

Visweswaren, K. (1994). *Fictions of feminist ethnography*. Minneapolis, MN: University of Minnesota Press.

Wagner, J. (1999). Visual studies and seeing kids' worlds. *Visual Sociology, 14*, 3–6.

Wasley, P., Hampel, R., & Clark, R. (1997). *Kids and school reform*. San Francisco, CA: Jossey Bass.

Weber, S., & Mitchell, C. (1995). *That's funny, you don't look like a teacher*. London: Falmer.

Weiler, K. (Ed.). (2001). *Feminist engagements: reading, resisting and revisioning male theorists in education and cultural studies*. New York, NY: Routledge.

Wilson, B., & Corbett, H. D. (2001). *Listening to urban kids. School reform and the teachers they want*. New York, NY: State University of New York Press.

Wittgenstein, L. (1976). *Philosophical investigations* (G. E. M. Anscombe, Trans.). Oxford: Basil Blackwell.

Part I

Why do visual research?

Research is always located within a particular research tradition and discipline. In this section three researchers reflect on visual research they have conducted with children, mobilizing different theoretical resources: critical pedagogy, hermeneutic psychology and post-structuralism. Each researcher discusses the reasons why she took up visual research methods and shows their application in a specific project of set of projects.

Chapter 2

'Play in focus'

Children's visual voice in participative research

Catherine Burke

In reflecting on a project which explored children's understandings of play, Catherine Burke suggests that critical pedagogy principles should guide the construction and design of research with children.

In this chapter, the question of how young children can become empowered as 'experts' and 'researchers' of their own play worlds will be addressed. The chapter is divided into three parts. First there is a discussion of factors that have shaped, and continue to influence, consideration of children as research subjects and researchers in their own right. Attention is drawn here to a critical reflection on dominant ideologies of childhood. Second, the discussion turns to considering the usefulness of the notion of critical pedagogy and emancipatory cultural practice in research with children. Here, the theoretical perspective of Paulo Freire is offered as a suggested frame of reference and practical tool. Finally, the chapter offers a critique of the author's own practice in an image-based research context.

Introduction

Childhood is shaped by adult attitudes, mythologies and beliefs, not all of which are entirely accurate but which reflect an adult need to know, protect and control children's lives. Many of these beliefs are commentaries on perceptions of risk, danger and hazard. In comparison with past generations, children out of sight are more often considered at risk while children out of adult control are considered a potential risk to themselves and others.[1] In general terms, such attitudes have seriously eroded children's access to certain materials, spaces and places for play considered by adults to be unsuitable. At the same time, there is often articulated among adults a nostalgic longing for the playthings and places of the past, such as den-building in natural habitats, street games in urban environments and playing traditional games in schoolyards.[2] Such is the popular contemporary view of childhood, particularly in the UK, and it is within this context that the research initiative to be described in this chapter was situated.

'Play in Focus' was a participatory photography project that positioned children of primary-school age as researchers of their own play worlds. Using simple technologies – pencils, drawing pads and disposable cameras – children between the ages of seven and eleven were engaged as investigators of their own spaces and places for play as they compiled a visual diary documenting one week's activities in November 2002. The participants were drawn from primary schools situated in two contrasting communities in West Yorkshire. One setting was a rather bleak 1960s high-rise housing estate that did not suggest, via its layout and architecture, rich opportunities for children's play; the other was a low-rise housing estate, built during the 1920s to support a then thriving mining community. The research demonstrated the capacities of children to take on the role and responsibilities of researcher, and certainly the visual tools employed were a motivating factor.[3] The results of the project have been described elsewhere (Burke, 2005), but here I want to reflect on some of the missed opportunities in the initiative. In particular, the chapter will reflect on the conditions under which the research process might have been transformed into one that enabled children to speak powerfully on behalf of themselves and others in their school and communities, and thus challenge prevailing notions of the status and condition of childhood.

Researching children's play cultures

One constant in the changing world of childhood is that children play. In whatever circumstances they find themselves, at home, on the way to school, in their lessons and in their organized breaks from class, they will play. Across all cultures and topographies and in circumstances as dire as found in some of the most war-torn parts of the world, short of starvation, children will play. Children's play is, therefore, one key to identifying childhood, and it is thus not surprising to find that anxieties about the state of modern childhood often include references to their play worlds. The space and place of children's play is, and always has been, a rich cultural landscape, infused with meanings that children make for themselves out of the materials and sites that occupy them. Such meaning-making may have been gleaned from previous generations of expert child-players who have used the same or similar materials or sites for their inventive play practices. Children's play is characterized by inventiveness and innovation through the capacities of the young to imagine the possibilities inherent in whatever comes to hand, and so it is not surprising that in recent times children and young people have embraced and developed the potentials offered by new information and communications media. However, the nature and culture of children's play is often poorly understood by adults who sometimes fear the consequences of children's free play in schoolyards, freedom to roam in urban environments or in new uncharted virtual landscapes via the Internet. The school, through this lens, is seen as a space where children can be contained and kept safe from the risky business of play, whether interpreted as 'stranger danger' in the streets or 'cyber-stalking' in online environments. Since the development of school as a modern institution, the spaces and places for children's play have become more defined, confined and surveyed.

Assumptions about children and the state of childhood shape attitudes that frame research design. The sociologist Berry Mayall suggests that, in research,

> children have been taken for granted, within traditional paradigms … (as) … adults are happy with their power over children and over childhood, and do not wish to face challenges to those powers inherent in serious analysis of the social status of childhood.
>
> (Mayall, 2003)

Yet, we know from a range of studies, some of which are described in this book, that if we offer children the time, tools and trust in a research context that address issues relevant to themselves and their peers, they can rise to the challenge and offer us valuable insight into their worlds of experience and meaning-making. An important, and overlooked, levelling dimension of photography as a research tool is that, unlike traditional forms of literacy, it captures perspectives on experience in a format that adults and children can produce with similar levels of technical skill.

Visual methods offer accessible, flexible and inclusive tools fit for purpose. Photography, in particular, can offer ways to engage individuals and groups in cross-generational dialogue and meaning-making. The subordinate social and political status of the child is thereby potentially surmountable and his or her contributions to community dialogue and development facilitated. New means of communicating a visual voice are emerging almost daily, and children having access to screen-based communications technologies are turning to photography and film, framing their play and creating rich visual documentation as a form of playful expression.[4] Children's play as performance is thus framed and logged, at least temporarily, as never before.

The schoolyard or playground was a product of the design of the modern school, and continues to be a significant space in young children's lives. However, the spaces, places and materials of children's play have rarely featured as the principal foci in educational research studies, since most research has been concerned with developing knowledge and understanding of the teaching and learning process.[5] Contemporary scholars, such as June Factor in Australia and Marc Armitage in the UK, have illuminated the hidden culture of school-based play, partly through visual representation and the use of archive photography. In *Tree stumps, manhole covers and rubbish tins. The invisible play-lines of a primary school*, Factor has shown how the physical features of a primary-school playground are incorporated and adapted for their own purposes by children in their free play (Factor, 2004). In the UK, Marc Armitage has emphasized the relevance to children of design features in the school grounds in nurturing play (Armitage, 2001; 2005). These and other research initiatives that offer children the chance to illuminate aspects of their lives, often invisible to the adult eye, are valuable, especially where misunderstanding or misinterpretation of children's behaviour is concerned. Such approaches can reveal the meanings, feelings and personal histories interwoven into children's places. What to adults might seem to be insignificant, an obstruction or an 'eyesore', is often shown to be of vital importance to children.

Paolo Freire and visual methods of enquiry into children's worlds

In 1973, while conducting a literacy project in a barrio of Lima, Peru, the Brazilian educator Paulo Freire asked the people questions about their lives and struggles but requested the answers in photographs. Freire already knew, through experience of working with non-literate peasants, that visuals and photographs, especially if they were made by the people themselves, could play a key role in helping them reflect on their own lived experiences, clarifying and articulating their discontent, and framing their ideas for change. When asked to describe 'exploitation', a child produced a photograph of a nail in a wall. This confused the adults until it was revealed, through the process of dialogue, that it represented a particular aspect of exploitation within the experience of children employed as shoe-shiners.[6]

Since the 1970s, partly inspired by the critical pedagogy legacy of Paolo Freire, a number of adult educators, visual sociologists and anthropologists have placed visual methods at the heart of their practice in order to illuminate the familiar and release the voice of the previously unheard and allow different stories to be told. Placing the camera in the hands of those who are experts in their own lives in a context that encourages the documenting and sharing of their own reality through photographs is variously termed 'photo voice', 'talking pictures' or 'visual voices'. But while there has been a trend in recent years to allow children to speak of their experience with a visual voice, there have been few studies that have explicitly conceptualized this in terms of the political status of childhood. Latin America continues to play a role in developing the concept of visual rights, with some important projects designed to challenge preconceptions and empower children and young people.[7]

In designing conceptual and theoretical frameworks for visual research with children and young people, therefore, we might choose to consider the notion of visual rights in order to bring together questions of truth, meaning-making and change. Towards this objective, we might want to ask, what right do we have as adults to know the hidden worlds of children's culture and to have them illuminate this through visual means? We may wish to access this knowledge to advocate on their behalf in order to bring children's voices more powerfully into the process of policy development.

However, given that play is a key element in children's culture, we need to consider how the subversive, hidden, intimate aspects of their play can be both recognized through research but enabled nevertheless to continue, untrammelled by adults' propensity to want to know and control all aspects of children's lives. A Freirian perspective can remind us of the importance of respecting the richness of children's own culture while revealing tensions arising from unequal relationships of power in the research setting.

'Play in Focus': methodological challenges, power and place

'Play in Focus' was a case study within a larger project designed to investigate and evaluate children's and young people's informal and formal play opportunities in East Leeds, Yorkshire, England. The objective of the case study was to attempt to bring into focus the detail of primary-school age children's play in the spaces and places they occupied. The task, using simple cameras to document their own sites of play over a period of one week, was offered within a framework that, through pre-task discussions, established trust, commitment. responsibility and fun.

Once the photographs had been developed, conversations were recorded with the photographers in small groups in their classrooms, and the recorded talk and the photographic diaries formed the research data.[8] This has been analysed and discussed elsewhere, but here I want to draw attention to the importance of what did not happen, what was not recorded and what, on reflection, might have been a valuable contribution to knowledge had the research been framed somewhat differently. Missing from the data is the record of conversations between children and (myself as) adult researcher that occurred during the initial planning stages where a collective understanding of the intention of the activity was generated and where notions of rights, responsibilities and the relationship between research and change began to be explored.

Carrying out research with children in school space and time offers benefits but poses challenges. Access to children of similar age can be facilitated fairly easily through communication with teaching staff, who can organize participation and appropriate permissions. However, as a context for research, the school is problematic as it wields a powerful cultural influence on the behaviour and imagination of those who occupy its spaces; adults and children alike. School sets its own rhythms of time that children learn early and (unless they resist) cleave to. 'Play in Focus' was located both inside and outside of school space and time, but since it was initiated from within the classroom, the children carried out their tasks as schoolchildren rather than as younger and smaller members of the community. Thus, the frame of reference brought by the researcher – that they as children were the experts and knowledge-producers – did not sit comfortably alongside their own expectation of themselves as schoolchildren.

Placing a camera in the hands of the child as both subject of research and co-researcher in educational contexts is a practice not without its challenges. First, one has to overcome the prevailing assumption that knowledge is owned, controlled and transferred to others by adults. It was important to discuss problems that might face the children in retaining ownership and control of the camera for a full week, keeping the cameras out of the hands of parents, friends and older siblings in the home context, and teachers in the school context. An important early stage in the research process was therefore to work towards an understanding that children's knowledge of their play worlds was owned by them and that they were indeed the experts. However, children are constantly engaged in learning to be children and they are themselves caught up in discourses of childhoods. To be invited to resist or refute this, especially within the context of school, is certainly an unfamiliar notion to them.

Conversations about images

Photo elicitation is the coupling of words and images, allowing for an interaction between the two. The images may be found or made: in this instance, they were made by children who were invited to talk about them. The research was exploratory and, as such, conversation could have been allowed within a completely unstructured free narrative approach or in a more structured context. In this study, to allow the interests and views of both the child and the adult to be considered in dialogue, a simple structure was imposed. First, the images were laid out randomly, allowing the child photographer to react. The 'magic' of seeing the photographs for the first time and finding out if they had worked was palpable. Digital photography allows almost instantaneous viewing and reflection on the product. In this case, cheap disposable cameras were used. The fact that children had to wait a period of two weeks before seeing their photographs certainly altered the nature and quality of the conversation. For example, no images could be immediately rejected; all had the potential to carry meaning and be explained.

After a complete survey of their individual photo-diary, the photographer was invited to choose just one image and to talk about what it showed and why they particularly liked it. This was straightforward, apart from the difficulty of limiting the choice. Once this was discussed thoroughly, the adult researcher chose one image and invited the child to talk about it. The choice of the second image was based on a hunch that the adult's view of the image or ways of understanding the meaning of the photograph might be challenged by the child. Another factor influencing the choice of the second image was in order to balance the child's choice. Hence, if the child had chosen an indoor site, I tried to counter this by choosing an image of an outdoor site.[9]

The images and the conversations about them revealed some surprising perspectives and certainly challenged many of the conventional notions about the state of children's play. For example, more photographs were taken of outdoor landscapes than of indoor spaces, although bedrooms did feature strongly. Many images captured territories that could only be revealed as significant through dialogue. A closely studied patch of grass that filled the frame prompted a conversation about the varieties of grass that could be used for different games (Figure 2.1). At certain times of the year, grass cuttings could be used for building purposes. Forbidden places and risky terrains were included (Figure 2.2), and discussion about these was tempered by children's own knowledge of how their images documented transgression.

Adult expectations might have been that children would have photographed indoor spaces mainly associated with computer-based media. However, overall, more children photographed open spaces than any other category.[10] Open spaces also featured highly in their conversation, often throwing light in the detailed description of these spaces for play. In these in-between or non-places are to be found the requirements for play; large open recreational spaces for running around, playing ball games and constructing 'buildings', dens or hideaways; high spaces made from hills and mounds where friends can meet, sit, talk and view activities below.

Often, in open spaces in the school grounds, very detailed and complex games are played as indicated here by a seven-year-old girl simply commenting on one open space.

> Right, that's the nature area near that and that's the wishing well and people put stuff in it and pretend it's gonna blow a bubble and a lot of people run around in it and do lots of stuff.

Not always used for running about, open spaces provide opportunities for meeting and talking with friends. Particular features in open spaces such as prominent spots or lamp posts hold significant meaning and trigger memories in relation to play and friendship. Indoor and outdoor play within closed, intimate or private spaces is an important strand of children's preferred play experience,

Figure 2.1 'Grass' (Bobby).

Figure 2.2 Forbidden and risky terrains...

as illustrated by their photographs. When asked to choose a photograph to talk about, many children chose to focus on a closed space. There could be a number of reasons for this but an important element seemed to be the sense of enclosure and privacy such spaces provide, whether in a back garden, a bedroom, a cupboard or a car. Intimate, explorative and dramatic play, such as dressing up, could take place in what appeared to feel safe, private spaces where children were known and loved. Several children photographed the interior or exterior of their family cars.

The schoolyard or playground played a large part in the children's photographic collections. The children who produced by far the most images of school ground spaces were those who had access to a space where adults had seriously considered the promotion of children's play in the playground design and redevelopment. It contained many informal, 'natural' areas, trees, bushes and rough grassy areas. Parents, friends of the school, teachers and children had constructed a play feature, a 'Shitara', and several children were prompted by their photographs to explain the fantasy games that happened daily at this space. The disadvantage with this well-considered site for children's play, as articulated by the children who photographed it, was that it was not possible for them to visit there after school hours.

Formal spaces for play, parks and playgrounds did not feature often in the photographic diaries, and in fact amounted to only 3 per cent of all photographs. The children reported that parents prevented them from going freely to local parks unless accompanied by parents or older siblings. Some commented on the play equipment in the parks as being uninviting as it was age-limited – that is, the space dictated, through its equipment, the age of child who should inhabit it for play.

A quiet road with parked cars on either side would not appear to be a land-

Figure 2.3 'Water'.

scape for children's play, but the photo-narratives helped to illustrate the liveliness of these spaces for children for whom play out of doors is an important part of their lives. This is not always random activity and there is clear evidence of traditional games being played in such spaces, such as 'Kerby'.[11] Such consistency of play pursuits over time, in spite of the problems posed by motor cars, indicates the well-being of a communicated live culture of play.

Given that the research was carried out in the context of densely populated suburban neighbourhoods, it is significant that such a large proportion of the images and discussion drawn from the photographic diaries featured the use and appreciation of natural materials and environments. Water found along pathways as puddles invites play; the local 'beck' attracts; a stream in the park with a pipe allows for paddling and balancing (Figure 2.3). Water featured in 4 per cent of children's collections, usually as informal landscapes for play. However, children delighted in describing the importance of bathrooms, baths and showers as spaces for play. Spaces featuring trees and bushes were highly important in discussion, and significant categories of spaces for play. For one child, a tree in an otherwise bleak square between houses was of great significance. The tree had become transformed through play, and was a 'seat' for another child and a 'cellar' for storing goods. One day, however, when the children visited the tree, half of it had been chopped down, causing some distress (Figure 2.4):

> That bush, we made a den in there, me, A (another child), and my sister,...
> but now all that side there has been chopped down so it's a bit harder and
> A's favourite seat what was up here it's been ... that's half chopped off.

Natural materials support imaginative play inside and outside of school grounds. 'Shops' were situated along the bushy boundary of one school ground, providing leaves, twigs and bark to 'sell' to customers. Stones and pebbles were used to decorate special spaces in ways that probably adults were unaware of.

The evidence of the photographic diaries of these two sets of children between the ages of seven and eleven offers a clear message. Children are well able to research and reflect on their own lives and the spaces they inhabit. They have a rich detailed knowledge to offer and when provided with an appropriate and relevant opportunity are able to contribute to the contemporary debate on the nature of childhood, the impact of the communications media, the issue of parental protection and the permanent importance of play in children's lives. The photographic narratives they produced argue the case that children's greatest needs are for safe open spaces, access to natural materials, freedom to meet, and some ownership of spaces which harness privacy, intimacy and creativity. Although the two communities were contrasting in terms of relative poverty, economic activity, levels of property ownership and other social factors, the project revealed that children had more in common across boundaries than otherwise.

Children as participants in research: intent, context and theory

So, in this particular study, how was the visual voice of the child enabled, empowered and recognized as of value to more than themselves and potentially to their peers and wider school and neighbourhood communities? Did the research framework operate to provide the conditions through which a deep and sustained reflection on the contemporary political and social status of children could be achieved? Did the children's efforts to show their play worlds achieve anything in altering attitudes, mythologies and beliefs about the condition of childhood?

Figure 2.4 'The tree that got chopped' (Adam).

Enabling the visual voice of the child to articulate and define their spaces for play revealed much that countered prevailing notions held by adults about children's preoccupations. This from-the-ground-up approach 'avoids the distortion of fitting data into a predetermined paradigm; through it we hear and understand how people make meaning themselves, or construct what matters to them.'[12]

Potentially, the research was rich in possibilities, but few of these were actually achieved. The constraints of time, space and culture of the essentially hierarchical institution of school worked to limit what was achievable. The project was short-lived and was not sufficiently embedded in the community of school and neighbourhood to realize its emancipatory potential. The role of the academic in such community interventions can be, as was the case here, limited. It can stimulate activity, but there is a need for a greater degree of continuity and sustained engagement in advocating on behalf of children and childhoods in communities where traditional ways of seeing the young are entrenched.

Visual research and critical pedagogy, with and for children?

Freire suggested a three-stage approach – curiosity, action and reflection – in designing pedagogical interventions, and we can adapt such a framework for research with children. These three stages were regarded by Freire as crucial in developing and constituting tools for critical thinking and transformative action within an approach that acknowledged the inequalities of power that framed their lives. So, where does a consideration of Frierian critical pedagogy sit within an appreciation of contemporary paradigms of research with children and with the construction of new visual-based research methodologies? We know that children and young people can be consulted and participate well in sharing their knowledge, identifying problems and designing solutions. Together, adults and children can devise approaches and methods (including visual methods) to generate data and analyse findings in order to facilitate change.

However, the intention that adult researchers bring to the activity, their sense of the possibilities of challenging attitudes, mythologies and beliefs largely determine the outcomes. For anything more than the surface to be scratched, a long-term engagement developing rich narratives of interpretation through dialogue across generations, situated in a commitment to realizing the social, cultural and political roots of inequalities and disadvantage is required. Only this, coupled with the degree to which the activity is sited and embedded in the local cultural context, will determine the level of criticality brought to the event.

Conclusions

Participatory research with children can be framed in many different ways, not always entirely in the interests of children as individuals or as a group. Significantly, within educational contexts, claims made about the outcomes of such engagement with children usually focus on the development of individual skills in child participants. Critically, within a Freirian perspective, the subject is primarily viewed as expert in their own world, already rich in knowledge, fashioned to the cultural context in which they operate. Such knowledge and expertise, realized through identification with others who share a common culture and situation, is invisible or at best disregarded by the outsider (in the case of childhood, the adult) and is transmitted within and between generations of the subject principally by means other than through written text – through visual communication, through music, song, performance and play.

The study, 'Play in Focus', sits within a growing body of evidence and associated literature that suggests strongly that children, even very young children, can be accurate and valuable communicators and recorders of their lives and their worlds. There are parallels here with early examples of Freirian critical pedagogy with working-class communities established in the UK since the 1970s, where the photo-voice perspective has been used with adults within a liberatory or emancipatory frame of reference. The historian Harry Hendrick has argued that 'the absence of a universally recognized political condition for children is crucial in explaining the kind of history to which they have been subjected to date' (Hendrick, 1997, p. 55). We might take this argument further and conclude that without a recognized political voice and presence, children will continue to be seen as less than equal to the adult in participatory projects.

Critical reflection on the consequences of taking children seriously coupled with the introduction of visual research methodologies has brought into play a new body of practice that challenges the prevailing paradigm of children and adult relations in research. This paradigmatic shift is characterized by an acceptance that children and adults 'see' and interact with their worlds in distinctive ways that may be obscured from one another, not only through cognitive developmental differences but also because they inhabit different cultural worlds offering dissimilar power and social status. For Freire, photography was a useful tool for developing critical dialogue between the photographer and others. Through photo elicitation, the photograph's narrative becomes itself a participatory site for wider story-telling, spurring others in the school or the wider community to reflect further, adding their own narratives, discuss and analyse the issues that confront them. The 'Play in Focus' project had the potential to fulfil this vision. However, such a level of openness to criticality and sustained attention to facilitate layering of re-interpretation could not at this time be achieved within the structures of time, space and cultural expectations of school-based research. A richer outcome might have been possible if, at the outset, a participatory framework that set out to critically question assumptions about childhood held by children and adults alike had been established.

Notes

1 For an example of how the media has taken up this concern, see the *Daily Telegraph* campaign to halt 'death of childhood', 13/09/2006.

2 There have been several schemes to introduce traditional games into school playgrounds motivated by the view that children do not play like they did in the past. 'Playground Fun' is one such project, based on a website aimed at getting children outside playing games. See www.playgroundfun.org.uk – by Culture Online, part of the Department for Culture, Media and Sport (launched July 2005).

3 The children were given a drawing pad, a pencil, a disposable camera and a set of their own photographs to keep. They were as delighted with the pad and pencil as with the camera.

4 The phenomenon of 'YouTube' www.youtube.com is an example where every day thousands of short video shots of children's own personal playful view of their worlds are uploaded for free informal public consumption.

5 During the 1950s and 1960s, the culture of children's play in the spaces and times set aside from formal learning was, for the first time, the subject of detailed ethnographical study. Iona and Peter Opie explored children's school-based culture in the British Isles through the language and lore of playground games and rituals (Opie & Opie, 1959).

6 The children's shoe-shine boxes were too heavy to carry and therefore they rented a nail on which to hang them for the night (see Boal, 1979).

7 See, for example, the Fotokids project in Guatemala City, www.fotokids.org (accessed 2006–12–11). At the 'Visual Rights' conference, held in San Paolo, Dec, 2006, scholars and practitioners met to explore multiple perspectives and different interdisciplinary 'frames' for carrying out collaborative photography projects with youth. A set of core questions included: how can photography mobilize or paralyse adults working for the rights of youth? How do youth use photography as a sense-making and aesthetic tool?

8 The children were enthusiastic participants in the research. In total, thirty-two children produced 639 images. The number of images successfully produced by any one child ranged from four to twenty-eight. There was very little difference in the number of images produced according to age: on average the older children produced nineteen images while the younger children produced twenty images. All children appeared to understand the task and carried it out appropriately.

9 All conversations occurred between myself, the child photographer and one other child who was present and who was encouraged to take part in the conversation, ask questions and add information. The rationale was that in this way the children would be more at ease with one another and be encouraged to respect each other's point of view while acknowledging their sharing of a common culture. Each discussion was recorded.

10 Open spaces formed 16.05% of the total number of photographs, followed closely by school grounds, 16%.

11 'Kerby' has been played by generations of children since the construction of roads with raised kerb stones.

12 Caroline Wang from the Photovoice website, see www.photovoice.com/

References

Armitage, M. (2001). The ins and outs of school playground play: children's use of 'play places'. In J. C. Bishop & M. C. Buckingham (Eds.), *Play today in the primary school playground: life, learning and creativity* (pp. 37–57), Philadelphia, PA: Open University Press.

Armitage, M. (2005). The influence of school architecture and design on the outdoor play experience within the primary school. In C. Burke (Ed.), *Paedagogica Historica Double Special Issue Containing the School Child: Architectures and Pedagogies, 41*, Issues 4&5.

Boal, A. (1979). *The theatre of the oppressed.* New York, NY: Urizen Books.

Burke, C. (2005). 'Play in focus'. Children researching their own spaces and places for play. *Children, Youth and Environments, 15*(1), 27–53.

Factor, J. (2004). Tree stumps, manhole covers and rubbish tins. The invisible play-lines of a primary school. *Childhood, 11*(2), 142–154.

Hendrick, H. (1997). *Children, childhood and English society, 1880–1990.* Cambridge: Cambridge University Press.

Mayall, B. (2003). *Sociologies of childhood and educational thinking* (Professorial Lecture). October, 2003. London: Institute of Education.

Opie, I., & Opie, P. (Eds.). (1959). *The lore and language of schoolchildren.* Oxford: Oxford University Press.

Chapter 3

Creatively researching children's narratives through images and drawings

Ruth Leitch

The researcher, Ruth Leitch, draws primarily on hermeneutic framing and creative, therapeutic psychological resources to show how image-making and narratives work dynamically to help children in Northern Ireland frame their personal and social experiences and ensure that their 'voices' are seen and heard.

This chapter illustrates how the creation of visual images, such as drawings, collages and posters by children and young people, can lead to rich individual and collective narratives that enhance differing approaches to research. The studies discussed provide an entrée to how metaphors, stories and narratives of children's experience are made more readily accessible by the use of visual image-making than by alternative, verbally-oriented methods of investigation. The premise of the chapter is that drawings, sensitively used *with* children in research, have potential for helping them to narrate aspects of their consciously lived experience as well as uncovering the unrecognized, unacknowledged or 'unsayable' stories that they hold. These stories focus on broader political and social issues affecting their lives as well as the more personal, private and emotional ones.

Researching children's and young people's narratives

Narratives and story-telling emerge from a distinctly different research tradition from that which has explored the use of children's drawings and artwork. Children's drawings have been collected as data and used extensively for many years in the clinical and diagnostic research tradition of psychology and psychotherapy (see, for example, Linesch, 1994). There are relatively few studies (with the exception of, for example, Weber & Mitchell, 1995; Kendrick & McKay, 2002; Harrison, Clark, & Ungerer, 2007) that have used drawing as an innovative, alternative way to understand children's knowledge and experience, and even fewer where children are invited to be co-interpreters (or narrators) of their own images (Leitch & Mitchell, 2007).

By contrast, narrative research in childhood has variously focused on the structure and form of narratives (Stein, 1986); the content of children's stories (Paley, 1990); the acquisition of narrative skills (Baldock, 2006); and how narratives change with age (Bruner, 1990). From a developmental psychology perspective, Nelson's (1986, 1989) seminal work on children's scripts demonstrated how even young children constantly tell stories about their experience and that particular stories grow out of general scripts they create about events. As is the case with scribbling and making marks, the ability to narrate arrives early, almost as soon as the child acquires language, and children have been shown to participate in and listen to stories before they can tell stories of their own (Bruner & Lucariello, 1989).

Children lead 'storied lives' (after Bruner, 1990), elements of which are deeply private, sometimes imaginal, often ambiguous and always socially embedded. Within a research framework, McLeod (1997, p. 31) usefully distinguishes between story and narrative. 'Story', he suggests, is an account of a specific event while 'narrative' is a more structured story-based account of happenings, containing within it other forms of communication above and beyond the story-line, such as commentary, illustration, moral and emotional reactions. Currently there are only subtle distinctions between the terms, and in the studies to follow, 'story' and 'narrative' are used interchangeably.

Within a constructivist framework, Engel (2005, p. 199) suggests that, increasingly, children's narratives are explored for the insight they offer into children's experience of their worlds. Narrative research is more often concerned with creating understanding *with* children rather than 'revealing it' and with the roles of 'teller and told' being shared and jointly created. Through these processes, where they have the opportunity to narrate for themselves and be their own audience, children have occasion to articulate perceptions, emotions and viewpoints which are latent or less conscious as and when they emerge. With this in mind, Rogers, Casey, Ekert and Holland (2005, p. 159) discuss the importance of children dealing with emotionally difficult issues through speaking metaphorically and how there they found evidence of:

> a poignant elusiveness in children's narratives when they began to speak about difficult and disturbing relationships in their lives or when they evaded speaking directly about these relationships but spoke metaphorically about them nevertheless.
>
> (Rogers *et al.*, 2005, p. 159)

The use of narrative research methods with children has thus also become of increasing interest as a means of giving 'voice', treating them as active subjects, and recognizing that they may have distinct perspectives on a wide variety of issues, including those which may be emotionally sensitive but nonetheless important. In the same way that a visual image can powerfully evoke a storyline, as Vygotsky (1978) indicated, so too can the spoken or written word (through story, myth, poetry or dialogue) amplify an image. What drawing and visual image-making add to the narrative process is that children and young people can be engaged holistically, creatively and practically in an activity that connects with the imagination (Anning & Ring, 2004). Image-making provides an opportunity to represent experience, a tangible process and product, within which stories are inherent, or out of which stories are (re)created. It is this rich dynamic which is illustrated in the following research examples.

Thus, despite their differing research roots, the study of children's drawings and children's narratives can be considered as gradually coming together under the general umbrella of creative methods. Until now, little attention has been paid in educational and social research to the relationship and synergy between the visual and verbal and how visual methods, such as drawings, can act as stimuli to children's and young people's narrativization, and vice versa.

Creatively researching children's narratives: four illustrations

What follows is a series of research examples of how drawings and image-making have been linked with narrative and used *with* children and young people across a variety of differing types of research studies, two of which are large-scale and two of which are smaller-scale, ethnographic-type case studies (Table 3.1).

A *Using children's drawings and associated narratives as data for policy in a large-scale audit*

The incorporation of drawings in research is commonly associated with small-scale ethnographic studies in which the express purpose is to sustain engagement with the child or young person in order to ascertain in-depth understandings of their experiences of particular phenomena. This study on Children's Rights in Northern Ireland, however, exemplifies the way in which drawings and other creative approaches were used as methodology in a large-scale, commissioned research study[1] aimed at consulting children and young people on the state of children's rights and welfare in Northern Ireland. What the children told the research team through drawing pictures, writing stories, designing posters and discussion groups, subsequently informed the Commissioner's strategy to improve children's lives on such issues as education, family life, health, wealth and material deprivation, leisure, youth justice and policing (Kilkelly, Kilpatrick, Lundy, Moore, Scraton, Davey, *et al.*, 2005).

Over 1100 children and young people (aged between five and eighteen years) expressed their views by the following creative methods, designed to be child-friendly and appropriately adapted to levels of understanding:

• *Individual drawings*
  Following a class discussion on what children considered to be unfair in their lives, pupils were asked by the research team to draw a picture

Table 3.1 Summary table of research studies using visual images and narratives

	Research study	Focus	Visual methods	Narrative	Outcomes
A	Large scale audit N=1167	Children's rights and priorities	Impromptu drawings Group posters	Stories: written and oral	Informing policy and strategy on children's priorities for action
B	Large scale participatory N=180	Political conflict and breaking a 'culture of silence'	Collages	Collective narrative Individual commentaries, poems and stories	Informing citizenship education
C	Small scale action inquiry using case study N=6	Understanding anger and self-management	Impromptu and critical incident drawings	Individual stories of anger and transformation	Young people's web-site Changing school policy on EBD[1]
D	Small scale phenomenological case N=10	Impact of sudden paternal death in families	Kinetic family drawings	Bereavement narratives	Understanding children's experiences of bereavement

Note
1 EBD: Emotional and Behavioural Difficulties.

highlighting the ONE issue they would like the Commissioner to address. Each picture was accompanied by a short spoken or written narrative describing the meaning and intention of their picture.

- *Group posters*
  Groups of at least four pupils focused on a particular issue (e.g. health, schools, leisure, crime/policing, etc.) and created a conjoint poster ensuring that everyone's ideas would be represented. The posters were also supported by individual written/spoken text.[2]
- *Stories*
  Stories were used across all age groups. Children and young people were free to write about personal issues that were particularly important to them in relation to the themes of the research.

Inherent to qualitative inquiry is the inevitable challenge of how best to analyse and represent creative data. Questions arise regarding how much to allow children's images and narratives to 'speak for themselves' such that their language and symbols are not completely redescribed and reshaped through adult interpretation (Fielding, 2004, p. 298). Nevertheless, there are circumstances when children's voices may be best heard through synthesis. In this study, in order to create a generalized children's narrative that would have impact at policy level, content analysis of the visual and written data permitted collective priorities to be mapped and carry weight. The interpretive process involved children's imagistic and narrative data being carefully summarized such that it would speak directly to policymakers. For example, the main issues and priorities from the children's and young people's voices on the theme of education were identified as *lack of voice in schooling and leisure,* and *pressure of work, bullying* and

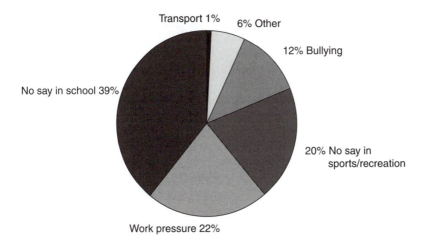

Figure 3.1 Children's priorities in relation to schooling: collective narrative (Kilkelly *et al.*, 2005, p. 17).

transport, the collective significance of which is depicted in Figure 3.1. Not having a say in the decisions made about them was identified by Kilkelly *et al.* (2005) as being the single most important issue to children and young people across all aspects of their lives, and one of the key findings identified by the study.

At the same time, the research team was committed to researching within a children's rights framework (UNCRC, 1990) and thus ensuring that minority issues were also heard and represented. They achieved this by including creative statements, combining image with children's declarations and aspects of their stories.

Thus, the final research report retained children's individual and group images/posters and narratives that made influential, incisive and inclusive statements across the study. These contributed more than simple illustration or decoration. For example, the poster in Figure 3.2 highlights the strongly held views by children from special schools regarding school transport. This issue was raised by only 1 per cent of the total sample (thus was a factor that could easily be ignored statistically), but by the majority of children and young people from the special schools sector.

In this geographical region, yellow-painted buses single out children with special educational needs as different, and were considered by them as stigmatizing. These pupils, in their narratives, were highly critical of the yellow buses. They commented:

> Get rid of the yellow custard bus; it's embarrassing.
>
> (Boy, aged fifteen, p. 29)

> We don't come home at the right time, it's too slow the banana bus ... we're embarrassed on that bus. We hide under the seats.
>
> (Girl aged fourteen, p. 14)

Figure 3.2 Illustrative drawing 1: 'The Yellow Bus'.

In the final analysis, it is unlikely that conventional research methods such as interviews and/or questionnaires alone would have provided the means for children and young people across the board to 'give voice' so powerfully and poignantly.

This study demonstrates how creative research methods can be incorporated centrally and with effect in a large-scale study such that:

- images alongside the generalized analysis of children's priorities ensure that, in particular, more easily marginalized issues are highlighted and the voices behind these can 'speak for themselves'
- individual and collective issues find their way directly on to the agendas and action plans of policymakers and assure children's rights.

B *Using collage in a large-scale research and development project on the impact of political conflict*

Veale (2005) describes examples of the ways in which creative methodologies, including drawings and drama, have been used effectively and sensitively in a large-scale community regeneration project in Rwanda in order to understand their experiences of 'vulnerable' children post-conflict. For ethical reasons, personal narratives were not sought but the use of free drawings was found to yield visual images of individual experience that the children were prepared to talk about.

The research and development study reported here by Leitch, McKee, Barr, Peake, Black, & White (2006) illuminates the widespread use of collage in a participatory study of a similar socially and politically sensitive nature in Northern Ireland. It explored young people's (aged eleven to sixteen years) realities and views on the recent and ongoing political and community conflict, in which many personal narratives were embedded. Like Veale (2005), this study was less concerned with the generation of knowledge and more focused on transforming opportunities and services for children and young people, in this case through 'opening up' conversations *by* and *with* young people.

Collage was used as a primary data source but also as a stimulus to pupils' narratives (both explicit and latent) about the political conflict. Even ten years post-ceasefire, this issue remains cloaked in a 'culture of silence' that has been described as acting as a community coping mechanism (Smyth, 1998) or 'safety valve' (Cairns, 1987). Although this silence may have served a purpose, it has reinforced children growing up in contexts where fears about traumatic violent experiences are not openly discussed, leaving the young person to internalize fears and emotions (Smyth, 1998). Additionally, key to a society emerging from conflict, discussing issues related to prejudice, sectarianism and difference and the consequences of the conflict now form a core element of the formal expectations of the curriculum on Citizenship (CCEA, 2006). However, the teaching of these areas has, understandably, been found problematic by teachers and thus studiously avoided.

'Collage' is a creative technique where different materials, artefacts and objects are pasted on a surface to create an artistic composition on a particular theme or topic (Butler-Kisber, 2007). Unlike drawings, using collage as methodology does not generally stimulate individual concerns about artistic ability. This is a particularly important consideration when undertaking image-based or creative research with adolescents who may be resistant to drawing tasks, given the commonly identified 'adolescent plateau' in artistic development (Lark-Horovitz, Lewis, & Luca, 1967). As part of their natural defence, rendering drawings may be viewed as 'too childish'. Selecting materials, images and phrases from magazines and newspapers to symbolize views on any issue seems to be a more immediately engaging and practical process for many at this age stage – especially when it comes to portraying matters of a more sensitive nature.

Collage, in this case, was found to act as a 'safe container' (Kramer, 1975) when used with individual pupils in schools and with cross-community groups of pupils. The process of collage-making encouraged symbolic expression by young people who produced collages that were rich, varied, powerful representations of deeply-held but frequently unarticulated hopes, confusions and fears (see www.enablingyoungvoices.org). Using collage allowed the young people to narrate not just generalized or partisan positions regarding the conflict (though these were in evidence) but also personal narratives of the conflict that were emotional and moving. These art images also seemed to create sufficient security and energy for conversations 'across the divide' of the two main religious groups, focusing on reconciliation and peace-building.

Despite commonly held views that children and young people born post-ceasefire have little or no awareness of the political conflict in Northern Ireland and have been relatively unaffected by it, the opposite was more frequently found to be the case, as the collage (Figure 3.3) and associated narrative vouch-safe.

Figure 3.3 Illustrative drawing 2: collage on What do 'the Troubles' mean to you?

Narrative excerpt:
Basically, it's [the conflict] just created a division, you know. Our town is split, like, right down the middle. If you are wearing a uniform in a different community, you could get beat up. Growing up here, if there weren't the Troubles, there'd be more mixed schools. You're also restricted in what you can say and where 'cos you don't want to offend people ... like at cross-community events, people are, like, banned from wearing, like, Celtic or Rangers tops and stuff like that 'cos it'll obviously offend someone ... If something does happen [in your community] you are just that scared, you don't want to tell anybody in case that stuff does happen again in the future ... and if you say anything, they'll come back and hit you or something...

(Lee,[3] Year 11)

While the young people frequently and voluntarily took the opportunity to narrate to each other, and to the adults involved, the intentions, stories and meanings integral to their collages, ongoing ethical and group agreements had to be negotiated to ensure safety for some of the voices to speak up. Although, the apparent 'visual message' of a collage may have appeared self-evident, it was important for researchers not to interpret or jump to assumptions about the statements being made. Rather, by creating a child-centred focus on the symbolic content of each collage, many embedded stories – sometimes persuasive, sometimes fragmented, sometimes painful, sometimes hopeful – were uncovered. Many of these linked personal biographies to the social, educational and political contexts in which these young people found themselves.

Thus, through individual and collective telling of stories, associated poems and prose related to their images, it was evident that, as Summerfield (1999) suggested, impact, suffering and traumatic memories are part of the socially distributed reality. Through the use of creative methods, some of the silence was broken for these young people. Additionally, stories are powerful tools for change (Frank, 1995), and through confrontation with their own and others' images many young people felt strongly about how they were disenfranchised from having a serious role to play in building a peaceful future. As one sixteen-year-old girl in a focus group commented:

Doing this work has made it okay to talk openly about your feelings and as young people we can really contribute to making a difference. It's sad we haven't been asked till now.

Within the particular focus of this study, collage was found to:

* engage young people in a fuller and more authentic participation in the research process
* act as a 'safe container' for difficult and ambiguous feelings and ideas to be expressed creatively without fear of judgement

- communicate visually young people's ideas on the violent situation, and helped to interrupt the 'culture of silence' surrounding the issue for young people:
  - by bringing to the surface individual views, stories, events and feelings that had been latent or inarticulate
  - through sharing what had previously been considered 'unsayable' or easily silenced in educational or cross-community contexts
- afford a means to cross-community engagement towards building a peaceful future in which young people felt they had rights and a role to play.

C Using drawings in small-scale action research on anger management with young people

Creative methods have been increasingly advocated in smaller-scale action research studies, in which students are invited to act as co-researchers with their teachers in the quest for development and change at local school level. Innovative methods, including visual research methods are recommended (MacBeath, Demetriou, Rudduck, & Myers, 2003) as increasing motivation and having the potential to reveal important insights unable to be elicited by more traditional, verbal-oriented research methods in such studies.

A small-scale participatory inquiry by McVeigh (1997) illustrates how one pastoral teacher worked with a small group of post-primary students (Years 9–11), as co-researchers using impromptu drawings to improve the experiences of some young people and to rewrite the discipline policy for the school. Where students are engaged as co-researchers, the young people act as both informants and as researchers themselves with teachers supporting and facilitating the process. Here, the teacher-researcher negotiated with students who were identified by the school as 'aggressive' (verbally and/or physically abusive to peers and teachers, using threats, throwing tantrums, damaging property, throwing furniture, etc.). The research goal was to develop a safe and trusting framework in which the young people would be willing to engage and work collaboratively with the teacher-researcher and explore their own experiences of anger and aggression and issues relating to what needed to change.

Impromptu (as opposed to truly spontaneous) drawings are defined by Furth (1988, 2002) as drawings that are stimulated or inspired by a suggested theme although no specific subject matter is specified. Through impromptu drawings, he argues, we can see how 'the inner situation can be projected onto the outer world and how the outer world affects the inner world' (Furth, 1988, p. 24).

The inclusion of impromptu drawings as a means of story-telling, the promise of one-to-one attention and the opportunity to improve the lot of others similarly labelled by the school as disengaged and volatile were viewed as motivating features by these pupils. Russell and Bryant (2004) maintain that internal representations of behavioural episodes are represented in narrative form.

Through illustrating critical incidents of anger and aggression from their bio-graphical lifelines (e.g. incidents at primary school, at home, in their neighbour-hood), these young people voluntarily developed and shared narratives of anger and aggression, providing insights into their own emotional and behavioural processes and how various social and educational factors reinforced or provoked these patterns (Figures 3.4, 3.5).

In the context of their ongoing relationship with the teacher-researcher, some students found sticking with the process severely challenging. However, the majority of these previously alienated pupils worked progressively to distinguish factors which they considered triggered and maintained their aggressive

Figure 3.4 Illustrative drawing 3: Cathy's impromptu drawing, 'Getting angry'.

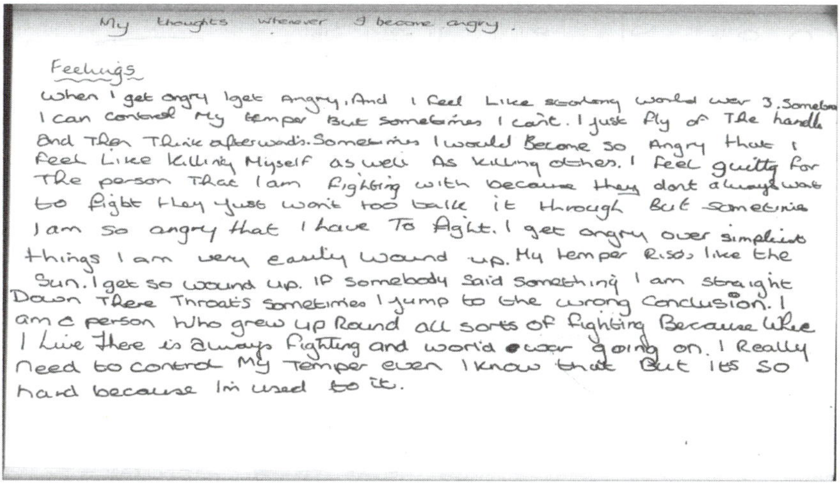

Figure 3.5 Cathy's narrative account.

behaviour (labelling, injustice, timings, shaming), and recommended how these might be better handled for themselves and others by the school. Insights arising from individual impromptu drawings developed into collective narratives that contributed to challenges for the school system itself, and the development of school policy on the positive management of aggressive behaviour that formed the basis for in-house teacher development.

Children's engagement with creative approaches is particularly pertinent for those committed to participatory approaches concerned to promote more active and democratic research involvement with children in the co-construction of knowledge (MacBeath et al., 2003). Within this orientation, creative methods, including drawings and storying, can safely mediate communication between children and adults, lowering the power differential, and act as catalysts for change rather than simply as data sources in themselves. The shift in focus has the result of placing less attention on analysis of creative product(s) and more attention on the dynamic relationship between researcher(s), participants as co-researchers and the artefacts they create.

Within the particular focus of this study, drawings as a participatory research tool were found to:

- be a key part of the research process in which sufficient trust was established and negotiated in an ongoing fashion
- provide structure for the safe expression of strong, often negative feelings (anger, frustration, indignation, rage) about critical experiences and events
- lead to the creation, co-creation and re-creation of narratives of injustice, perpetration and in some cases reparation, most of which had been previously 'unsayable' and, in some cases, 'unthinkable'
- provide a means by which these marginal, disenfranchised voices could articulate contributions towards change and system improvement for self and others.

D Use of kinetic family drawings in understanding the impact of childhood bereavement in families

Despite the widespread acknowledgement of creative methods as being more empowering, research on emotionally sensitive issues in the lives of children, such as bereavement or loss, has largely centred on clinical or therapeutic populations and within a diagnostic framework (Fristad, Jedel, Weller, & Weller, 1993; Parkes & Weiss 1988; Sanders, 1982). As Dawes (2000) has argued, however, children in such studies are traditionally positioned passively and often represented as 'traumatized', 'lost' or 'damaged', which has not necessarily served them well.

Leitch, Lavery, Kilpatrick and McMahon (1996) report a study with school-children (twelve to eighteen years) that explored their understandings of the impact of losing a father on their family relationships. The design employed more therapeutically oriented methods of kinetic family drawings (KFD: Burns & Kaufman, 1970) and regressed family drawings (RKFD: Furth, 1981, 1988). Both are simple drawing techniques used to stimulate discussions on relationships within a family. KFDs focus on action, symbols and relationships in a family present-day, and RKFDs capture family action at earlier stages in development. In this case, each student was individually requested to draw a picture of the entire family before the death of the father (RKFD) and again at the time of the study (KFD), without the use of stick figures. They were given A4 paper, coloured crayons and as much uninterrupted time as they needed. When they had finished they put a title on their drawings, and were invited to amplify and narrate their images privately with the researcher on one or two occasions.

The images and narratives provided insight into the ways in which family dynamics were altered that were both subtle and complex following the death of a father in childhood. Each narrative of loss was unique, yet collective themes could be identified across the images and associated stories. For instance, although some relationships in the family became closer, in general family members were perceived by the participants as becoming more separate, with strong feelings of isolation persisting following the death. Whether or not the remaining family members could communicate about the death itself appeared to be a key factor with regard to perceptions of closeness and distance in the family, with young people demonstrating the felt need to shield the mother from their own or her strongly felt emotions.

The images by Patricia, aged sixteen, illustrate how increasing personal and social distance was represented before and after the death of her father when she was eight years old (Figure 3.6, 3.7). This shift in family dynamics was evident across all participants' KFDs and RKFDs, and the accompanying narratives told stories of how this related to loss and change of identity and relationships within the family.

Figure 3.6 Illustrative drawing 4: Patricia (RKFD), 'Happy families'.

Figure 3.7 Illustrative drawing 5: Patricia (KFD), 'Growing up'.

Patricia's accompanying narrative of loss:
Life before his death I call 'Happy Families' altho' I wouldn't say I had a really close relationship with my dad, like, as I was only eight but he always took us everywhere. Life is certainly not as good now … sometimes I feel sorry for myself because I am the one something awful has happened to. It came as a complete shock. I waited a long time for him to come home but of course he never did, and, at the funeral, Sharon [twin-sister] and me took turns to cry. We tried to share the responsibility of looking after our mum who didn't cope at all with the death and that goes on … I know she finds it very hard bringing up three children on her own. I feel under a huge pressure all the time to be good and conform so as not to upset her. I know she feels vulnerable and worries all the time that people will accuse her of failing as a single parent if we misbehave. Sharon and me both feel we need to shelter mum and Karen [younger sister] and so we try not to share our fears or worries at home so as not to cause her any distress. The worst thing is that I feel left out and neglected because Karen's still clingy and takes up all mum's attention.

Using drawings in this study sheds light on aspects of these young people's experience of bereavement that they would have otherwise found difficult to articulate and which had resonance with others in similar circumstances. Using impromptu family drawings in this way facilitated and structured these young people's reflections about previously silenced and painful issues in a safe manner and, through the process of storying, opportunities were provided for re-framing their perspectives and reactions to their loss. It also taught those who work with young people something distinctive about these children's experiences of family dynamics as a result of sudden paternal loss.

Using family drawings in this research:

- permitted children to represent and story past and present scenarios within a safe ethical context
- provided a means for expressing the 'felt sense' of children's stories of loss and change outside a therapeutic context
- created tangible records that young people could refer to, reflect upon and explore verbally (or not) as they felt disposed
- allowed for re-framing of family system dynamics and opportunities for self-change.

Summary and future considerations

These four studies demonstrate a breadth of differing types of research designs that incorporate children's image-making as central to the generation of children's stories and narratives. Both large and small scale, they serve to illustrate how image-making and narratives can be used sensitively and synergistically *with* individuals or groups of children and young people to generate both powerful individual stories and collective narratives that have impact for differing audiences.

Used sensitively with children and young people, the combination of image-making and children's narratives in the four studies reinforces that such creative research methods:

- can be used within a range of research approaches of differing scale and with varying purposes, methodologies and audiences
- place the child/young person at the centre as 'expert' on their own worlds, focusing on their own meaning-making
- engage children and young people's creative tendencies and are intrinsically motivating and inclusive
- combine universal and naturally occurring and interdependent activities for children and young people
- can communicate the inner (emotional) and outer (social) worlds of children and young people individually and collectively
- present tangible and dynamic 'products' that can be revisited and revised and that generate literal and/or metaphorical and symbolic visual and verbal data
- possess latent capacity – as children picture inner experience they frequently become more verbally articulate
- render emotional experience and difficult issues less threatening (for self and others)
- provide opportunities for more participatory democratic research processes that hold the potential for change and transformation.

Nonetheless, despite the evident claims arising from these and other studies in this tradition, the use of images to engage children's creative narratives also raises a number of concerns that need to be taken into account. Until recently, the use of drawings and stories have been viewed as either (i) part of the accepted toolkit of educational methods, therefore not requiring any specialist knowledge or experience in their usage, or (ii) associated with clinical and therapeutic approaches to working with children, e.g. within art therapy or narrative therapy, and therefore only to be used by trained clinical professionals. Either view has potential problems and limitations. Undoubtedly, creating images and stories is a truly simple, engaging and universal pedagogical approach that has had a lasting effect in education. This standard usage reinforces some of the main rewards for incorporating them into research designs with children and young people. Children know what to do and what to expect and yet, within a research framework, the process can work somewhat differently, taking researchers into children's socio-emotional worlds outside the borders of normal classroom discourse and practice.

Within therapeutic paradigms, it has been widely accepted that drawings and storying can also be symbolic expressions or projections of subjective (or unconscious) factors (Silverstone, 1997). Simple line drawings and sketches, for example, hold the potential for participants to access unexpected emotions and feelings that may prove overwhelming and, as such, require anticipation and a skilful, caring approach should this occur. Wadeson (1980, p. 9) talks of 'how unexpected things may burst forth in a picture or sculpture', and such occurrences might easily have happened in studies C and D. This places an onus on researchers, from the outset, to reflect carefully upon their ethical purposes, experience, training and capacities for facilitation and support when considering the inclusion of image-making and narrative in their studies with children and young people.

Reflecting on studies A–D, it seems advisable for researchers incorporating images and narrative inquiry to extend their understanding and judiciously build upon the knowledge and experience from educational and therapeutic fields and the arts regarding the appropriate use of creative methods. This will permit those who engage in research with children to expand their methodological repertoires but, more importantly, be sensitized on how to create safe, trusting and ethically sound research contexts in which to use creative methods, whether these are large or small scale. Building the necessary and sufficient conditions was a crucial element to the effectiveness in all four studies.

The following issues are considered to have been critically important in the creative combination of image and narrative in research.

1   *Informed consent and ethical considerations*
    As part of the process of gaining full informed consent by children and young people, it needs to be made clear to participants from the outset that drawings and any other creative approaches are integral to the research process. Children should be appropriately informed about the purpose(s) of such creative activities; what will be expected; what materials will be

involved; any benefits and potential drawbacks. If they agree to participate, they need to understand explicitly how the images or creative artefacts or their stories will be used during the research and afterwards, including their potential use for dissemination purposes. Thus, if drawings are to be used differently than agreed explicitly by the children at the outset, then researchers will have to return to the participants to request permission for this additional usage.

2   *Creating a 'safe container' in the research process*
Bion (1962) talked of the importance of developing a relationship as a 'safe container' for others to engage in reflective processes, and Kramer (1958) emphasized the 'art object' as a 'container of emotions'. What Winnicott (1996, p. 54) adds is the importance for art-making of the creation of a 'potential space' where a 'good enough' and significant other person provides a relationship that enables the person to play in order to find themselves. A key element of the four studies was setting a respectful yet natural and collaborative atmosphere for the research tasks. Clarifying boundaries, articulating who will be involved, what will happen and anticipated timings were all found crucial in creating safety – especially in cases where the researcher is a previously unfamiliar adult. Additionally, since some children and adolescents are diffident about their artistic ability, a common theme in studies A–D was that participants benefited from careful reassurance that there were no right or wrongs; that they should try to relax and enjoy the task, and that whatever they produced would be of value and interest. They found that, in relation to pupil voice and the question of *who gets heard*, it is crucial that higher value is not necessarily paid to drawings or images considered to be of greater aesthetic merit. The important focus is the storying and witnessing of the life of each unique art image, however articulate or inarticulate this may be.

3   *Responding dynamically to children's images and narratives*
Children's images and symbols need to be respected and responded to; children also need to be given the opportunity to express and explain their response in follow-up interview-type situations, and be encouraged to take the initiative as necessary to help them create a meaningful contribution to the research context. One particular benefit of children creating visual images, reinforced by studies A–D, is that it avoids the need for the researcher to determine the 'right' question(s). Rather, what seems fundamental, when researchers invite children to reflect on/story their own drawings, is that they are genuinely interested in hearing their ideas about what is going on in the image and what meaning(s) they are making of them and to recognize and facilitate a context in which the child or young person becomes an audience to themselves.

In respect of the research process, it is important to have consideration of the interactive, ongoing, dynamic that ensues once image-making is incorporated into the research relationship. This is illustrated in Figure 3.8, which character-izes the three-way dynamic engagement between researcher, participant and image. The essential difference from standard eye-to-eye interviewing or focus groups with children is the presence of the third party, the visual image itself. Schaverien (1999) differentiates the 'life *in* the picture' (image-making process) from the 'life *of* the picture' (final publicly shared product). Image-making and how it is conducted is a crucial step in the research process, and needs to be thoughtfully handled to ensure that participants 'put life into their pictures'. The visual representation as product, however, is tangible, and as well as expressing (consciously or unconsciously, articulately or inarticulately) the child's or young person's intentions, impressions and experiences, it can also be moved, changed, touched and, unwittingly at times, abused. In this sense, 'the life of the picture' requires also to be treated respectfully and handled with care.

Within the ongoing research relationship, the drawing or image as artefact mediates and has considerable influence on the researcher and participant(s). By facilitating and holding a safe, listening space, the researcher enables the partici-pant(s) to story, narrate or dialogue with the image(s), thus allowing layers of meanings and significance to emerge. This storying may be in verbal or written form. Through spending time with the visual image and its symbolic contents, this fundamental dynamic leads to an enhancement of the narrative process such that children and young people 'largely make sense of their experiences and communicate their experiences to others, in the form of stories' (McLeod, 2002, p. 104). In some cases, new insights and awareness will be gained for those involved.

In smaller-scale, in-depth studies (such as C and D), this dynamic process can be an intense one, during which young people construct and reconstruct various

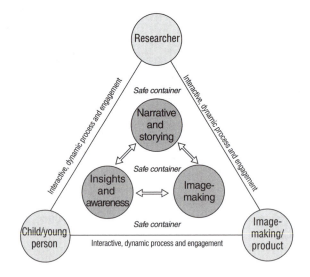

Figure 3.8 Creative research dynamic.

aspects of their inner or outer worlds within the containment of the research context. In the larger studies (such as A and B), similar principles should apply but the process will be duly moderated and the intensity diluted without loss of sensitivity or quality of data.

Shedding light on children's personal experiences and social issues in depth undoubtedly requires interpersonal skill, sensitivity and humility. Moving from the use of drawings and into stories of emotional sensitivity cannot be assumed to be something that derives from conventional research training alone. These methods are therefore best undertaken by those researchers who have strong empathic and interpersonal understanding, and who have been exposed themselves to the use of the arts. As interest in creative research methodologies expands, it is worth considering the value of specialist research guidance being developed to ensure safe, ethical and child-centred practice in their application. The step to researching creatively, using visual image and narrative, is a small but nonetheless significant one, and, in the light of the studies illustrated and the spirit of Beloff's words:

> I would suggest that not only young people but even some children have got some things to tell us that could put life into their marks on paper ... We should sometimes be prepared to dismount from our high horses and just sit around, talk, look, feel.
>
> (Beloff, 1980, p. 175)

Notes

1   The research was commissioned by the first Northern Ireland Commissioner for Children and Young People (NICCY) in 2003. The Commissioner is independent of Government but must report to Parliament about the outcome of work undertaken by the Office. The research comprised an audit of children's rights in Northern Ireland, and evaluated the law, policy and practices which impact on children's lives against the standards in the UNCRC and other international human rights covenants, and the outcomes were to inform a comprehensive strategy on children and young people in the Province.
2   On advice from specialist teachers, the wording, font and layout of poster tasks were amended appropriately for children with mild and severe learning difficulties (see *NICCY Schools' Report: an analysis of research conducted with school children* for details www.niccy.org/uploaded_docs).
3   Pseudonyms are used throughout.

References

Anning, A., & Ring, K. (2004). *Making sense of children's drawings.* Maidenhead: Open University Press/McGraw-Hill Education.

Baldock, P. (2006). *The place of narrative in the early years: how the tale unfolds.* London: Routledge.

Beloff, H. (1980). A place not so far apart. Conclusions from an outsider. In J. Harbinson,

& J. Harbinson, J (Eds.), *A society under stress: children and young people in Northern Ireland* (pp. 167–176), Ilminster: Open Books.

Bion, W. (1962). *Learning from experience.* London: Heinemann.

Bruner, J. (1990). *Acts of meaning.* Cambridge, MA: Harvard University Press.

Bruner, J., & Lucariello, J. (1989). Monologue as narrative recreation of the world. In K. Nelson (Ed.), *Narratives from the crib* (pp. 73–97). Cambridge, MA: Harvard University Press.

Burns, R.C., & Kaufman S.H. (1970). *Kinetic–family–drawings (K–F–D),* New York, NY: Brunner/Mazel.

Butler-Kisber, L. (2007). Collage in qualitative inquiry. In G. Knowles & A. Cole (Eds.), *Handbook of the arts in qualitative inquiry. Perspectives, methodologies, examples and issues* (pp. 230–242). Thousand Oaks, CA: Sage Publications.

Cairns, E. (1987). *Caught in the crossfire. Children and the Northern Ireland conflict.* Belfast: Appletree.

Council for the Curriculum Examinations and Assessment (CCEA) (2006). *Revised Curriculum for Northern Ireland.* Available online at www.ccea.org.uk/ (accessed 26 October 2006).

Dawes, A. (2000). Creative methodologies in participatory research with children. In S. Greene & D. Hogan (Eds.), *Researching children's experience: approaches and methods* (pp. 253–272). London. Sage Publications.

Engel, S. (2005). Narrative analysis of children's experience. In S. Greene & D. Hogan (Eds.), *Researching children's experience: approaches and methods* (pp. 199–217). London: Sage Publications.

Fielding, M. (2004). Transformative approaches to student voice: theoretical underpinnings, recalcitrant realities. *British Educational Research Journal, 30*(2), 295–311.

Frank, A.W. (1995). *The wounded storyteller. Body, illness and ethics.* Chicago, IL: University of Chicago Press.

Fristad, M., Jedel, R., Weller, R., & Weller, E. (1993). Psychosocial functioning in children after the death of a parent. *American Journal of Psychiatry, 150*(3), 511–522.

Furth, G. (1981). The use of drawings made at significant times in one's life. In E. Kubler-Ross (Ed.), *Living with death and dying* (pp. 63–95). New York, NY: Macmillan.

Furth, G. (1988). *The secret world of drawings – Healing through art.* Boston: Sigo.

Furth, G. (2002). *The secret world of drawings. A Jungian approach to healing through art.* Toronto: Inner City Books.

Harrison, L.J., Clark, L., & Ungerer, J.A. (2007). Children's drawings provide a new perspective on teacher–child relationship quality and school adjustment. *Early Childhood Research Quarterly, 22,* 55–71.

Kendrick, M., & McKay, R. (2002). Uncovering literacy narratives through children's drawings. *Canadian Journal of Education, 27*(1), 45–60.

Kilkelly, U., Kilpatrick, R., Lundy, L., Moore, L., Scraton, P., Davey, C., Dwyer C., & McAlister, S. (2005). Children's Rights in Northern Ireland. Belfast: Northern Ireland Commissioner for Children and Young People. Available online at www.niccy.org/uploaded_docs (accessed 29 December 2006).

Kramer, S. (1958). *Art therapy in a children's community.* Springfield, IL: Charles C. Thomas.

Kramer, S. (1975). *Art therapy.* New York, NY: Schocken Books.

Lark-Horovitz, B., Lewis, H.P., & Luca, M. (1967). *Understanding children's art for better teaching.* Columbus, OH: Charles Merrill.

Leitch, R., & Mitchell, S.J. (2007). Caged birds and cloning machines: how student imagery 'speaks' to us about cultures of schooling. *Improving Schools, 10*, 53–71.

Leitch, R., Lavery, M., Kilpatrick, R., & McMahon, J. (1996). The effect of sudden paternal death on young people and their family relationships: some implications for practice. *Child Care in Practice, 2*(3), 15–27.

Leitch, R., McKee, D., Barr, A., Peake, S., Black, G., & White, J. (2006). *Enabling young voices: a research and development project on the impact of the Northern Ireland political conflict. Report to the Department of Education (NI)*. Available online at www.enablingyoungvoices.com (accessed January 2006).

Linesch, D. (1994). Interpretation in art therapy research and practice: the hermeneutic circle. *The Arts in Psychotherapy, 3*, 185–195.

MacBeath, J., Demetriou, H., Rudduck, J., & Myers, K. (2003). *Consulting pupils. A toolkit for teachers*, Cambridge: Pearson.

McLeod, J. (1997). *Narrative and psychotherapy*. London: Sage Publications.

McLeod, J. (2002). *Qualitative research in counselling and psychotherapy*. London: Sage Publications.

McVeigh, C. (1997). *Aggression in adolescence: an exploration of the phenomenological experiences of aggression in secondary school pupils*. Unpublished MEd dissertation. Queen's University Belfast.

Nelson, K. (1986). *Event knowledge. Structure and function in development*. Hillsdale. NJ: Lawrence Erlbaum Associates.

Nelson, K. (Ed.) (1989). *Narratives from the crib*. Cambridge. MA: Harvard University Press.

Paley, V. (1990). *The boy who would be helicopter*. Cambridge, MA: Harvard University Press.

Parkes, C.M., & Weiss, R.S. (1988). *Recovery from bereavement*. New York, NY: Basic Books.

Rogers, A.G., Casey, M., Ekert, J., & Holland, J. (2005). Interviewing children using interpretive methods. In S. Greene & D. Hogan (Eds.), *Researching children's experience: approaches and methods* (pp. 158–175). London: Sage Publications.

Russell, R.L., & Bryant, F.B. (2004). Minding our therapeutic tales. Treatments in perspectivism. In L. E. Angus & J. McLeod (Eds.), *The handbook of narrative and psychotherapy: practice, theory and research* (pp. 211–227). London: Sage Publications.

Sanders, C.M. (1982). Effects of sudden versus chronic illness death on bereavement outcome, *Omega, 13*(3) 227–240.

Schaverien, J. (1999). *The revealing image. Analytical art, psychotherapy in theory and practice*. London: Jessica Kingsley Publishing.

Silverstone, L. (1997). *Art therapy – the person centred way*. London: Jessica Kingsley Publishers.

Smyth, M. (1998). *Half the battle. Understanding the impact of The Troubles on children and young people*. Londonderry: INCORE.

Stein, P. (1986). *A model of story-telling skills*. Boston University Conference on Language, October, 1986.

Summerfield, D. (1999). A critique of seven assumptions behind psychological trauma programs in war affected areas. *Social Science and Medicine, 48*, 1449–1462.

United Nations Convention on the Rights of the Child (UNCRC) (1990). UN General Assembly Resolution 44/25 New York. United Nations. Available online at www.unicef.org/rights/HRToday (accessed 30 August 2005).

Veale, A. (2005). Creative methodologies in participatory research with children. In S. Greene & D. Hogan (Eds.), *Researching children's experience: approaches and methods* (pp. 253–272). London: Sage publications.

Vygotsky, L. (1978). *Mind in society: the development of higher psychological processes*. Cambridge. MA: Harvard University Press.

Wadeson, H. (1980). *Art psychotherapy*. New York, NY: John Wiley Press.

Weber, S., & Mitchell, J. (1995). *That's funny you don't look like a teacher*. London: Falmer.

Winnicott, D.W. (1996). *Playing and reality*. London: Routledge.

Chapter 4

Visual methods and policy research

Julianne Moss

Qualitative researcher Julianne Moss draws on poststructuralist *and* critical theories of research and knowledge production to situate and reflect on her Australian research into inclusion. She works with a normative sense of justice and equity but also with/against the provisionality and partiality of truth and meaning.

Introduction

In recent years as a qualitative researcher working in Australia I have used visual data sources captured through digital methods to understand the complexity of diverse student needs. Designing policy and curriculum studies, my interest lies in how difference manifests in education systems and, once inside schools, how understandings of diversity work amongst early career teachers, experienced teachers, students, policymakers and parents. I take up the challenge of doing research during the 'seventh moment' (Denzin & Lincoln, 2003, p. 3) of qualitative research, the moment that Denzin and Lincoln state is concerned with the 'moral discourse, with the development of sacred textualities ... critical conversations about democracy, race, gender, class nation-states, globalization, freedom and community' (Denzin & Lincoln, 2003, p. 3).

Methodological positioning

In this chapter I report on two small-scale studies. The first study, the middle-school project, focuses on Grade 7, a stage of the middle years of schooling, in a comprehensive secondary school. The second is an ongoing policy review of inclusive schooling. Both studies were carried out in Tasmania, the smallest and only island state of Australia. My methodological orientation is enacted through critical and democratic research practices. I emphasise the importance of being alert to issues of identity and difference and the limitations of research that aims to promote the hierarchy and exclusivity of existing cultural arrangements for researchers and the researched.

In qualitative research, it is possible to interpret texts, including images, from the 'linguistic tradition which treats text as an object of analysis itself' (Ryan & Bernard, 2003, p. 259). Methodologically my position is closer to the sociological tradition, through the production of texts as free flowing, the 'windows into experience' (Ryan & Bernard, 2003, p. 290) of students, parents, teachers and policymakers during times of curriculum change. Ryan and Bernard (2003) show in detail how these differing analytical approaches are used in qualitative research. I, however, see these approaches as being a potential continuum in a research design and, particularly when we are using visual methods, the separation is debated although questionable.

As Marcus Banks, a visual social anthropologist, pointed out over a decade ago, whilst visual data has become of concern to the social sciences in two ways, first through visual records produced by the researchers (examining pre-existing visual representations) and second through visual documents produced by the participants under study (studying society by producing images), significantly 'this dichotomy between the observer and the observed has begun to collapse (as it has across the qualitative social sciences more generally)' and has resulted in 'a third kind of visual record or more accurately representation has emerged: the collaborative representation' (Banks, 1995).

Having engaged with the 'never-ending struggle for social justice' (Lather & Smithies 1997, p. 50) over three decades of practice in education, I have also been concerned to see how socially just values are enacted by education researchers. How do researchers design and construct collaborative representations? What challenges do these types of representations pose for qualitative research and education research in particular? I have spent as many of my working years inside school systems and policymaking bodies as I have spent studying and working in higher education. My prior experience and positioning makes me alert to the effect of the researchers' stance and positioning on their methodological orientation. I persist in developing and refining methods that can be used in small-scale studies by practitioners, who more often than not are engaging in research to complete a higher education qualification. Despite the burgeoning qualitative literature, visual methods remain under-represented in the field of education.

Researching two policy stories

I understand visual data as sources that allow readers and viewers of research to assemble the complications of the lived experience and cultural meanings from image. Visual sources can be read through *form* and *content*. 'Form and content', as Banks (2001, p. 51) points out, are 'analytically separate-able but inextricably linked'. Typically, *form* can be understood through questions such as, what is the 'meaning' of this particular angle, design, motif, colour, assemblage, performance? Who is the person/group in the visual? *Content* of image asks who produced the image or performance, and for whom? Why was this image taken or made of this particular person, and either kept or discarded? It is also useful to consider how *form* and *content* are juxtaposed. Is one privileged over the other, and if so in what particular social context/s? The ambiguities encountered in an image are not obstacles to 'understanding' but a cause to hesitate, inviting, for example, memories and metaphors derived from everyday experiences, 'the distinctive texture of social relations in which it [image] is performing its work' (Banks, 2001, p. 51).

The two studies detailed in the chapter, although originating from differing research designs, generate data through digital processes, via cameras (35-mm, digital or disposable) and develop them into a documentary record through scanned images or participant-created images enhanced by multimedia effects. In both cases, working as a qualitative researcher in education I regularly remind myself that:

- analysis of these data occurs throughout the research
- research methods are inseparable from theory
- theory and analysis are also inseparable from each other
- visual data can uniquely engage the researcher and the researched in spatial performances, moving bodies, conversations and action in collaboration or through traditional researcher/researched relationships
- visual data and the subsequent analysis draws not only from familiar territory, in my case curriculum and policy studies, but from a wide range of fields, including narrative theory, 'technoliteracy', cultural studies and visuality
- I am sometimes blind to the encounters I am experiencing; ethically my reflexivity is paramount and I know new ethical challenges are being created
- I am a learner making the most of interdisciplinary processes, particularly as I work and rework over extended periods of time the intertextual experiences of generating, analysing and producing accounts
- no single visual approach is a neat fit; there are as many takes possible within visual methods as there are with any qualitative method
- pictures and images are differing constructions; theories of visual culture inform these distinctions
- there is order to my processes; I generate, assemble, analyse, review and perform my findings dependent on the research problem, but I remain alert to the dynamic and interaction of these processes.

In my research using the visual, I set out not to impose a single storyline to the sequence of the images that I assemble as text – to do so would inhibit or deny their own language and manner of construction as active constituents of aesthetic production. With each of the studies I have continued to allow the multiple meanings of the sequence of photographs collected from the research sites to continue to circulate. I regularly use the gallery of images from each study as part of my teaching and, in the study of inclusive schooling, have continued to gather imagery from the local press and official systems documents. Circulating these data through conference presentations, academic publication and teaching about curriculum and inclusive education, I have found visual sources to be readily taken up and questioned by other readers and viewers. Be it a policy or curriculum story, these data work to unsettle. It is important to stress that I do not view the visual unproblematically. In the wider field of visual culture, it is recognised that visual culture, like material, oral or literary culture, can be an 'instrument of domination' (Mitchell, 2005, p. 350).

Both studies use 'framed' digital format photographs as data. I deliberately scare the word 'framed' as I am wary of being framed, in this case by realist accounts that merely see image as representation of data used to illustrate the text or elicit student responses that take on the character of the interview. Photograph, as Bach (2007, p. 284) notes, is a verb. Photographs and imagery are ambiguous, people make and take images that matter to them. As John Berger asserts, 'this is why the visual is astonishing and why memory, based upon the visual, is freer than reason' (Berger, 1972, p. 133). In advocating his stance I am attempting to respond to the claims of the literature, particularly in the field of inclusive schooling, where research should recognise 'the complexity and plurality of perspectives, voices and interests and the need for researchers to make them explicit' (Booth & Ainscow, 1998, p. 246), the movement away from the essentialist traditions of the special education field, a field that so often assumes authority in mediating discourses of diversity, inclusion and exclusion.

The social science literature identifies multiple methods that researchers deploy when using imagery and photographs (Briski, 2005; Rose, 2001; Stanczak, 2007). These methods equally can be used with small or large numbers of participants and research sites, and typically engage singularly or in combination with approaches such as collecting images, creating images, constructing intertextual formats that embody image and text, narrative formats, video and performance texts. Perception and meaning can be understood as a product of psychological, physiological and cultural contexts (Schirato & Webb, 2004, p. 14). Beyond accounts of what disposes researchers to account for how form and content are produced, 'our cultural history and trajectories naturalise certain values and ideas and effectively determine our worldview' (Schirato & Webb, 2004, p. 14).

The next section of the chapter describes how I have gone about policy and curriculum research across two different sites and problems over the past decade. I highlight how schools are cultural sites and thus when represented through image are windows to 'selection, omission and frame; signification and evaluation; arrangement; differentiation and connection; focus and context' (Schirato & Webb, 2004, p. 21).

The middle-school project

The middle-school study sought to identify issues significant to the development of teacher education programmes and the middle years of schooling. The middle years of schooling refer to a period of schooling between years 5 and 9, well known as a time for young people to disengage with schooling. Working with a fellow teacher-educator, I designed a study that required re-engagement with the classroom experientially, an opportunity to confront our understanding and perceived deficits of our work and the practice of teacher education curriculum development. We looked to the teaching profession to stage our being in the classroom, rather than out of the classroom, giving us the political and cultural opportunities to reach for differing identities as teacher-educators. Looking beyond restrictive practices set up by binary oppositions of teacher-educators as being in/out of the classroom and in/out of date, we were confronting our exclusion from the realm of practice and our professional identity. In our roles within a university Faculty of Education, we were spending too little time in direct teaching roles in schools and we wanted to redress this imbalance. Prior to our university appointments, our identity formation included two decades of continuous service to the teaching profession.

In the middle-school project the images were produced by student researchers. The PowerPoint assemblage was a part of the data produced through a critical ethnographic study. The students shot, selected and assembled the images into a PowerPoint show, which they publicly exhibited to their peers. These data and the act of producing the moving imagery proved to be, and still are, the most powerful and transferable element of the research study. Our Tasmanian graduate teacher education programme commenced in 1997 and was one of the early two-year postgraduate programmes developed in Australia. We knew first hand the limitations of our programme, and elsewhere have written an account of the difficulties of implementing other ways of working when resourcing is small and the operational demands privileged (Moss, Fearnely-Sander & Hiller, 2001).

The data production in the middle-school project derived from an authentic and rich perspective, and was informed by a longstanding knowledge of Tasmanian government education. I had taught in neighbouring schools a decade earlier, and had prior knowledge of the demographic and social issues that confronted teachers in this context. Our focus was around the questions *what* to teach, and *how* to teach a pre-service teacher education programme broadly. In particular, we wanted to make reference to the middle years of schooling and the Tasmanian context where the local Department of Education was in the first year of a community-based curriculum consultation process that led to the values and purposes statements, the curriculum design platform of the Essential Learnings (Department of Education Tasmania, 2000) curriculum.

In order to achieve our research aims, we entered the school in the manner that any of our pre-service teachers would, joining a school staff for the practicum experience. We found ourselves taking responsibility for teaching a Grade 7 class in a school that was beginning to implement a middle-school programme. We wanted to explore how our students' preparation as pre-service teachers might be reinforcing or perpetuating practices that served to alienate the next generation of teachers we were trying to engage. Our teaching time was restricted to the 'core' periods of English, Studies of the Society and the Environment (SOSE) and Maths, due to the pressure of our university commitments. The teaching load was, however, that of a practicum period, a 0.8 teaching load. We had wanted a nine-week period in the school as our internship, but instead we had to opt for a shorter four-week period as the research funds granted were halved. Interestingly, it was the university teaching relief that was reduced in our budget. At the end of each teaching session at the school, a research assistant debriefed us and our narratives were recorded and transcribed.

The interview data formed the first layer of the research narrative describing our experiences in the culture of an emerging middle school. As teacher/researchers we also had our field notes, lesson planning documentation and samples of student work. Each of us developed a portfolio of work with our Grade 7 students. The portfolios were developed around the rich task we developed as classroom teachers with our two classes of Grade 7 students. My class also developed a visual narrative of school life as understood by them. The thirty-nine digitised images were entered into a PowerPoint presentation and captioned by the students. Other narrative accounts obtained through recorded semi-structured interviews were transcribed and entered into NVIVO.[1] These narratives were contributed by a pre-service intern, a recent graduate of our programme, a teacher with nine years' experience (also a graduate of our institution), a support teacher and the school principal. Transcribed interviews were offered to the key informants for verification. One participant elected not to have the interview recorded, but instead gave permission for the research assistant to record field notes. The transcript narratives were then bound into a single volume for each teacher/researcher to analyse, whilst the research assistant produced the NVIVO conceptual mapping of the data.

NVIVO is highly suitable for small-scale projects such as ours which produced data from semi-structured interviews, school documents, newsletters, policy statements, student work samples and visual imagery. The research assistant coded segments of text, and recalled these segments later to analyse specific instances of situations as well as to cross-reference data from one coded segment to another. Data were left in single node form, leaving them readily available for further interrogation. These nodes are reflected back not as categories for reduction but as ways to interrogate how each of us makes sense of our situation, our views and actions and our particular stance. This method matched the phased nature of our encounters with the data. Times for carrying out the project are defined through our institutional contexts. Research waits until teaching is finished, and school personnel also are subject to organisational demands and cycles – for example, the school principal who supported our entry into the school was on long-service leave during the first school term of 2002, the term following the completion of the data production period.

Collaboratively we examined the research assistant's coding and interpretation and re-read this against their interpretations. The first analysis included scrutiny of the transcribed narratives of the two teacher educators, the pre-

(a) The lockers

(b) The Grade 7 area: Pullen's Garden

(c) The 'stands'. Grade 7 girls hang out there during recess and lunch

(d) ... some of the sculpture work

Figure 4.1 'Another way of telling'; The Middle Years Project 2001.

service intern, the recent graduate, the experienced teacher, the support teacher, the school principal and the visual imagery produced by one Grade 7 class. Student work samples were excluded at this first stage of the analysis. These data, we believed, would be particularly useful in exemplifying the pedagogical dimension of the research.

Our efforts, despite the limitations of a compromised time-frame are intended to live out and signal the importance of the research tensions acknowledged and urged by Wideen, Mayer-Smith and Moon (1998). In their review and critique of ninety-three empirical studies on learning to teach, they urge research in teacher education to be characterised by researchers who

> reflect on their research and openly comment on the implications and possible conflicts created by instructors and researchers ... [and] applaud these researchers for explicitly acknowledging the dilemmas that face those who do research with the subjects they teach.
>
> (Wideen *et al.*, p. 163)

Each of us would concur that this was probably the most professionally rich experience of our years to date in teacher education.

Reviewing this study five years on, and the student data, I concur with these initial thoughts, particularly the place and significance of the visual narrative produced by the student researchers. This study could have been completed without the student data, but it has been the reflection back of this data that I have used over and over in teacher education and presentations to school leaders that has provided the epistemological nudge to see the social context of schooling as integral to curriculum development, school change and the design of pre-service teacher education.

This study used the visual as one of the multiple data sources, and adds to the debate in the field of visual methods whether the visual should be treated as the primary object of analysis or as one of the available methods that can be used to study our social and cultural worlds. In this study the visual afforded us an opportunity to analyse the middle-years students' perspective, to build insights into how they understood their experience of schooling. Their visual analysis of the context of learning proved not only to be an important link to the curriculum work we were teaching and developing during the period, but also provided a place for us as teacher-educators to confront the absences of student bodies in this particular story of schooling. The photographic lens, through the eyes of middle-years students, was recording a set of cultural rules and practices. Schooling was symbolised through empty open spaces, locked rooms with an isolated desk and chair, sites for pleasure and consumption. Detached, regulated student identities that applaud the canteen, the visual art, music and technology rooms get photographed. Places that support pleasure, conversations, the arts and bodily engagement through sport are on offer as sites where worthwhile student trajectories appear. The bodily presence of students was invisible but very visible behind the lens as they selected, arranged, framed connections and disconnections to their context of schooling.

My account of the second study, a policy study of inclusive schooling follows. Through an image-based research design, the study offers a productive alternative for researchers who aim to disrupt the dichotomous other of inclusion/exclusion.

Researching inclusive schooling policy in Tasmania

The second policy study began as my PhD research and remains an ongoing pre-occupation. The PhD research was designed and developed in response to the events that have occurred in Tasmanian schools since the implementation of the Inclusion of Students with Disabilities (ISDP) Policy. Between 1994 and 1998, the ISDP was drafted, released and implemented. The research design draws on narratives from the key informants, parents, teachers and policymakers to tell the tales of the 'story series'. Between the stories are visual intertexts. The 'eye' of the camera, adds another data source. Using visual narrative, the cultural world of schools becomes a powerful semiotic source from which data could be produced. In the PhD thesis, these disparate data texts are used to unsettle social knowledge about inclusive schooling and open up possibilities for further analysis. The 'story series', the data stories of the key informants and the inclusion of my research narrative and the movement backwards and forwards between these texts and visual intertexts were developed and fingerprinted by myself as the researcher. The photographs from the traditions of photojournalism narrate a visual text of the sociocultural, professional and systemic world of the key informants, teachers, parents and policymakers.

Broadly, the research consists of story-telling that uses two distinct forms of texts, the literary and visual. This is a demonstration of the linguistic and sociological traditions intermixing with each other. In the thesis, these visual texts are referred to as image-based texts and occupy a space that I have named after Lather and Smithies (1997, p. 47) as 'intertexts'. Sometimes these two types of narrative forms are entangled by other story lines. Sometimes I am a participant, at other times I am an observer, sometimes I am both of these. Within the thesis, sometimes the narratives merge, at other points there is a deliberate separation by the intertexts. The image intertexts are part of the cultural tradition of the special education knowledge tradition, a representation of schooling for students with disabilities from 1967 to 1998.

All in all, this text is a part of the 'narrative turn' and 'textual turn ... literary and cultural studies that now tend to be labelled postmodernist and poststructuralist' (Gough, 1998, pp. 59–60). Intentionally located at the entry of the data production, for those of us who can see, the combination of image and text constitutes, as Chaplin (1994, p. 3) endorses, one of the most effective means of communication. This conscious use of visual texts arises in my own narrative through an initial schooling in the visual arts as a secondary-school art teacher.

The insertion of a second narrative form, the visual, has two purposes. The first is to suggest that image-based research is a significant but under-utilised methodology in educational research. The second is to show, through the gradual threading of visual storylines into the thesis text, how image-based texts work as a powerful data source in research that focuses on social change. Also, what I am arguing is that image and text are not in opposition to each other. Texts are constructions through which we recognise and mis-recognise. Mitchell (2005, p. 351) writes of 'the visual construction of the textual field', rather than the 'social construction of the visual field' (2005, p. 351). Image in the contemporary study of culture is not heralded as iconoclastic; visual culture and visual images are, as Mitchell states, ' "go betweens" in social transactions, as a repertoire of screen images or templates that structure our encounters with human beings' (Mitchell, 2005, p. 351).

The interactions between image, voice and text, I also finally recognised, were what St Pierre describes as 'response data' (St Pierre, 1998, p. 4). Through the threading of response and narrative, images, split texts of researcher and informant working on a single page, layering one story with another, 'foregrounding the exquisite proliferation of subjectivity that was enacted before my very eyes as my participants both constructed themselves and were also being constructed within responsive relationships' (St Pierre, 1998, p. 4), this was a woven research method. Visual intertexts constructing the social history of schooling for students with disabilities interrupted the available narratives. The visual intertexts in my study are used to recount the available history within Tasmania and to draw other ways of problematising and reconceptualising the discourse and practice from the work described as inclusive schooling.

The use of photographs as historical method and texts aiming for social change is not a new phenomenon in the disability field. In 1966, Burton Blatt, and Fred Kaplan published *Christmas in Purgatory: A photographic essay*. In this visual text Blatt and Kaplan captured the life of thousands of intellectually disabled children and adults who were institutionalised (Christensen & Rizvi, 1996, p. 1). This work brought attention to the wider injustices experienced by

Parent voice 23rd August 1996
My son has significant global developmental delay, complicated by poor muscle tone and fluctuating hearing loss. His language delay is severe, and he has a moderate intellectual disability. The cause for all of this is unknown. He receives six hours aide time, and is at kindergarten for ten hours each week. He sees the district speech therapist once a month – illness, excursions and strikes permitting. We are a family with a commitment to the state school system, and have worked hard to support our state schools. I have always been firm believer in equity, social justice and giving people a fair go. Had the inclusion policy not been in place, I would have actively worked for it. One of the questions I am most suspicious of is 'Wouldn't your son be much better off in a special school?'

(a)   (c)

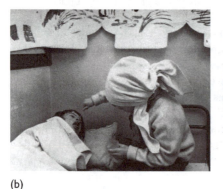

(b)

(d) ... some of the sculpture work

Figure 4.2 Educational facilities in Tasmania (a) for 'handicapped' children, 1967; (b) for children with special needs, 1973; (c) Parent voice, 1996; (d) Inclusive schooling, 1998.

people and children with disabilities, at a time when students with disabilities were excluded from the right to participate in normal educative processes.

I am currently researching the decade following the first phase of the policy implementation beyond 1998, that was the site of the original study. Much has occurred in Tasmania during the ensuing decade; there has been another major policy review, the Atelier Report (Essential Learnings for All, 2004) and a Ministerial statement on 'refining' the curriculum (Department of Education, 2006). This statement in essence signalled the end of Essential Learnings as they were initially conceived. In 2006, the state of Tasmania had a small number of separate special schools with a significantly reduced number of students. Compared to 900 at the beginning of the 1990s (Moss, 1999, p, 175), now just 132 students attended segregated settings. This endpoint, however, is not without its challenges, as my continuing research indicates, but demonstrates that one system radically altered its system of delivery.

Mitchell (2005) argues that the 'life of images is not a private or individual matter. It is a social life … They [images] form a social collective that has a parallel existence to the social life of their human hosts, and to the worlds they represent' (p. 93). Thus there is much to be gained by developing research designs that are longitudinal in nature – one of my aims in continuing policy research informed by visual method into the first decade of the twenty-first century.

Intertextuality and policy research

I argue, through the visual and 'text' work set out in the chapter, that visual forms developed from pixels and images are important sources of knowing that can contribute to reviewing policy and curricula aimed to achieve inclusive and socially just learning contexts. For the reader, images are displayed to elaborate the complications of what it is that is going on in classrooms, confronting how we understand school communities claiming to honour diversity and disability.

Theorising inclusive schooling has in recent times begun to link with broader theories of schooling and cultural politics. How unequal relationships in research practices remain hidden and obscured are questions that 'researchers' of inclusive schooling cannot ignore. Whilst some recognition of these issues has appeared over the past decade and some examples of changed practices have evolved, recognition of the centrality of these issues I assert is not central to the theorising of inclusive schooling, as Reid and Knight (2006) have also noted. Through questioning the meanings of appearances, borders of essentialist traditions can be reframed. Interactive and dialogical methods supported by the pixels of visual forms displace panoptical systems and invite the participation of the subject in a range of discursive practices – the sociocultural, the political and historical.

My research practices in both studies attempt to break apart the normative assumptions of policy that pervade the rapid advance of the inclusive schooling discourses. 'Policy is both text and action, words and deeds, it is what is enacted as what is intended ... (p)olicy *as* practice is "created" in a trialectic of dominance, resistance and chaos/freedom' (Ball, 1994, pp. 10–11). Positioning policy within this methodological frame, policy becomes an ongoing intertextual process, bringing into view the social relations in which 'texts' are embedded. Visual methods, like a picture are 'a very peculiar and paradoxical creature, both concrete and abstract, both a specific individual thing and a symbolic form that embraces a totality ... For whatever that picture is ... we are ourselves in it' (Mitchell, 2005, p. xvii). Positioning image as a key data source and using methods that radically rather than incrementally displace the dominant role of the researcher would seem to be an important aim for educational researchers interested in disrupting either/or categories.

Part of my interest in understanding visuality in policy and curriculum inquiry is to signal that these fields and methods alert us to the importance of carefully analysing the paradigm possibilities and interpretive tools that over the past two decades have been taken up in the social sciences. I have long struggled with the limitations of the dominant orientation of research traditions that, despite their judgment by the academic community as having integrity and quality, are rarely taken up on the inside of schools by practising teachers and leaders. International contributions to curriculum and pedagogy are predominantly theory-laden; teachers rarely locate and translate research-based knowledge to inform their pedagogy (Grimmett & MacKinnon, 1992; Huberman, 1985; Richardson & Placier, 2001). It is recognised that educators are not translating research into classroom practice (Kennedy, 1999; Langemann, 1996; Raths & McAninch, 1999). Educational research has too little influence on improving classroom teaching and learning. As Hiebert, Gallimore and Stigler (2002), comment:

> In spite of the continuing efforts of researchers, archived research knowledge has had little effect on the improvement of practice in the average classroom ... As teachers begin to examine their students' learning of the curriculum, for example, they rarely search the research archives to help them interpret their students' conceptions and misconceptions, plot their students' learning trajectories, or devise alternative teaching practices that are more effective in helping their students master the curriculum...
>
> (Hiebert *et al.*, 2002, p. 3)

Researchers who aim to take on approaches that include the voice of others and build practices where students get involved as student researchers or co-researchers, however, need to be reminded of the potential limitations in these approaches unless there is an informed and reflexive researcher at work. Lather, citing Ellsworth notes the inherent dangers of liberatory attempts that reproduce themselves; 'How do our very efforts to liberate perpetuate the relations of dominance?' (Lather, 1991, p. 16).

What I am illustrating and arguing in this chapter is that if we are to understand more deeply the multiple realities that construct schooling and shape educational opportunity, visual method has unrealised methodological potential, particularly as time and space compression invade social contexts. Rapid technological and social change have coincided with the growth of the interdisciplinary fields such as critical race theory, disability studies, queer theory and identity politics more broadly. 'Students' as a category or as subjects are placed within differing constructs or stage of development identity. As Baker notes and questions – '[if] "ability" and "disability" collapse under the contradictions inherent to their relationship in the text (where a text can be anything from a classroom to a test), then how can a pathway of normal development ever be described?' (Baker, 1999, p. 825).

My cautionary tale when working from localised practices is that we must remain sharply cognisant of the explanatory power that paradigms have and hold over our research. Images are not innocent practices. Their production must be questioned. Images are not simply realist tales that 'other' research subjects. If we are to take up the possibilities, researchers will need to engage with the politics of representation, not the least being their epistemological position as knowledges morph[2] rapidly.

Visual methods introduce the spectacle of the classroom and catapult realist policy forms. If image is a trap for our gaze, and knowledge of representations from visual sources is the now, a methodology of the visual will be how education researchers can view and review representations of subjects and selves held by policy formations. In our global world, how is education repressive? Visual methods developed in collaboration with our research participants have the potential to shake the authority and authorial canon of research production. The continuous presence of subjects and discursive inter-relationships produced both in a time and over time are inherent to the practice of visual culture.

Changing cultures of schooling requires us to undo an entrenched material and social reality. Lessons learned from visual culture affirm the central place of subjectivities (Doy, 2005) and the means to analyse image. As education researchers, we need to pay closer attention to the field and spaces that visual culture generates.

Notes

1 NVIVO details are available at http://www.qsrinternational.com/.
2 'morph(3) (transitive and intransitive verb) morph [mawrf] *1. transform from one image to another* to transform one graphic image on screen into another or others, through the use of sophisticated computer software, or to be transformed in this way *2. transform quickly* to cause something to change its outward appearance completely and instantaneously, or to undergo this process' Encarta Dictionary: English (UK) (accessed online 2 January 2007).

References

Bach, H. (2007). Composing a visual narrative. In D.J. Clandinin (Ed.), *Handbook of narrative inquiry: mapping a methodology* (pp. 280–307). Thousand Oaks, CA: Sage Publications.

Ball, S. (1994). *Educational reform: a critical and poststructural approach.* Buckingham: Open University Press.

Baker, B. (1999). The dangerous and the good? Developmentalism, progress and public schooling. *American Educational Research Journal, 36(*4), 797–834.

Banks, M. (1995). *Visual research methods.* sru.soc.surrey.ac.uk/SRU11/SRU11.html (accessed 27 January 2007).

Banks, M. (2001). *Visual methods in social research.* London: Sage Publications.

Berger, J. (1972). Problems of socialist arts. In L. Baxandall (Ed.), *Radical perspectives in the arts.* Harmondsworth: Penguin.

Blatt, B. & Kaplan, F. (1966). *Christmas in purgatory: a photographic essay on mental retardation.* Boston, MA: Allyn & Bacon.

Booth, T., & Ainscow, M. (1998). *From them to us: an international study of inclusion in schooling.* London: Routledge.

Briski. Z. (2005). *Born into brothels: photographs by the children of Calcutta.* New York, NY: Umbrage Editions.

Chaplin, E. (1994). *Sociology and visual representation.* London: Routledge.

Christensen, C., & Rizvi, F. (1996). *Disability and the dilemmas of justice.* Buckingham: Open University Press.

Denzin, N.K., & Lincoln, Y.S. (Eds.). (2003). *Collecting and interpreting qualitative materials* (2nd ed.). Thousand Oaks, CA: Sage Publications.

Department of Education. (2006). *Refining our curriculum, curriculum statement.* 10 October. Hobart, Tasmania: Department of Education.

Department of Education Tasmania. (2000). *Essential learnings.* www.education.tas. gov.au/ocll/publications/valuespurposes.pdf (accessed 11 November 2004).

Doy, G. (2005). *Picture the self. Changing views of the subject in visual culture.* London: IB Tauris & Co Ltd.

Education Department of Tasmania. (1967). *Educational facilities in Tasmania for handicapped children.* Hobart: Education Department.

Education Department of Tasmania (1973) *Educational facilities in Tasmania for children with special needs.* Hobart: Education Department.

Essential Learnings for All. (2004). *Report of the Review of Services for Students with Special and/or Additional Educational Needs.* A Review commissioned by the Tasmanian Department of Education June 2004 Atelier Learning Solutions Pty Ltd www.education.tas.gov.au/__data/assets/pdf_file/83173/finalreport-june29.pdf (accessed 29 April 2006).

Gough, N. (1998). Understanding curriculum systems. In J. Henderson & K. Keeson (Eds.), *Understanding democratic curriculum leadership* (pp. 47–69). New York, NY: Teachers College Press.

Grimmett, P.P., & MacKinnon, A.M. (1992). Craft knowledge and the education of teachers. In G. Grant (Ed.), *Review of Research in Education 18* (pp. 385–456). Washington, DC: The American Educational Research Association.

Hiebert, J., Gallimore, R., & Stigler, J.W. (2002). A knowledge base for the teaching profession: what would it look like and how can we get one? *Educational Researcher*, *31*(5), 3–15.

Huberman, M. (1985). What knowledge is of most worth to teachers? A knowledge-use perspective. *Teaching and Teacher Education*, *1*(3), 251–262.

Kennedy, M.M. (1999). *Ed schools and the problem of knowledge*. In J.D. Raths & A.C. McAninch (Eds.), *Advances in teacher education*, Vol. 5; *What counts as knowledge in teacher education?* (pp. 29–45). Stamford, CT: Ablex.

Langemann, E.C. (1996). *Contested terrain. A history of education research in the United States, 1890–1990*. Chicago, IL: Spencer Foundation.

Lather, P. (1991). *Getting smart. Feminist research with/in the postmodern*. New York, NY: Routledge.

Lather, P., & Smithies, C. (1997). *Troubling the angels. Women living with HIV/AIDS*. Colorado: Westview Press, Harper Collins.

Mitchell, W.J.T. (2005). *What do pictures want? The lives and loves of images*. Chicago, IL: University of Chicago.

Moss, J. (1999). *Inclusive schooling. Contexts, texts and politics*. Australian Digital Theses Program (available at http://tux.lib.deakin.edu.au./adt-VDU/public/adt-VDU20040524.162132).

Moss, J., Fearnley-Sander, M., & Hiller, C. (2001). *Techno hero fiasco*. In G. Webb (Ed.), Kogan Page Series of Case studies of Teaching in Higher Education, Case studies of Teaching with Technology (pp. 151–161). London: Kogan Page.

Raths, J.D., & McAninch, A.C. (Eds.). (1999). *Advances in teacher education*. Vol. 5: *What counts as knowledge in teacher education?* Stamford, CT: Ablex.

Reid, K., & Knight, M. (2006). Disability justifies exclusion of minority students: a critical history grounded in disability studies. *Educational Researcher*, *35*(6), 18–23.

Richardson, V., & Placier, P. (2001). Teacher change. In V. Richardson (Ed.), *Handbook of research on teaching*, 4th ed. (pp. 905–947). Washington, DC: American Educational Research Association.

Rose, G. (2001). *Visual methodologies. An introduction to the interpretation of visual materials*. London: Sage Publication.

Ryan, G.W., & Bernard, R.H. (2003). Data management and analysis methods. In N. Denzin & Y. Lincoln (Eds.), *Collecting and interpreting qualitative materials*, 2nd ed. (pp. 259–309). Thousand Oaks, CA: Sage Publications.

Schirato, T., & Webb, J. (2004). *Reading the visual*. Crow's Nest: Allen & Unwin.

Stanczak G.C. (2007). *Visual research methods*. Thousand Oaks, CA: Sage Publications.

St Pierre, E. (1998). 'The work of response in qualitative inquiry'. Unpublished paper presented at the American Educational Research Association Annual Meeting, San Diego.

Wideen, M., Mayer-Smith, J., & Moon, B. (1998). A critical analysis of the research on learning to teach. Making the case for an ecological perspective inquiry. *Review of Educational Research*, *68*(2), 130–178.

Part II

Processes, possibilities and dilemmas

This section brings together a series of chapters which present aspects of visual research that challenge researchers: What do I do to get children and young people to use visual tools? How do I make sense of what is happening? How do I understand what I am looking at? What are the ethical pitfalls in working with images? What can get in the way of my goal to have children and young people speak through visual means?

Chapter 5

Teaching children to use visual research methods

Kaye Johnson

This chapter makes explicit the ways in which a class of children was taught to work with visual research. The researcher, Kaye Johnson, was the school principal, whose overall research project was to work with children to change aspects of the school that they identified. The pedagogic scaffolding ensured that by the time the children began the action research component, which involved making photographs, they had considerable expertise in the visual elements of the research.

Introduction

The research context

I am the principal of a government primary school attended by 450 children and situated in the western suburbs of Adelaide, South Australia. The school began in 1878 in a three-roomed building with the headmaster living in the adjacent cottage. In the 130 years since that small beginning, the school claims a proud history of outstanding academic, cultural and sporting achievement and is well known for its provision of quality education for deaf and hearing-impaired children.

My interest in the sense children make of their school-places results from having spent most of my life in schools, initially as a child, then as a primary-school teacher and now as a school principal. My long-term involvement in primary schools led to my awareness that children experience places differently from adults, and that adults do not ask children about their perceptions of places. My observations have been confirmed by researchers who have shown that adults often do not recognise children's places (Rasmussen, 2004), nor do they enquire into students' perspectives, especially those of primary-school age children (Prout, 2001). As a principal recently appointed to my second school, I was interested in exploring with the children their perspectives of their school places. I anticipated that children's perceptions would provide me with new insights, would challenge me to question some of the assumptions about children's experiences of school and would allow me to discover new ways of working with children. I therefore designed research which would engage children as co-researchers into their everyday school places.

My research valued children's knowledge about their places and provided opportunities through visual research for them to share their perspectives. This chapter tells the story of co-researching with children using visual research. It focuses on the processes I used to help children become researchers – a story that is rarely told.

The research was divided into three interlinked projects. The first project invited children to represent through artwork and photography the school places they like and those they want to talk about. The second project invited children in small groups to interpret their photographic representations from the first project. Many of the places in which western children live, play and learn have been designed by adults to facilitate the controlled development of children (James, Jenks, & Prout, 1998). One such place, the school, regulates children's activities inside the buildings as well as in the playgrounds. Indeed, the spatial organisation, structures and processes of schools may have controlled children's development to such an extent that children's abilities to perceive, appreciate and connect with place may have been dulled (Fisher, 2004; Gruenewald, 2003). The small-group interviews explored children's understandings of the relationship between the physical places of the school and their positioning within the school.

The third project built on the first two projects, which had invited children to identify the places in the school they wanted to change. This enabled children to use action research methodologies to form partnerships with other stakeholders and to implement those changes. It allowed the children to act on their interpretations of their visual data about their school places. It empowered them to make immediate changes to their school places and thus transform their positioning in their own school. Although this research is located in a specific context, it contributes to a wider analysis of children's place(s) in schools. It was explicitly concerned with change which would improve individual and collective well-being for the children at my school, as well as having implications for wider educational practice.

The focus of this chapter

This chapter describes the pedagogic approach I used to enable children to become competent co-researchers so that they could explore their place(s) in their primary school. I invited children in Years 4 and 5 at my primary school to represent, interpret and respond to their everyday school experiences by creating photographs and artworks of 'places we like' and 'places we need to improve'.

I was aware of research which assumes that children are incompetent, treats them as incompetent and which then produces findings which confirm that incompetence (Alderson, 2000; Buckingham, 2000). I acknowledged children's capabilities and valued their unique perspectives while recognising their need to develop specific skills and expertise in visual research methods. I therefore decided to explicitly teach the research skills and processes that children would need to become active, confident co-researchers.

The pedagogic approach I adopted had three phases:

1   Discovering children's existing understandings about research and making connections with children's experiences and current knowledge
2   Exploring with the children the use of ethnographic techniques of data collection, i.e., the creation of visual representations of aspects of their everyday school lives
3   Providing information about my research interests, the purposes of the proposed research and raising ethical issues of coercion, confidentiality, rights and responsibilities of co-researchers.

This chapter focuses on the second of these phases, i.e., teaching about visual research methods. It:

•   describes the purposes of using photographs and drawings as research tools
•   explores the use of my own photographs of the school to encourage the children to 'read' visual representations
•   examines the use of picture books to raise children's awareness of the ways in which visual compositions communicate with the reader/viewer
•   demonstrates children's competence in using new technologies and extending their existing expertise to create visual representations of their school places.

My work suggests that children benefit from explicit teaching about research and can become competent co-researchers who contribute their unique insights into life in schools by using visual research methods.

A pedagogic approach

While children have the lived experience, the intellectual capacity and the social competence to engage with research, the twenty-two children who participated in my project had limited experience of research. I believed that if these children were to become co-researchers – that is, if they were to work as partners in collecting the material, contributing to the analysis of that material, and identifying possible action (Fielding, 2001) – they needed to be explicitly taught about research. They needed to learn about research by transferring their existing abilities to becoming researchers as well as acquiring new skills and dispositions relevant to research.

I designed strategies to make explicit to children the purposes of my research and my reasons for inviting them to participate. Further, I planned to make all aspects of the research relevant to the children by connecting new information

Figure 5.1 Child's representation of the 'big tree'.

about research with their current understandings and expertise. I anticipated that such a teaching approach would increase children's appreciation of the role of the researcher. Finally, I planned to talk with students about their authority during the research process with the intent of securing their positive engagement. On this basis, I facilitated a series of workshops prior to children agreeing to participate in the research. These workshops were designed to:

- provide information to the children in ways which connected with their understandings about research
- create spaces for them to talk about, reflect on, and to ask questions about the research
- treat children as competent and able to make informed judgments, and
- teach specific skills, in particular the use of visual representations in research.

Using visual representations as research tools

I invited children to become co-researchers by creating visual representations of their school places. I asked them to produce artworks and photographs for four main reasons.

First, the visual representations could be analysed as sources of data (Chaplin, 1994). Although not traditionally included in ethnographic studies, artworks, and indeed a range of cultural items, can be analysed to learn more about the participant's everyday experiences. Children's photographs and artworks would freeze their perceptions of aspects of their school life and provide:

...a way of 'fixing' the fluidity of the lived school environment sufficiently for me to explore questions.

(Karlsson, 2001)

Initially, I concentrated on the content of the photographs and artworks, that is, I focused on the layer of representational or denotative meaning. Next, I analysed the layer of symbolic or connotative meaning of the photographs and artworks. To do this I adopted the analytic approach of Kress and van Leeuwen (1990), whose descriptions of visual grammar and the semiotics of images have informed recent work in examining the multimodal nature of texts.

Second, the use of visual images in this research was inclusive of the abilities of all children. It enabled all children who wished to participate to 'have a say', to reflect on their daily lives, to identify issues of concern, and to make informed judgments. The use of artwork and photography enabled children to develop expertise in having their 'voices heard'. Because words were not the privileged source of data, children who were deaf and communicated with AUSLAN (signed language), those with identified language disorders and those who did not speak fluent English were able to participate.

Third, the use of visual images allowed the children to construct the information and gave them greater control of the research processes. Children participating in this research shaped the images of their school by selecting the content and the composition of the photographs, so it can be said that they 'made' rather than 'took' photographs (Chaplin, 1994). Later, they also selected and ordered the photographs for discussion, thus contributing to the direction of the research. Then children analysed and interpreted their own artworks and photographs.

This approach counteracts the likelihood of 'othering', which can occur when a researcher attempts to understand the culture by directing the photography and organising the photographs/cultural artefacts for discussion. Visual methods where the children generate their own visual representations enable collaboration with the researcher, thus reducing the unequal power relationship and promoting children as co-researchers rather than simply as participants in the research.

Finally, the children's artworks and photographs invited the viewer into the children's worlds and provided insights into their daily school experiences. Their visual representations challenged the viewer to consider the children's school places from their perspectives. Even so, the children's artworks and photographs provided incomplete pictures of their school places and provoked questions to be explored with their creators about their perceptions of these places, their access to them and their activities within them. I did not intend children's representations to become photographic or visual evidence objectively recording scenes from the schoolyard. Rather, I acknowledged the representations reflected the photographers' and artists' points of view and related individual children's stories (Harper, 1998; Prosser, 1998).

Figure 5.2 Child's perspective of explicit teaching time in the classroom.

Ethnographic research workshops

While the children had extensive experience in creating artworks as part of their everyday school lives, they had not used visual representations as a means of research. I now summarise the ethnographic research workshops in which I taught children to use photographs and drawings as research tools.

Photographs as research tools

Within days of my appointment to my current primary school, I had taken many photographs of the school to record places I considered attractive, those which surprised me and those I disliked. I had documented these places when I looked at the school through eyes which were not dulled by becoming familiar with the school's physical geographies and its practices and protocols. My intention was to develop tools which would assist me to be reflexive. I had planned to refer to these photographs throughout my tenure to recall my first impressions of the school and its operations and to challenge myself to look again at that which had become normalised.

Although I was cautious about constraining children's thinking and their later selection of images, I decided to share with the children my photographs as a way of:

- introducing them to the huge amount of information contained in visual representations
- encouraging them to carefully scrutinise and 'read' the photographs
- challenging them to recognise that photographs are representations created by the photographer.

I made multiple, enlarged copies of some photographs so that the children could peruse them as a class group and hypothesise about each image. Children's individual responses to the photographs were interesting and provoked much debate. The photographs of the staffroom with its padlocked cupboards and fridges generated lively discussion. Children's suggestions about my reasons for photographing this place included 'to show how many people use it because of all the cups'; 'to record it as a messy room with stuff everywhere'; and 'perhaps you wanted a before-and-after shot to show the changes'. The children focused solely on the material conditions. They were surprised to hear that I had recorded this place because I wanted to talk about all the padlocks. I had taken the photograph because of my interest in the ideological aspects of this place (Gruenewald, 2003), sometimes known as the moral geographies of place (Fielding, 2000). The organisation of the staffroom space legitimised and reproduced the authority of particular adults. The locking of fridges and cupboards and the entrusting of the only key to a school assistant who had worked at the school for more than twenty years made a strong statement about the ownership of the room, access to resources and authority. The refusal to admit students and parents to this room, made clear by the large STAFF MEMBERS ONLY signs posted on the windows and doors, further maintained this control.

The children's responses to a photograph of the fence with its locked gate and instructional signage identified objects in close proximity to the fence. They suggested that I had focused on 'the attractive trees, the library behind the fence; and the asphalt play area'. Again, children concentrated on the material aspects of place, identifying those objects and places they had experienced and about which they had personal knowledge. They were surprised to hear that I had been dismayed by the large number of signs and had wanted to record them for later discussion. Several students hadn't even noticed the signs in the photographs and rechecked them in the schoolyard to verify their existence. Children accepted the signage as non-controversial and appeared to believe that such signs were 'natural'. My purpose was to teach children to critically examine the representations. I challenged them to look beyond the material characteristics and to identify ideological and sociological aspects of place as they viewed the photographs.

I further structured children's examination of my photographs to enable them to hypothesise about the interaction of the portrayed objects. While a photograph of a school place might be intentionally focused to reveal a particular object, it will automatically reveal others. This characteristic is defined as the polysemic nature of photographs (Ball, 1998) and permits the viewer to analyse the relationships between the objects. The photographs I had shared with the children had been created by me to focus on a particular school place. However, they simultaneously revealed other places and invited analysis of the relationships between the places. I had intended the photograph of one of the school's four entrances surrounded by signs to stimulate debate about the kind of place people were creating in their positioning of rules and instructions, that is, to direct the attention of the viewer to the sociological and ideological aspects of place. The children's interpretations of the images relied heavily on their experience of the other objects captured with the signs, especially the basketball court and the library. Their focus was directed initially to their knowledge of this place and they overlooked other information. I used these photographs to challenge children to closely observe and to think critically about the visual representations.

To further develop close scrutiny of images, to promote critical viewing of photographs and to invite discussion about aspects of place, I introduced a sequence of three questions (Johnson, 1999). I asked:

1 *What* can you see? Describe the objects in the photograph.
2 *So what* does this really mean? What does it tell us about what is valued? Is this a concern? For whom?
3 *Now what* is our response?

I asked children to form small groups, to examine a randomly selected photo from my pack and to answer these questions. This task assisted children to recognise that in any photograph photographers consciously select the subject, deliberately frame the image and convey their points of view (Pink, 2001). While the groups responded quickly to the first question and were confident in their scrutiny, they were more hesitant in their suggestions about the perspective of the photographer. By contrasting the children's interpretations of the photographs with my purposes in creating the visual representations, I demonstrated that the meaning of a photograph is co-constructed by the maker and the viewer. The children enjoyed further exploring the images using these questions and discussing their (the viewers') responses with me (the photographer).

Picture books

I adopted a literature-based study to further develop children's awareness of the ways in which visual representations communicate with the viewer/reader. I invited children to explore the links between pictures and the places they represented; to consider the ways that illustrations reveal specific perspectives; and to contemplate how drawings and diagrams reveal relationships.

Figure 5.3 Child's detailed pencil drawing of cleaning the classroom.

Visual representations communicate information

The images in Jeannie Baker's (1991) *Window* were invaluable in focusing children's attention on the detailed information contained in visual representations. Using no written text and relying solely on the artistic technique of collage, this book depicts the view from the window of a child's bedroom throughout that child's life. The window is the frame through which the changing outside place of the developing suburb is monitored.

As I shared this book with the class, the children's astute observations stimulated much discussion about the simultaneous creation and destruction of place. Unlike their responses to my photographs of school places, children's comments revealed careful examination of the represented places. Such scrutiny can be attributed to children's recent practice in 'reading' visual information as well as to their lack of familiarity with the represented places. Their attention to the detail in the illustrations allowed them to identify the exploitation of both people and environments. Children's observations of the window itself showed their appreciation that the foreground of ever-changing artefacts was reflective of the child's growth and the passing of time. This book raised their awareness of the ways in which visual compositions communicate with the reader/viewer. The children readily engaged with Baker's artistic technique of collage because of its realistic representation of the place with the use of lifelike colours, natural materials and sequential progression.

Visual representations reveal specific perspectives

The illustrations in *Stickybeak*, written by Hazel Edwards and illustrated by Rosemary Wilson (1998), demonstrate that places are experienced from particular perspectives. This tale of an inquisitive duckling escaping from a box and exploring the house of its new owners enabled the children to look at the everyday home places from the perspective of a tiny creature which could not make sense of its environment. Although designed for much younger children, the illustrations in this picture book allowed the children to view the house through the duckling's eyes. Everyday kitchen objects loom large and incomprehensible, while floor surfaces become treacherous terrains to be negotiated. During the first reading of *Stickybeak* many of the children enjoyed the challenge of perusing the illustrations prior to hearing the text in an attempt to guess what the duckling was observing. As they individually re-read the book and were able to examine the illustrations more closely, children's amusement at the duckling's escapades transformed into empathy for the small creature and its confusion.

I could have selected any example of an emancipatory project which used visual images to convey the need for change to allow children to discover the influence of art and photography in identifying and challenging current perspectives. One such powerful example is the exhibition produced by The Pavilion Women's Photography Centre, Leeds (Chaplin, 1994). Instead, I elected to use a picture book with a non-human main character with which all children could identify. The children's reactions to the predicament of the duckling allowed them to acknowledge the effective role of illustrations in communicating emotions, in expressing points of view and in presenting an argument.

Visual representations convey reciprocal relationships

The annotated maps and detailed coloured pencil drawings in *My Place*, written by Nadia Wheatley and illustrated by Donna Rawlins (1987), introduced children to the complex reciprocity between people and places. The visual representations in this book made explicit links between people as makers of place, and places as makers of people. Several whole-class readings and discussions, as well as perusal of sections of this book by individual children, were required for children to explore the visual representations and to discover how they revealed the interdependence between people and places. The illustrations, maps and diagrams allowed the children to discover that 'the individual is not only influenced by but also influences the environment' (Matthews, 1992). The visual representations in each double-page summary of a decade in the history of the location demonstrate the connection between place, identity and cultural experience. Each apparently discrete illustration challenged the children to be

Figure 5.4 Child's view of the classroom from the ceiling.

conscious of the interaction between people and place within that decade and to recognise the human decisions which changed that place. The graphics in this book invited the children to identify how the changed place constrained or enabled the interactions and activities of the people living there. Further, the images of the arrival in this location of particular ethnic groups required the children to acknowledge the effects of specific cultural practices both on the place and on the people.

As children interpreted the visual representations of this book, they were able to trace the influence of one decade upon another. The diagrammatic representations clearly revealed the longer-term links between human decisions; their impact on the material aspect of place; and their consequent influence on the culture – that is, the sociological and ideological aspect of place. Choosing to read the book from the end to the beginning, i.e. backwards, from the time of white people coming to Australia until the bicentenary in 1988, impressed on several children that the current ecological and political aspects of place had not been inevitable but were the outcomes of human decision-making. The children noted that the detailed maps at the end of the book showing the location of factories, businesses and shops were in marked contrast with the open spaces of the earlier maps. The realistic colours of the illustrations enabled the children to identify how cultural groups imposed their knowledge and experience in the place, and how this impacted on others for hundreds of years later.

Children's competence in using visual research methods

I now describe the research constraints on the children's creation of visual representations of their school places. I then comment on the way children used their learning from the ethnographic workshops. Finally, I highlight the importance of visual research methodologies in allowing children to use their existing expertise and in enabling all children to participate.

Children create visual representations of their school places

At the conclusion of the preliminary workshops, those children who consented to participate in the research were invited to create individual visual compositions of the school places they liked. There were no limits on the number of artworks they could produce or restrictions on the media they could apply. The twenty-two participants created more than eighty artworks, experimenting with artistic techniques such as ink and water colour, collage and wax resist, as well as pastels, acrylic paints, felt-tipped pens and coloured pencils. Many of the children trialled different techniques they had learned during the year during the school-wide specialist visual arts programme. Some of their more detailed creations took several hours to complete. There was no proscription about the size of the artworks and children selected the size paper they decided would suit the subject, thus varying the sizes of their creations. Some of the larger artworks measured more than a metre in length and presented challenges for safe storage, while the smallest representations were the size of pages from exercise books.

While the artworks represented places children liked, the photographs could represent places children wanted to talk about as well as those they liked. Unlike the lack of restrictions on the individual artworks, there were three constraints imposed on the children's creation of photographic data because of the design of the research. First, they were required to work in small teams because of the limited number of digital cameras available. Had unrestricted class time been available, it may have been possible for each child to create individual photographic representations of her or his school places. Because this was not the case, children were asked to form self-selected teams of three or four to create their photographic images. The self-formation of research teams, while allowing the children some control over the way they worked by enabling them to choose with whom they conducted their research, presented some initial challenges. However, with the assistance of the class teacher, the selection of teams and collaborative interaction was soon established.

Second, I consciously restricted the number of photographs which could be produced by each team because I wanted the children to make deliberate selections of places they planned to represent prior to taking the photos. Rather than having children capture many places and then decide which ones were relevant, the research design required teams to re-examine the school's physical environment before agreeing on a list of the ten places they planned to photograph. Mindful of the advice of Pink (2001), that photos which are discarded are as important as those that are selected, I sought to make the process more manageable for the children as co-researchers and to have them make some decisions prior to creating their representations. In this way, in their analysis of the photographs the children could concentrate on the reasons for including places rather than needing to focus simultaneously on the reasons they discounted some photographs. Prior to receiving a digital camera, each team recorded their list of 'photo opportunities' and the name of the student who would photograph each place and stored it in their research team folder.

Third, I had asked the children not to photograph other children and adults in the school. As part of the workshops explaining this research project and the children's roles within it, I had taught them explicitly about the ethical issues of consent, confidentiality and the well-being of all children at the school. For these reasons, I had stipulated that children and adults were not to be included in the photographs of the school places. This restriction had not applied to their artworks. Rather, children had been encouraged to include other people in their visual compositions of the school places they liked.

Children apply their learning from the workshops

When creating their individual artworks, some of the children imitated the artistic techniques they had learned during the ethnographic research workshops.

Several children were so impressed with Baker's use of visual images to convey her message that they emulated her collage technique to represent dimensions of their school places. Like the illustrations in *Window* (Baker, 1991), children's collage was definite and used bold colours, thus conveying strong attachment to the depicted objects, as revealed in Figure 5.1. Such positive attachments by children to aspects of place were first documented by Hart (1997), and are sometimes known as affective geographies (Boler, 2002).

The illustrations in *Stickybeak* (Edwards & Wilson, 1998) influenced many children's visual representations of the places in the school, and they made explicit the perspectives of young children in the school setting. Figure 5.2 reveals that the young focus on the floor and lower part of the walls. This illustration captures the widespread cultural practice of bringing young children together on the mat for explicit teaching times and for sharing circles. It clearly communicates to the viewer that young children may spend large amounts of time looking at their teacher's legs and footwear and unable to see the teacher's face.

The visual representations in *My Place* (Wheatley & Rawlins, 1987) inspired several children who imitated the drawings in coloured pencil to show the reciprocity between the people and places. One of the children's drawings (see Figure 5.3) emulates the detailed style of Rawlins and includes the pattern of the carpet, as well as labels on the drawers and individual ceiling lights. Other children adapted Rawlins' maps to create diagrammatic representations of their places. These illustrations are examples of natural mapping, where children adopt 'a downward eye-in-the-sky perspective' (Matthews, 1992). Figure 5.4 reveals the artist's strong sense of connection with the classroom by including the children's work displayed on the walls as well as on the desks and on a line stretched across the room. This focus on children's work demonstrates the artist's identification with this place as a place of learning and thus emphasises the sociological aspect of place. The absence of the teacher's desk, chair or whiteboard suggests that the creator of this visual representation sees this as a children's place (Rasmussen, 2004) rather than one that is dominated by the teacher.

Children use existing expertise

Inviting children to use the range of classroom art materials to show places they liked allowed them to use some of the techniques and technologies with which they were familiar. At my primary school, the presentation of children's learning through visual art forms was encouraged by all classroom teachers, as well as being further developed by a specialist visual arts teacher. This research approach enabled children to use their considerable skills in visual communication. Other researchers have noted that visual compositions and other forms of art, a routine part of children's daily school experience, have been an under-utilised means of producing data with children (James et al., 1998). They acknowledge, too, children's ability to interpret visual images, to analyse critically their content and cultural meanings (Kress & Van Leeuwen, 1990; Van Leeuwen & Jewitt, 2001). While they may not verbalise their use of composition, setting, point of view and realism, children intuitively employ these techniques in their artistic creations and photographs. As Kress and van Leeuwen note: 'Children, very early on, and with very little help, develop a surprising ability to use elements of visual grammar' (Kress & Van Leeuwen, 1990, p. 18).

Others using visual research methods have broadened the notion of existing expertise from technical skill in creating data to include knowledge of the topic being researched. Wendy Ewald (1985), whose research required her to teach Appalachian children to use Polaroid cameras, considered children's awareness of their environment as their existing expertise. While she taught them the technical skills of photography, children already had the knowledge of their surroundings. In this way, she believed that her research built on children's current competence: 'Children can become eloquent in an unfamiliar medium if they are asked to tell us about what they know intimately and what crucially affects them' (Ewald, 1985, p. 118).

Children who participated in my research had extensive experience and ability in communicating through artwork, but had little practice with digital cameras. Like Ewald's image-makers, they had specific knowledge about their places and quickly became proficient with the new technology.

Inclusive methods

The use of visual images in this research was inclusive of all the children by enabling them to convey their understandings in forms other than oral and written text. It meant that words were not the favoured source of data. Drawings and photographs: '...can show characteristic attributes of people, objects and events that often elude even the most skilled wordsmiths' (Prosser, 1998). Visual representations facilitated the active engagement of students from non-English-speaking backgrounds, those who were deaf or hearing impaired, as well as those children who had communication/language disorders.

In her work with non-English-speaking migrant and refugee children, Christine Igoa (1995) found that by integrating verbal and visual texts, children were enabled to reflect on and share aspects of their cultures of which they were proud as well as provide insights into the reasons they left their home-lands. Similarly, I found that the creation of artworks enabled several of my research participants for whom English is not their first language to communicate their perceptions of their places in the school. The two particip-ants in my research who are hearing impaired and who communicate mainly through AUSLAN signing were confident in the use of art as a vehicle for sharing their feelings and preferences and were able to participate in this first research project. Figure 5.5 is an example of the artwork created by one of the hearing-impaired children, and clearly communicates his pleasure at being in his favourite place, with the play equipment. His use of bold colour, the demand for the viewer to enter into an imaginary relationship with the happy child and the inclusion of the swings, slippery dip and climbing bars on a frontal plane shows a strong affective connection with this place. The use of visual research methods allowed several other children who had difficulty in conveying their emotions and thoughts in verbal forms to fully participate in this project. The self-assurance of these children when using visual forms of expressing their ideas demonstrates that 'Images allow us to make kinds of statements that cannot be made by words' (Harper, 1998).

Summary

My explicit teaching of visual research methods enabled Year 4 and 5 students at my school to become co-researchers and to explore their school places.

Children participating in the research project described in this chapter used artworks and photographs to communicate information about their everyday

Figure 5.5 Child's representation of the playground.

school places, to reveal their specific perspectives of their experiences in these places and to demonstrate their reciprocal relationships with their school places. The visual representations became sources of data, challenging the viewer with their possible multiple meanings and interpretations (Pink, 2001; Prosser, 1998) and inviting the viewer to see something different in the familiar school places. The children's photographs and artworks thus created new ways of understanding aspects of everyday school life and generated opportunities for reconstructing school places.

The use of visual images allowed children to be co-researchers and to take greater control of the research processes because they selected the content and composition of their photographs. Further, the children selected and ordered the photographs for discussion. They used their photographic representations as catalysts for relating their knowledge of their school places. In the third project, the children analysed and interpreted the visual representations to determine what action they would take to change their places in the school. Finally, the visual images created by the children in the first research project were used to illustrate the need for change to other stakeholders during the third project. As a result of their presentations to the school's Governing Council, those places identified by the children as most needing change (toilets, the development of a vegetable garden, the entrance to the school and the pool) received priority in the budget for the following year. The children's visual representations realised their transformative potential by challenging adults to look at the school, its operations and the relationships between its members through the children's eyes.

References

Alderson, P. (2000). Children as researchers. In P. Christensen & A. James (Eds.), *Research with children. Perspectives and practices.* London: Falmer Press.

Baker, J. (1991). *Window.* London: Julia MacRae Books.

Ball, M. (1998). The visual availability of culture. In J. Prosser (Ed.), *Image based research.* London: Falmer Press.

Boler, M. (2002). *Creating space for the imagination. Youth writing their lives in the inner city.* Berkeley, CA: University of California.

Buckingham, D. (2000). *After the death of childhood.* Cambridge: Polity Press.

Chaplin, E. (1994). *Sociology and visual representation.* London: Routledge.

Edwards, H.,& Wilson, R. (1998). *Stickybeak.* Melbourne: Penguin.

Ewald, W. (1985). *Portraits and dreams. Photographs and stories by children of the Appalachians.* New York, NY: Writers and Readers Publishing.

Fielding, M. (2001). Students as radical agents of change. *Journal of Educational Change, 2*(2), 123–141.

Fisher, K. (2004). Revoicing classrooms: a special manifesto. *Forum, 46*(1), 36–38.

Gruenewald, D. (2003). The best of both worlds: a critical pedagogy of place. *Educational Researcher, 32*(4), 3–12.

Harper, D. (1998). On the authority of the image: visual methods at the crossroads. In N.K. Denzin & Y.S. Lincoln (Eds.), *Collecting and interpreting qualitative materials.* London: Sage Publications.

Hart, R. (1997). *Children's participation.* London: Earthscan

Igoa, C. (1995). *The inner world of the immigrant child.* Hillsdale, NJ: Lawrence Erlbaum Associates.

James, A., Jenks, C., & Prout, A. (1998). *Theorising childhood.* Cambridge: Polity Press.

Johnson, K. (1999). Reflections on collaborative research from the realms of practice. *Change: Transformations in Education, 2*(1), 12–24.

Karlsson, J. (2001). Doing visual research with school learners in South Africa. *Visual Sociology, 16*(2), 23–38.

Kress, G., & van Leeuwen, T. (1990). *Reading images.* Geelong, Victoria: Deakin University Press.

Matthews, M. (1992). *Making sense of place. Children's understandings of large-scale environments.* Hemel Hempstead: Harvester Wheatsheaf.

Pink, S. (2001). *Visual ethnography. Images, media and representation in research.* London: Sage Publications.

Prosser, J. (Ed.). (1998). *Image based research: a sourcebook for qualitative researchers.* London: Falmer Press.

Prout, A. (2001). Representing children: reflections on the children 5–16 programme. *Children and Society, 15*(3), 193–201.

Rasmussen, K. (2004). Places for children – children's places. *Childhood, 11*(2), 155–173.

Van Leeuwen, T., & Jewitt, C. (2001). *Handbook of visual analysis.* London: Sage Publications.

Wheatley, N., & Rawlins, D. (1987). *My place.* Melbourne: Collins Dove.

Chapter 6

Gender and being "bad"

Inner-city students' photographs

Marisol Clark-Ibáñez

Marisol Clark-Ibáñez studied the costs of being "bad" in an inner-city school in the US. Her goal was to address a gap in the literature: while there is currently considerable effort going into investigating the academic and social costs for "bad boys," there are few specific case studies about "bad girls." In this chapter she presents the findings of the study and discusses how utilizing photo-elicitation interview methodology enhanced her understandings of the students' experiences, gained through a school-based ethnography.

Introduction

The chapter has two goals. First, I will share findings about gender and the students who were labeled "bad" in an inner-city school. Second, I will illustrate how a project that began as ethnography became a meaningful project and garnered better data once I involved the students in a photo-elicitation interview project.

To elaborate upon the first goal, I compare the experiences of two fourth-graders, Dante and Pati, who were deemed the "bad" students in their classroom. Although there were numerous costs to "being bad" in school, I found that Pati, the bad girl, was worse off than Dante, the bad boy. Masculinity, in particular urban poor masculinity, seemed compatible with being bad in school. Boys in general were punished for breaking school rules, not for breaking gender norms. In contrast, Pati the "bad" girl was breaking school rules *and* diverging from expectations of femininity. Girls who get into trouble in school seem to have more to risk than do boys. The consequences of being a "bad" girl were harsher punishment, less academic support, and less reform or social help for her problems when compared to the "bad" boy.

This current study of students "being bad" originated from a larger school ethnography that compared classroom interactions on the basis of gender, language, and ability (Clark-Ibáñez, 2005). I had noticed specific gendered interactions that differed for the two students who experienced the most negative interactions from students and teacher. I wanted to comprehend the extent to which schools operate as gendered institutions. However, relying on one methodology, in this case ethnography, would have prevented me from deeply understanding the students' experiences.

For the second methodology, I conducted auto-driven photo-elicitation interviews, an approach that asks research participants to take photos and then requires the researcher to interview the participants about their images. PEI and ethnography are an ideal methodological match. In the summer after I completed my ethnography, I began a photo-elicitation project with the students who participated in my ethnography. Dante and Pati both participated. I felt that the lives of the children in my study were too complex to be understood through only their schooling experience (Clark-Ibáñez 2004). For the purposes of understanding the lived experiences of the "bad" students, it was essential to analyze their photographs and hear the way they understood their lives.

Gender and inequality in school

Gender and schooling continue to be a critical issue, but must be understood in a nuanced way. In particular, *gender inequality is experienced by both girls and boys but in different ways.*

In general, boys are faring poorly in school. Academically, boys perform less well than do girls in writing, reading, and mathematical reasoning (Smith & Wilhelm, 2002). Overall, according to results of the National Assessment of Educational Progress, low-scoring boys in 1998 scored lower than they did in 1992 (ibid.). When we specifically examine minority boys, the situation is grimmer. Boys of color have more negative interactions with teachers and schooling than white or Asian boys (Sadker & Sadker, 1994). African-American and Latino boys are subject to stereotypes and biases in school. African-American males are placed in special education at higher rates than all other students and are more likely to be suspended (Davis, 2001). In one study, 70 percent of African-American high-school boys reported that they were frequently suspended for minor offenses, such as wearing hats or lacking school supplies (Berry, 1994). Race can affect boys' learning (Smith & Wilhelm, 2002). In almost every category of academic failure, African-American boys are disproportionately represented (Davis, 2001).

One key to understanding their academic decline is that boys explicitly break school behavioral norms. Boys are much more likely to receive detention or punishment, or to be sent to the principal's office (Sadker & Sadker, 1994). One study found that 88 percent of suspensions involved boys (Meyenn & Parker, 2001). Discipline problems in schools most often concern boys, and they enact most of the violence in schools (Connell, 2000). Since a positive self-concept leads to students' success in school, punishment may have negative effects on boys' academic performance (Taylor, 1997). Also, using de-merits and sending students to the office reinforces a hierarchical system of power and threat rather than encouraging students to take responsibility for their own behavior (Meyenn & Parker, 2001). Dante, the "bad" boy in the present study, was an African-

American fourth-grader and had a very low socio-economic status. He received the most negative interactions (i.e., punishments, isolation, putdowns, and sent to the office) and was in the lowest academic ability group. Dante reflected the plight of boys who get into trouble, yet when compared to his female counterpart, he was privileged in significant ways.

Girls, in general, have made some gains in academics. Yet, I do not frame the boys' failure as girls' success, because this is not a zero-sum game and research continues to document the negative experiences of girls in the classroom. Girls receive less overall teacher attention and less specific feedback from teachers when compared to boys (AAUW, 1992; Garrahy, 2001; Lundenberg, 1997; Sadker & Sadker, 1994). Boys monopolize space in the classroom and dominate classroom discussion (Francis, 2000). Crawford and MacLeod (1990) find that gender-biased classroom interaction decreases females' confidence and intellectual achievements.

Research finds that girls of color have additional challenges in school. Latino and African-American girls leave high school at higher rates than white females do (Flores-González, 2002; Ginorio & Huston, 2000; US Department of Education, 2002; Vives, 2001). Pati, the "bad" girl featured in this study, was a Latina from a very poor family. Her sisters had already dropped out of school, and Pati, given her extremely low academic ability, may follow the same fate.

Gender and being "bad"

For the purposes of this chapter, I am concerned with young people specifically labeled as "bad" and how they fare in school. Anne Ferguson (2000) wrote an in-depth ethnography about bad boys where she explored the role of masculinity in both academic and behavioral consequences. She analyzed the intersections of power, agency, race, and gender among African-American young boys. She compared the identity construction of black masculinity for a group of fifth-grade "bad boys," who were constantly being sent to the office for detention, to "school boys," African-American male students who did not get into trouble. Ferguson found that being labeled as "bad" shaped the bad boys' "tough" identity and that saving face and peer support were crucial to acting out their bad boy status.

Her thought-provoking analysis helped me identify and better understand the "bad" versus "school" boys in my fieldwork. It left me wondering, where do the "bad girls" fit into the picture? How does the gender literature handle girls who are labeled "bad?"

Few studies explore the consequences for girls who act outside of traditional gender norms. Powerful gender dynamics are played out at school. Gender is embedded in the institutional arrangements through which a school system functions and organizes social practice and interpersonal interactions (Connell, 2000). Arnot (1982) finds that "gender codes" convey messages to students that are embedded in school processes that define "appropriate" models of masculinity and femininity. The school in the present study conveyed and enforced traditional gender roles; a gender code operated clearly and strongly. Of course, students adjust, negotiate, rebel against, or try to modify gender codes (Connell, 2000). When PEI shifted the focus from school to home and community, the students' predicaments and struggles become clearer.

Room 24: an inner-city classroom

Room 24, the inner-city classroom where I conducted this study, was in 89th Street Elementary, a large inner-city elementary school. The school had low standardized test scores, endured major scrutiny from the district for its teaching and testing practices, and had a majority of teachers of color, half of whom had emergency credentials. The student population consisted of 60 percent Latinos and 40 percent African-Americans, and 90 percent of the students at each school qualified for free or subsidized school breakfast and lunch.

The teacher of Room 24, Mrs Belle, was in her late twenties and African-American. She had an emergency credential for teaching and focused on performance and public speech in her classroom, which was her major in college. Mrs Belle had a loose classroom management style with significant "down time," and she experienced much criticism from the African-American female principal.

Identifying "bad" students

There were several ways I identified the "bad" students in the classroom. First, I analyzed over 450 pages of ethnographic fieldnotes that I wrote throughout the academic school year. Then, I systematically coded for negative interactions between teacher and student. Dante averaged six negative interactions per week, compared to an average of two for all the boys in the classroom. Pati experienced twelve negative interactions per week compared to an average of two for all the girls in the classroom. Second, "bad" girls or boys had little or no positive interaction with Mrs Belle. Third, they were in the lowest ability group. Fourth, they had no friends in the classroom.

Two students fit this description in Mrs Belle's class. Dante, African-American, had a small frame, bright eyes, and closely cropped hair. He was energetic and enjoyed doing back-flip somersaults. Although the school did not require a uniform, because of abject poverty Dante wore the same clothes every day: blue pants and white polo shirt.

Pati, a Latina, was chubby and her dark bobbed hair framed her round face. Her raspy voice could easily switch from Spanish to English. She liked bringing treats to school to share with others. There were signs that things were stressful at home for Pati, who came to school wearing skirts with hems that dragged on the floor and jackets hugely oversized.

The costs of being "bad"

While both students were "bad," they had extremely different experiences in the classroom with their teachers, peers, and adult staff members.

Dante: a talent for trouble and social interaction

Dante spent half of the fourth grade at his own desk facing away from the classroom activities, yet this did not stop him from speaking out. Dante spoke out an average of eight times per week – the weekly average for 89th Street boys was three.

Despite being permanently isolated, Dante frequently wandered round the classroom and chatted with students. He ignored most classroom rules, and Mrs Belle responded by trying to ignore his behavior as long as she could stand it. Dante's relationship with his teacher can be summed up in the following interaction I captured in my fieldnotes: "Dante says to Mrs Belle, 'I don't care about you, looking at me like I was crazy...' [turning to Sergio] 'Sergio! You need to comb up your hair!'" Dante knew that his teacher had problems with him, yet he remained defiant. In the next breath, he turned to another male student to tell him that his hair needed combing. My fieldnotes were peppered with rebellion and practicality infused with a rough kindness.

Dante broke the classroom rules with a flourish, as seen in this example from my fieldnotes:

> Dante goes to sharpen his pencil after standing up and throwing his chair back so that it crashes loudly onto the ground. Mrs Belle says sharply, "Excuse me? Do I need to put that away? [Meaning his chair] That's the second time you've sharpened your pencil without permission this morning."

Not only did Dante break the classroom rule of sharpening his pencil after "prepare for the day" period (first thing in the morning), but he did so by loudly throwing his chair down. Dante behaved in ways that would inevitably cause him to get yelled at.

The following are just some examples from my fieldnotes of Dante's classroom behavior: he

- made creaky and other types of noises, clashing his coins around on his desk
- made "sex" noises – high pitched and rocking in his chair back and forth
- loudly and monotonously hummed and yodeled
- loudly moved his lips and mouth and intentionally fell off his chair with a loud bang, and
- jammed a thumbtack into his thumb and bled.

Dante acknowledged his outcast status and did not allow himself to be alone in his conflict with the teacher. Dante enlisted the support of the principal, who allowed him to be in her office, vent his frustrations, and run errands for her. The following is an excerpt from my fieldnotes of Dante explaining to me what he does in Principal Springsteen's office:

> Dante, when his group was doing the poem "Lemonade," he came over by me and told me he didn't want to go [back to his group]. He wanted to go to Principal Springsteen's [office]. I asked him why. He says that he goes there and tells him all the bad things that happen in class. I asked him, "Like what?" He repeats, "All the bad things." He tells me that he was sent to Principal Springsteen's office yesterday. I asked him why. He explained that Salvador had his pencil and wouldn't give it back but Mrs Belle got mad at him. I asked him what bad thing happened today. He said, "Tommy's sitting in my seat. He brang his seat everywhere he went. Andy wouldn't let me sit in my seat."

This excerpt shows that Dante was able to get out of doing work without getting sanctioned by the teacher. He was skilled at engaging me, an adult volunteer in the classroom, to hear what he had to say. He revealed that he supplied the principal with information about his teacher and what happens in the classroom. Throughout the year, the principal and Dante formed an alliance against Mrs Belle. This relationship had pay-offs: with Dante's help, Principal Springsteen created a garden program that included several other boys from Mrs Belle's classroom.[1] Mid-year, Dante officially became the principal's "apprentice."

Pati: frustrated and victimized

Pati never was invited to participate in any official school program or informal interventions. Mrs Belle showed concern and extra sternness toward Pati because she thought that was what Pati needed to thrive. For example, one morning on her way to work, Mrs Belle spotted Pati walking to school in a black Lycra mini-dress. Mrs Belle pulled her car over and told Pati to go home and change, that she could not wear that dress to school and that she would excuse Pati for her tardiness. Mrs Belle made an effort to call on Pati.

However, Mrs Belle's relationship with Pati steadily disintegrated as the year progressed. By the end of the year, Pati was permanently "isolated" and frequently told Mrs Belle, "I hate you!" Pati told me several times that she "wanted to die" and slapped herself, muttering "I hate myself."[2]

Mrs Belle lost her battle for "reforming" Pati. The culmination and cost of this loss occurred at the end of the year when Pati was involved in an incident on the playground at lunch recess. Two of her male classmates and eight other boys from another fourth-grade classroom attacked Pati, kicked her, called her fat, and threw fruit at her.

Mr Lopez, the vice-principal, called in Pati and the boys who attacked her. As we all stood in the crowded office, Mr Lopez asked her to tap the shoulders of each of the boys who were involved in the incident. Crying, Pati stood in front of each boy and tapped his shoulder. Mr Lopez sent Pati back to class. I remained in the office and observed Mr Lopez punished them for the rule of "no fruit on the school yard" rather than the rules of not harming another student. Mrs Belle did not get involved in the incident in any way. Both adults inferred "You know how Pati is," intimating that she deserved what she got.

Pati did not conform to gender norms for girls – she was aggressive and fought with others – and this cost her support when she was the victim in this attack. She did fight, but it was against eight boys – hardly a fair fight. Pati found no advocate in the teacher or vice-principal because they felt that she had brought the attack onto herself.

In contrast to Pati's experiences, when Dante got into trouble the principal created programs for him, such as a principal's apprenticeship and a garden club. Pati experienced similar treatment by her teachers, administration, and fellow students. She was frequently excluded from participating in classroom activities punished by her teachers, and lacked allies in the classroom or school.

Being "bad" and learning

The "bad" status affected their learning in the classroom, but gender rendered learning unequal between Pati and Dante.

Dante: learning despite being bad

Dante, for example, would frequently ask for his own hand-made worksheet. His teacher was so glad that he wanted to participate instead of being a disturbance that she created individualized worksheets and assignments for him, or assigned the aide or myself to work with him one-on-one. I never observed Pati receiving this level of individual attention. Dante's rebellious behavior paid off. Adults gave him more attention, and he occasionally scored the rarest of rare rewards in a public school setting – individualized work.

Dante's occupational aspirations reflected his pragmatism by weighing various options. In his journal, he wrote:

> It is going to take hard work and I can do hardwork. I want to be When I grow up I wovnt to Be a polece and If I Don't Past I want to Be a cumstruchiworker I want to Be a cumstruchiworker Becus I Like to Beld and I want to Be a polece so I can stop Bad.

Dante wrote that he wanted to be either a police officer or a construction worker. He reasoned that if he does not pass the exams or schooling to become a police officer, he can work in construction because he likes to build things. At the bottom of his entry, he drew two pictures: one shows two people with shaded faces (no features) under a sign that says "police" and the other a picture of himself, smiling with a hardhat next to piles of wooden planks under a sign that says "cumstruchenworker."

In another journal entry, Dante wrote what he liked about school: "I Like Math and to play gams for math and I Like to spell I might geta A or B or C on my test. I Love to have E.S.L." Dante writes about loving most the academic subjects, such as math, spelling, and "English as a Second Language," that all 89th Street students do on a daily basis.[3] Other students in the 89th Street classroom put "recess" or "get ready for dismissal" periods as the things they like most about school. Underneath Dante's entry, he drew a boy sitting at a desk with letters on it, another with a boy sitting at a desk doing math, and a final one with two boys sitting at a desk with writing in front of them. All the figures in his drawings are smiling. When responding to the journal question, "What do you *not* like about school?" Dante wrote: "nuten," meaning he liked school.

Dante chose to resist his teacher and her classroom rules. He accumulated social capital to varying degrees of success. Social capital depends on the function of a particular group or network. It can be the use, by members of a group, of information, tools, ideas, or assistance found in within the network of that particular group. Social capital implies reciprocal relationships. For example, Valenzuela (1999) finds that the successful Mexican immigrant high-school students form clubs and friendship groups, where, for example, *Amiga* A helps *Amiga* B with math homework and *Amiga* B reciprocates by allowing *Amiga* A to use her family's computer for an upcoming paper. Thus, students accumulate social capital and convert it to socially valued resources, such as good grades (Valenzuela, 1999, p. 28). In this study, Dante was the most successful. He was ultimately not denied (or didn't deny himself) participation in learning. In contrast, the *lack* of social capital and the *isolation* from learning characterize the "bad girls."

In terms of her relationship to learning and the classroom, Pati missed opportunities for academic growth due to her isolation in the classroom. Pati, at the beginning of the year, was angry because she did not know her numbers or how to read. One morning, Pati threw her math book on the floor and said, *"No puedo. No sé nada. Ni sé mis numeros!"* ["I can't do it. I don't know anything. I don't even know my numbers!"] Pati's journal entries were indecipherable; she did not know how to write in Spanish or in English. By the end of the year, she was just plain angry. Pati tried to engage in learning, but the lack of Spanish support in the classroom impaired her efforts.

Pati: missing out on learning

Pati seemed to have a fairly positive attitude about school. However, she was not given the same opportunities to participate as Dante, the "bad boy." For example, Pati wrote in her journal, "a mi me usta mi maesetar Mrs [Belle] y me uta Ms Ibañez. Per a mi me tar mu mael Los niño. e me uta lere" ["I like my teacher Mrs Belle and I like Ms Ibáñez. But I don't like the kids. I like to read."]

Pati chose a strategy of accommodation *and* resistance to deal with her deviant status. Sometimes she participated in class activities, but most of the time she did not or was not allowed to by her teacher. Thus, as the "bad girl," she lost out on social capital that might be accumulated by working with peers.

Stopping my analysis at this point would have yielded interesting findings. However, after the school year was over I had the opportunity and found the funds to create a photo-elicitation interview project with the students. Pati and Dante both wanted to participate. My understanding of their lives was significantly deepened after they showed me their photographs and explained more about their lives.

Photo-elicitation interviews

Photo-elicitation interviews are an ideal way to engage children in the research process. Children lead the pace, set the linguistic level of communication, and do not surpass their cognitive development. The images in PEI can produce story-telling responses rather than a potentially intimidating "question-and-answer" approach. Photos can improve the interview experience with children by providing them with a clear, tangible prompt. In my experience with PEI, children become experts as they explain aspects of their life or community, thereby disrupting the power dynamics between adult/researcher and child/research participant.

In my study, I had the fourth-graders take pictures, with a disposable camera, of what was important to them. Many had never taken photographs, and none of the children had ever had their own camera. Their lack of experience did not affect the quality of the images, and they viewed it as an exciting project that placed them at the center.

It is important to note that some researchers choose to take photos themselves to use as prompts in the interview. I noted my tendency to capture images that, as an outsider, I found unique or beautiful (e.g., Domino's pizza deliveryman on a bicycle and a meat store mural with the *Virgen de Guadalupe*) but lacked meaning for the children in my study (Clark-Ibáñez, 2007). Clark (1999) reports that photographs captured and introduced content area which otherwise (from an adult viewpoint) might have been poorly understood (or even overlooked). Therefore, I chose the "auto-driven" technique where children generate the images.

Once a child completed the picture-taking process, I picked up her or his cameras and developed double-prints at the local drug store. I took the photographs to the child's house to discuss them. I tape-recorded the interview, which lasted from half an hour to two hours. Sometimes the child was alone, because parents were away working, and other times many family members were present for the interview. Dante's and Pati's mothers had given me permission to do the interviews in the afternoon before they came home from work.

A logistical issue to be aware of is obtaining permission from the parents for the child to participate. I recommend that PEI studies be conducted through an institutional affiliation, when possible, because photographs may represent additional intimacy that may require more recruitment negotiation than "words-alone" interviews. However, the novelty of taking pictures would also create excitement about participating in a PEI study. Because I had already conducted a year-long ethnography project with the students, it was relatively easy to obtain permission from the students' parents. Careful planning, coordination, and relationship-building will enhance a PEI study.

"Bad" students with cameras

Pati and Dante were among the first to take their photographs. The process of PEI and the resulting images helped me understand how school and home are connected. PEI provided an important entry to the children's home, and the photographs explored the contours of their personal environments.

Dante: friend and brother

Dante instructed me to not come into his apartment complex before calling him; he needed to come down and escort me. Indeed, as we traveled under the overgrown, dried bougainvillea that clung to the wire-mesh gate, several young men nodded at Dante. As we climbed the cement steps to his apartment, he explained that they were drug dealers who lived in the complex. Dante explained that they do not like strangers, and especially anyone who might look like a Child Protective Services social worker – at which he smiled and looked pointedly at me.

We entered the one-bedroom apartment where Dante, his mother, his six brothers and sisters, his oldest sister's two children, his aunt, and her two children lived. Dante introduced me to his neighbor named Esther, an older African-American woman, who gave Dante and his young kin snacks after school while the adults worked. Our interview, which took place at the family dinette, lasted about an hour. I was able to understand the crowded and at times noisy conditions that prevented Dante from being able to complete his homework.

His photos revealed that Dante was a leader in his apartment complex. Dante reported that he walked the younger children home every day from school. His images focused on his friends and play. While Dante lacked friends at school, he played with the children in the apartment complex. He explained photographs of

Figure 6.1 "Friends playing in the yard."

his friends, "Mooga and Desinay and Tee," and revealed that in one of the photographs they were playing with water balloons (Figure 6.1).

The swings represented past fun times. Dante explained, "We was swinging too high, when I swung off ... I fell off and it broke." They transformed other property near the complex for their play area. He explained, "This is the wash-house. This is the mat we always play wrestling or something on ... But we don't hurt people. We play a fake." Other photographs captured details of his apartment complex: red flowers, stairs, snack table, barbeque pit, and trees (Figure 6.2). Dante took pride in revealing aspects of his community.

His home life was filled with many interactions with various members of the apartment complex. Dante explained his photographs with statements such as, "[This is a photo of] Janelle Diaz. And she wanted to take a picture. She my friend. She walks to school with me" and "this is Carla Clayborn house." His astuteness at school for accessing help and support from adults was now better understood when he explained the various members of his community and their relationships to him.

Pati: from bad to worse

Pati waited for me outside of her yellow two-story house and had created a sculpture in honor of my visit that was composed of wildflowers and shards of colorful ceramic laid out in a circle. Her front yard had a rusted truck with

Figure 6.2 "Pretty red flowers."

several inches of dog excrement piled underneath that Pati said had formerly covered the entire yard; it was another task Pati completed for my arrival. We sat in her spacious living room and began the interview perched on the velvety edge of the sofa. The guard dog outside barked while puppies locked in an empty room upstairs whined, whimpered, and ran around. To me, this seemed like a contrast of relative tranquility compared to Dante's house. Yet, by the end of the interview, I came to understand the isolation and loneliness Pati felt.

Many of Pati's photographs were taken from inside her house or from her front yard. She did not specifically reveal any reasons that she would stay close to home, but this style of photography was found in most of the girls in the larger study and seemed to indicate a gender difference in play-space boundaries (Clark-Ibáñez, 2004). She captured her surroundings and the people in her neighborhood at a distance (Figure 6.3), which was unlike Dante's immediate and close up study of his apartment complex.

Pati lived with her mother, her fifteen-year-old sister, and her pregnant seventeen-year-old sister. Her father was incarcerated for murder. Pati's mother worked at a paint factory. By the end of the year, her mother was pregnant by her married boss, who Pati referred to as her step-dad in our interview. Her familial relations seemed quite strained. She revealed that her sisters hit her and picked on her. Her sister, Nina, took photos with her camera and Pati explained, "She was saying bad things to me and she was taking everything, pictures.

Figure 6.3 "Views of Pati's neighborhood from a removed perspective."

[pause] Not everything. She only took two pictures." Pati reported that her mother, who she describes as a "nice mother ... even though she yells at me," had little impact on the bullying that Pati endured from her sisters.

The most important finding about Pati regarded friendship. Recall, Pati and Dante did not have friends at school. However, in Dante's case the PEI project revealed a lively and intimate social life at home. In Pati's case, it was the opposite. In fact, the pain of fighting with her best friend along with other troubled friendships with neighborhood girls affected her so deeply, we had to stop the interview at the end of the two-hour session because Pati was sobbing about not having any friends.

The majority of photographs focused on Pati's friend Jessica, with whom she had recently fought, but the content of the interviews was about the serious problems Pati was having with other girls in the neighborhood. At the time Pati captured the images, Jessica and Pati seemed to have fun playing around with the camera, such as posing as models (Figure 6.4).

However, they were no longer friends. Lupe reported that "[Jessica] was calling me a lesbian ... she was telling me bad things." Apparently Nina, Pati's sister, told Pati, "[I told] all your friends that don't be your friends cause you're a lesbo." Then, Pati explained that another friend, Jennifer, "called me a lesbian and then that I was a psycho and that's when I got mad and ... [I] hit her." To make matters worse, Pati reported that a neighborhood girl, Martina, had "been

Figure 6.4 "Jessica's modeling pose."

telling Jennifer and another girl that I steal things from them." The cumulation of telling these experiences resulted in Pati's sobbing and expressing much grief.

We don't know whether these friendship crises were temporary or represented a longer-term situation of rejection and anger. However, what was abundantly clear was the severe and deep impact the loss of connection and friendship meant to Pati. We know from the classroom data that Pati is what researchers term a "rejected child." These are children who do not have friends in school, tend to be aggressive, are disruptive and inattentive in school, and are less socially skilled and less sociable than average (Wright, 1999, p. 113). Dante fitted this category as well, but his home and community life may have been his saving grace. Pati, in contrast, seemed to have no space where she could enjoy safe and positive friendships.

Peer rejection is correlated with children at risk – children who are not accepted and who have difficulty keeping or making friends (Parker & Asher, 1987). They are likely to develop social and emotional problems in the future (Wright, 1999, p. 116). In a study that followed children from eighth grade to age eighteen, 60 percent of rejected children had either dropped out of school, experienced school suspension, or had a police record compared to 35 percent of average students (Kupersmidt, De Rosier, & Patterson, 1990). Thus, Pati's lack of friendships at home and school indicate more serious problems in the future. In contrast, Dante's homelife may cushion him from potential effects based on the lack of friendships at school.

Discussion

As a group, the bad boys and bad girls could be at risk of being dropouts. Flores-González (2002) found that school "leavers" developed a street identity (rather than a school one) because of the "lack of social respect, prestige, and rewards [in school]; their inadequate performance of the student role; and absence of meaningful relationships" (p. 42). In the classroom context, both "bad" students in this study lacked positive interaction with their teachers and were rarely rewarded. Both were in the lowest ability group and struggled academically. In the school context, Pati and Dante lacked meaningful peer relationships; however, Dante had adult allies. As a whole, both students are vulnerable to the factors that lead to dropping out of school (Bowditch, 1993). Then, when we take into account Dante and Pati's home life through the PEI, we see that Dante has a richer social life than Pati does.

In the school context, Dante operated just within the boundaries of Mrs Belle's expected behavior for boys while Pati operated outside of her traditional gender norms and suffered the consequences. Although their teacher believed in gender equity, she also believed that boys and girls learn and behave differently. Mrs Belle felt that inner-city boys, as a group, were in crisis, and admitted that she had a tendency to focus on them more than her inner-city female charges. Given the teacher's beliefs, the resulting classroom dynamic was that the boys spoke out more often, teachers called on them more often, and they were punished more often than the girls. (I conducted cross-tabulations not shown in this chapter.) Overall, Mrs Belle paid more attention, whether positive or negative, to boys than to girls.

In general, the teacher treated boys as active participants and girls as passive audience members. Most of the girls in both classrooms responded to their teachers by acting "sweet": waiting for their turn to speak, quietly chatting with one another, working together, and helping each other. Boys actively shouted out answers, got individual attention from their teacher, and were asked to help female students with their answers. Thus, the gender code operating in the classroom reinforced very traditional gender roles.

Pati, like many of the high-school "leavers" in Flores-González's (2002) study, was not rewarded for her "street identity." Her tough attitude, talking back to adults, and proud posture resembled her classmate Dante's; in contrast to Dante's case, school personnel did not see Pati's street identity characteristics as an asset. Pati fought at school, but was also left out of the programs designed for the boys who got in trouble. Connecting Pati to other girls at school through programs may have greatly helped her. Instead, her intervention was a psychological, monthly one-on-one appointment with a school counselor rather than a social intervention.

Two additional circumstances, revealed through PEI, add to the complexity of Pati's experiences. First, Pati was open about expressing her inner turmoil and her low self-esteem. Her self-portrait (Figure 6.5) revealed a sad expression. I asked Pati what this photo was about, and she replied, "Picture of me." When I asked her about her expression, she glumly stated, "Sad." In contrast, when I asked Dante about his self-portrait (Figure 6.6), he said, "I took a picture of myself ... Hmm, it turned out pretty."

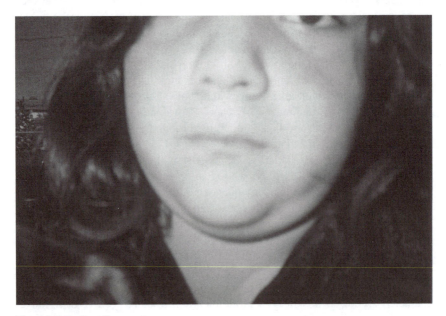

Figure 6.5 Pati's self-portrait.

Second, Pati was seen as perhaps even more deviant than Dante because her teacher held the image of Latinas as sweet, hard workers, and passive. Although Mrs Belle (African-American) fought to reform African-American girls' behavior, she felt that a typical black girl was angry and aggressive. From Mrs Belle's perspective, Pati operated outside of the realm of possibility for "how to be" a Latina student. Mrs Belle never directly called Latinas passive; however, 63 percent of her praise went to Latinas in her classroom for "sitting quietly." These different expectations point to a more complex and racially sensitive gender code than has been previously theorized.

Pati operated outside the boundaries of expectations for their racialized/ethnic-specific gender. She fought, talked back, spoke out, and ignored directions. She was an outlaw, violating the gender code of the classrooms, and as such endured the consequences – socially and academically. Dante operated within the boundaries of their gender roles – in particular, his gender roles as black, poor, urban young male. The schools were ready to respond and give more leeway to the boys enacting their "bad boy" identity, but showed themselves ill equipped and unwilling to support a "bad girl."

The case study of these students points to several important advances in understanding gender inequality in schools. Studies show that boys are punished more often than are girls; the classroom interactions analyzed in this study confirmed previous research. However, when we examine the experience of the boys and girls who are getting the most negative attention from their teachers, we see that "bad girls" have more to lose than do "bad boys." This study shows

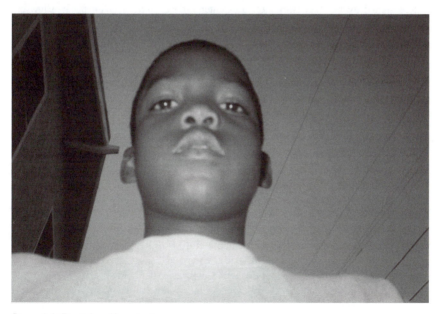

Figure 6.6 Dante's self-portrait.

that among these fourth-graders, gender and school context seem to make the difference and not the students' ethnicity or cultural background. Both students wanted to learn; however, the opportunity to learn and be part of the classroom seemed to depend on their deviant status, school context, and, most importantly, gender. The PEI's revealed that home life needed to be taken into account for trying to assist all students, boys and girls, who are labeled as "bad." Photo-elicitation interviews provided an ideal way to understand the ways in which children's social worlds outside of school helped or compounded experiences occurring at school.

Notes

1 Other programs were created for 89th Street students, such as the "recycling club" (the after-lunch garbage crew who worked with the janitors). Although none of these programs were explicitly for boys, they were the only ones invited to participate.
2 Concerned with the frequency of these comments, I reported Pati's self-abusive and self-loathing behavior to her teacher and the school counselor. The counselor made an effort to meet with Pati on a regular basis.
3 Native and non-native English speakers take English as a Second Language at 89th Street; staff felt it would enrich both groups' linguistic abilities.

References

AAUW. (1992). *How schools shortchange girls: the AAUW Report. A study of major findings on the girl and education.* Commissioned by AAUW Educational Foundation. Researched by the Wellesley College Center for Research on Women. Washington, DC: AAUW Educational Foundation.

Arnot, M. (1982). Male hegemony, social class, and women's education. *Journal of Education, 161*(1), 64–89.

Berry, S.R. (1994). *Instilling the thirst for knowledge. How to increase the academic performance of Afrikan American males.* Milwaukee, WI: Blackberry Creations Publishing Company.

Bowditch, C. (1993). Getting rid of troublemakers. High school disciplinary procedures and the production of dropouts. *Social Problems. 40*(4), 493–503.

Clark, C.D. (1999). The autodriven interview. A photographic viewfinder into children's experiences. *Visual Sociology, 14*, 39–50.

Clark-Ibáñez, M. (2004). Framing the social world with photo-elicitation interviews. *American Behavioral Scientist, 47*(12), 1507–1527.

Clark-Ibáñez, M. (2005). Making meaning of ability grouping in two urban schools. *International Review of Modern Sociology, 31*(1), 57–79.

Clark-Ibáñez, M. (2007). Inner-city children in sharper focus. Sociology of childhood and photo-elicitation interviews. In G. Stanczak (Ed.), *Visual Research Methods. Image, Society, and Representation* (pp. 167–196). Thousand Oaks, CA: Sage Publications.

Connell, R.W. (2000). *The men and the boys.* Cambridge: Polity Press.

Crawford, M. & MacLeod, M. (1990). Gender in the college classroom. An assessment of the "chilly climate" for women. *Sex Roles, 23*(n3–4): 101–122.

Davis, J.E. (2001). Transgressing the masculine: African American boys and the failure of schools. In W. Martino & B. Meyenn (Eds.), *What about the boys? Issues of masculinity in schools* (pp. 140–153). Buckingham: Open University Press.

Flores-González, N. (2002). *School kids/street kids. Identity development in Latino students.* New York, NY: Teachers College Press.

Francis, B. (2000). *Boys, girls and achievement. Addressing the classroom issues.* London: Routledge Press.

Ferguson, A.A. (2000). *Bad boys. Public school in the making of black masculinity.* Ann Arbor, MI: University of Michigan Press.

Garrahy, D.A. (2001). Three third-grade teachers' gender-related beliefs and behavior. *The Elementary School Journal, 102*(1), 81–94.

Ginorio, A., & Huston, M. (2000). *Sí Se Puede! Yes, we can: Latinas in school.* Washington, DC: American Association of University Women Educational Foundation.

Kupersmidt, J.B., De Rosier, M.E., & Patterson, C.P. (1995). Predicting disorder from peer social problems. In S.R. Asher & J.D. Coie (Eds.), *Peer rejection in childhood* (pp. 66–97). New York, NY: Cambridge University Press.

Lundenberg, M.A. (1997). You guys are over reacting: teaching prospective teachers about subtle gender bias. *Journal of Teacher Education, 48*(1), 55–61.

Meyenn, B., & Parker, J. (2001). Naughty boys at school. Perspective on boys and discipline. In W. Martino & B. Meyenn (Eds.), *What about the boys? Issues of masculinity in schools* (pp. 169–185). Buckingham: Open University Press.

Parker, J.G. & Asher, S.R. (1987). Peer relations and later personal adjustment. Are low-accepted children at risk? *Psychological Bulletin, 29*, 611–621.

Sadker, M., & Sadker, D. (1994). *Failing at fairness. How America's schools cheat girls.* New York, NY: Charles Scribner's Sons.

Smith, J.W., & Wilhelm, J.D. (2002). *"Reading don't fix no chevys". Literacy in the lives of young men.* Portsmouth, NH: Heinemann.

Taylor, G.R. (1997). *Curriculum strategies. Social skills intervention for young African American males.* Westport, CT: Praeger.

US Department of Education (2002). *The condition of education: 2000–2002* (available online at http://nces.ed.gov//programs/coe/).

Valenzuela, A. (1999). *Subtractive schooling: US–Mexican youth and the politics of caring.* New York, NY: SUNY Albany Press.

Vives, O. with K. McCray. (2001). Latina girls' high school drop-out rate highest in U.S. *NOW Times.* Fall.

Wright, D.E. (1999). *Personal relationships: an interdisciplinary approach.* Mountain View, CA: Mayfield Publishing.

Chapter 7

'Scrapbooks' as a resource in media research with young people

Sara Bragg and David Buckingham

Sara Bragg and David Buckingham conducted research into young people's responses to media portrayals of love, sex and relationships. Their research design featured scrapbooks (collages of cuttings, drawings and writings) which the young people kept. Bragg and Buckingham's reflexive stance is a helpful exemplar of the ways in which researchers must consider the limits of what they can 'see and say'.

This chapter explores the use of media 'scrapbooks' in research with young people. In the research project discussed here, participants created a mix of found-image collage and personal annotation or comment about their views of sexual media content. The article explains the evolution, rationale and implementation of the method, and comments on the form and content of the scrapbooks produced and how we approached the task of interpretation. It also describes how the method was subsequently adapted for classroom teaching, as a tool to promote reflective learning in sex and relationship education.

'Scrapbooks' in the context of research: aims and methodological issues

The visual research methods discussed in this article evolved in the context of a research project entitled 'Children, Media and Personal Relationships', directed by David Buckingham at the London Institute of Education in 2001–2003 (see Buckingham & Bragg, 2003, 2004). The research had quantitative elements, but was intended as primarily qualitative. It aimed to explore young people's responses to the portrayal of love, sex and relationships in the media, and thereby to intervene in public debates (or moral panics) about youth and sexual media.

Commentators on these issues too often assume that young people are passive victims of the media, and depict the media as corrupting their innocence by introducing them to sex too young, or as distorting their sexuality by commercialising it. In such debates young people's own perspectives are rarely heard, and the research hoped to amplify their voices and enable them to carry greater weight than they normally do. The research therefore needed to investigate young people's own understandings and perspectives, their media competences and practices of media consumption, and how they negotiated their way through an increasingly sexualised mainstream media culture. It took as its starting point a view of the media as more diverse and contradictory than public debate admits, serving therefore as one set of cultural resources amongst others on which young people could draw to learn about sex and relationships, to make sense of their lives and to construct their identities, including their gender and sexuality.

The research was commissioned and funded by a consortium of media regulators led by the Broadcasting Standards Commission. This meant that it needed to address the public service remit of these organisations and consider how to help develop young people's media coping strategies, in a contemporary context of deregulation where they can potentially access (perhaps more easily than in the past) sexual material deemed inappropriate for their age group. There were also a number of key ethical dilemmas raised specifically by working on both the topic and the age group: for instance, research should not introduce inappropriate sexual material, and it should not be intrusive. The research therefore needed to allow young people to find their own level of response and to have some control over what information they were prepared to share.

The methodology emerged in response to these aims and issues. We wanted to go beyond responses to surveys, which would be limited and address questions already identified by researchers rather than new ones raised by young people themselves. We also rejected the 'effects' agenda of much previous psychological research, which sought evidence of the media's (usually negative) effects on young people's values, attitudes or behaviour (Bragg & Buckingham, 2002). However, we did not want to rely only on interviews, which might provide limited access to the emotional and symbolic aspects of young people's experiences or their media-related modes of expression. David Buckingham's earlier research (see, for instance, Buckingham, 1993) had shown how group interviews often became dominated by interpersonal dynamics rather than the substantive issues in which we were particularly interested in this project. While this can be very interesting and revealing in itself, the challenge here was to find other visual or multi-modal methods, which could shift the balance away from the written or spoken word and provide a way to explore broader dimensions of young people's engagement with the media, as well as to put their voices and experiences at the centre of our concerns. Nonetheless, as we explain below, we are sceptical about some of the claims made about how far any approaches enable young people to 'speak for themselves', which is by no means a simple and direct process.

The eventual shape of the study involved working with 120 young people aged nine to seventeen (equal numbers of male and female participants), in two primary and two secondary schools in socio-economically contrasting areas. Participants were asked to complete the scrapbooks first, then interviewed in friendship pairs about them. This was followed by group interviews: a first round dealt with a two-hour video of extracts that we compiled and that participants had watched beforehand, and with advertisements that had been the subject of complaints to one of our funders, the Advertising Standards Agency. A second round of interviews with the twelve- and fourteen-year-olds only considered tabloid newspapers and teenage magazines. We also conducted focus groups with around sixty parents. This was followed by a survey of nearly 800 young people aged ten to fourteen, conducted in the same schools.

The idea of using scrapbooks – which we also called 'media diaries' – came from a number of sources. There is a growing literature on the use of visual media in sociological and anthropological research (Banks, 2001; Pink, 2001; Rose, 2006). However, given our backgrounds as media educators, recent school pedagogies – informed by Cultural Studies perspectives on media audiences – may have been equally relevant a factor (Buckingham, 2003; Buckingham & Sefton-Green, 1994). In studying the concept of 'audience' in Media Studies formal curricula, for example, students are encouraged to reflect on themselves as media audiences as well as studying others. This might involve logging their own media consumption or constructing 'media autobiographies', comparing these with others in the class, or developing surveys of friends and family members' media usage. The aim of this is to explore different research methods, to challenge easy assumptions about media 'effects' (which young people tend to attribute more easily to others than to themselves) and to achieve 'social self-understanding' – a socially located understanding of their own media consumption practices in the context of broader cultural and social relationships (Buckingham, 2003; Richards, 1998). In addition, there is a considerable body of research on young people's creative production, in both formal and informal settings, which suggests its potential in enabling 'identity work' and critical reflection, as well as more public forms of communication that have been seen as 'empowering' for young people (de Block & Buckingham, 2007, Chapter 7).

Media education practices had then already suggested the utility of approaches such as media diaries, and that they might be to some extent familiar to some of the older students with whom we were working. We hoped they might provide a different means for us as researchers to gain access to young people's perspectives and experiences, to achieve a more privileged 'inside' view than might be possible using other methods.

There were further reasons why they seemed to suit our purposes in this context. Some were *topic-specific*: in our culture, sex is popularly constructed and understood as a personal, private matter. The scrapbooks therefore enabled a more 'private' and individual form of communication than interviews, a form which would be less structured by their knowledge of (or guesswork about) us as researchers, could be carried out in their own time and allow young people to talk to us in ways they chose, about what they saw as important, relatively free from the peer pressure that a group task might involve. We hoped that the technique could also allow some access to responses that might be hard to articulate fully, especially where they dealt with emotions and the 'non-rational', or where participants lacked a fully developed vocabulary to discuss issues. However, the scrapbooks were intended not to be unduly personal or intrusive. The project was not about young people's own sex lives, and we rejected simplistic causal hypotheses about, for instance, the relation between certain forms of media con-

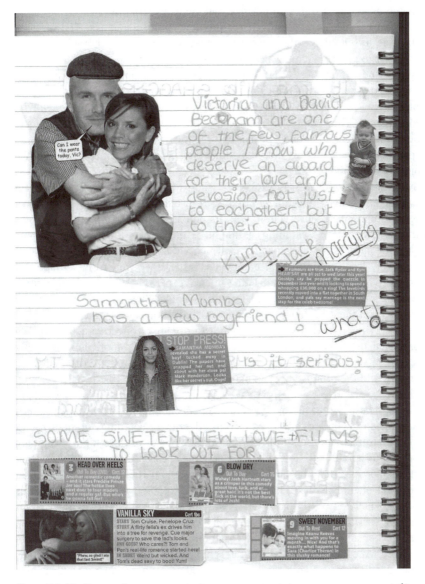

Figure 7.1 Hayley, twelve, uses magazine genre conventions to express empathy and involvement with celebrity relationships.

sumption and sexual activity, which might have necessitated gathering data on the latter. The idea of a media scrapbook meant the focus would be more clearly on young people's relation to the media than on personal revelations. Finally, we wanted young people to teach us, especially where we were not familiar with the media materials they might be encountering. The scrapbook meant they could include examples of advertisements, magazines, newspaper articles, and so on, allowing us to gain insights into their actual media experience.

There were also *project-related* reasons for using scrapbooks. The research took place in schools, as these were the most convenient site through which to reach a large group of young people. We did not want participants to produce only the kinds of responses that they thought would be appropriate in an academic context (such as, censorious ones). Although this remained an issue, as we explain below, we wanted to offer young people a range of ways to engage with media images. The scrapbooks potentially allowed them to play with ideas and different identities, to express pleasure in the media as well as to critique them, to produce both a record and reflection, thus bringing their voices into the project in more diverse ways.

Moreover, the project was a relatively short-term one, where we would meet young people only a few times. Funding restrictions meant it did not involve long-term participant observation, with its potential for deepening relationships with those we were researching, as might be the case in a more ethnographic project, or participatory approaches in which we could adapt our methods collaboratively in response to their comments. Instead, we worked in settings that were relatively unfamiliar for us, for intensive periods of a week at a time. Although we had contacted them through schools, they had to complete the 'tasks' we set them in their spare time, which also meant they had to do so on their own, as it would have been difficult to organise collective activities. We appreciated that there might be limits to young people's motivation in being involved in such a project (we relied primarily on the incentive of small cash payments and the promise of making their views known to 'the people who run the media'). The effect this might have on our methods became clearer when, in a piloting phase, we gave young people cameras and asked them to take photos of sexualised media around them, such as advertising hoardings on their routes around their neighbourhood, of their bedroom walls or of their family watching television at home. Although this approach has been used successfully in other contexts, here it did not produce worthwhile results; participants seemed unclear as to what pictures to take, and we were not available for them to clarify this with us. They may also have felt that such documenting of their lives for strangers was too intrusive. Since in any case we were interested in young people as consumers of media, it was as appropriate for them to reflect on found material as to create their own; and the scrapbook was a more familiar and thus 'safer' form. That is, whilst it could be used in longer-term projects, it also addressed the exigencies of our particular, short-term and focused aims.

Third, there were *age-related* reasons for using scrapbooks, which also addressed potential ethical dilemmas. The project aimed to elicit views from children as young as nine, to seventeen-year-olds, across a spectrum of academic achievement. It therefore had to enable them to participate at a range of levels. We stressed when we introduced the idea to participants that they should focus on the media that they regularly encounter in their own lives. In this way, we hoped that the content would reflect actual media usage rather than

Figure 7.2 Tania, ten, displays media literacy and knowingness about Britney Spears.

encourage young people deliberately to access more 'adult' material in a way that might cause concern to parents and teachers. We also hoped that the scrapbooks did not over-emphasise the need to be sophisticatedly literate or creative, since they involved cutting and pasting with annotations or drawings (see Figures 7.1–7.6).

The young people were recruited with the help of teachers in the schools we chose. Most volunteered after seeing a flyer distributed during tutor group time,

Figure 7.3 Todd, ten, evaluates media propriety.

no doubt attracted partly by the offer of cash; however, in some cases teachers actively encouraged particular students to be involved in order to make up numbers. Each young person had first to obtain parental consent for their involvement, and to sign a consent form themselves. Sara then visited schools to introduce the idea to participants and to answer initial questions, meeting them in their year groups (twelve young people at a time) and distributing the scrapbooks. We had, after much hunting and experimenting during the pilot phase, sourced an affordable blank, black-covered A4-size art book, which we hoped would be neither too gendered nor too intimidating in terms of the amount of pages provided. Participants were given a page of instructions that gave them some structure for the task. It asked them to keep the diary or scrapbook over a period of around a fortnight, in their own time, focusing on 'your views about how the media shows love, sex and relationships', and we gave a broad definition of the media. They were asked to include a page or so about themselves, their families, their media access and tastes. They were then to write either in the form of a daily account over about a week of 'anything that they saw in the media' that related to the theme of love, sex and relationships, or in general about their views, in both cases including relevant images where available.

They were also given assurances about privacy and confidentiality (although we should admit that we fell down on some of this; for instance, we said that we would ask their teachers not to look at them when they collected them for us, yet it turned out that some did nonetheless, provoking justified complaints). We then collected them from the schools to read before discussing them with their makers in pair interviews (with a nominated friend).

Outcomes from the scrapbooks: a range of 'voices'

From this initial outline of our approach, it should be clear that we ended up with a wealth of material. The most immediate use of the scrapbooks was to provide a stimulus or prompt for our first interview with the students. Having read them in advance, we were able to prepare a general set of questions about the process of making them, and some specific follow-up questions about elements we had found interesting, or to ask for clarification and further details. Even where some participants were unconfident about their opinions on sexual media, most were nonetheless able to complete a page about themselves, their families and their media preferences, which provided alternative starting points for the interviews. Unsurprisingly, in some cases, the voices that emerged through the scrapbooks were very different to those in interview – some wrote extensively in their scrapbooks but were shy in interviews, and vice versa. We would not claim that any version of the self our participants presented was more authentic than any other, but would instead see this as evidence that the methods gave us access to a wider range of voices than might have been obtained through interviews alone.

In considering how to interpret and read the scrapbooks, we explored their content, their form and their mode of address, or sense of audience. Some media obviously lend themselves better to the scrapbook idea than others. It worked well for print media such as magazines, advertisements, newspapers. It was less amenable to television, although many participants made creative use of listings magazines for images from soap operas, and in any case the programmes being discussed tended to be ones with which we were already familiar. It was less useful for films, music, computer games and the Internet, although some young people did download and print out images to illustrate all of these. Overall, however, it did give us a better impression of the kinds of texts young people were encountering in their daily lives. It also helped them communicate in a range of ways, not only in written form. For instance, some included their own drawings; the style of writing could also convey meaning, for instance in terms of what was highlighted, in capitals or in different colours. (One twelve-year-old girl wittily encapsulated her response to a 'sexy' image of the pop star Robbie Williams by placing an orange sticker with 'ugh' written on it over his groin area, and writing 'put it away!' next to it). The collage element of the task often conveyed rich and complex meanings: for instance, one fourteen-year-old girl cut out a teenage magazine picture of attractive young men headlined 'Lush Lads Ahoy!', and wrote underneath about her own dilemmas over having an older boyfriend, juxtaposing the celebratory approach of youth media and her more ambivalent feelings to add poignancy to each.

In analysing the voices that emerged, we had to take into account that such voices are multiple and shifting, shaped by how people are asked to speak, by whom, by what means, and in what context – which often involves a context of unequal power relations. People can occupy different identities or subject positions, according to these contexts. We therefore explored how voice was coded generically in the scrapbooks; that is, how our participants drew on the codes and conventions of forms (genres) that were familiar to them. We could identify a number of 'genres' through which young people responded to the task, which in turn gave us a sense of wider cultural repertoires and textual styles available to the young people who participated.

For instance, some students treated the scrapbooks as a school project, marked by the use of an 'essay-like' approach in which, for instance, they would address each of the concepts (love, sex and relationships) separately, as if it were an essay title they were 'breaking down' into its various components, as teachers often exhort students to do. Occasionally they would apologise for poor presentation or spelling, addressing us as disapproving teachers rather than friends. They also adopted the kind of tone they thought would be deemed appropriate – often one that was distant and moralistic, involving a language of 'critique' that mobilised media-negative concepts such as 'stereotyping' or the idea that 'sex sells'. For instance, Lori (fourteen) handed in a meticulous and well-presented book, writing at the end, 'well before I started this project I was really quite naïve as to how the media portrays love, I didn't really think about it at all', before going on to explain that she has now 'learnt a lot' and looks at the media in a far more 'critical' way. Rather than taking this account at face value, we read it as a prime example of the 'school genre', in its narrative of enlightenment and progress through study of a topic. Such responses may be the product of the implicit demands of the research and school context, rather than telling us about young people's everyday media experiences. They were often at odds with

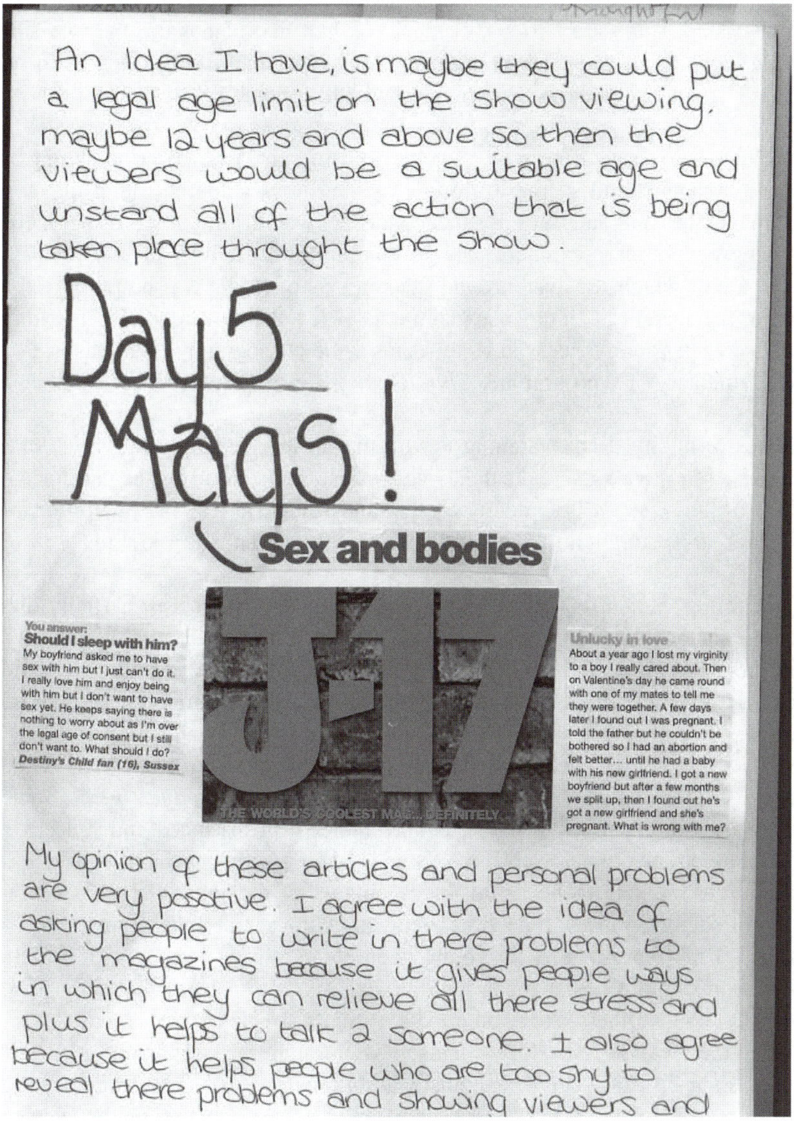

An Idea I have, is maybe they could put a legal age limit on the show viewing, maybe 12 years and above so then the viewers would be a suitable age and unstand all of the action that is being taken place throught the show.

Day 5

Mags!

Sex and bodies

J·17

You answer:
Should I sleep with him?
My boyfriend asked me to have sex with him but I just can't do it. I really love him and enjoy being with him but I don't want to have sex yet. He keeps saying there is nothing to worry about as I'm over the legal age of consent but I still don't want to. What should I do?
Destiny's Child fan (16), Sussex

Unlucky in love
About a year ago I lost my virginity to a boy I really cared about. Then on Valentine's day he came round with one of my mates to tell me they were together. A few days later I found out I was pregnant. I told the father but he couldn't be bothered so I had an abortion and felt better... until he had a baby with his new girlfriend. I got a new boyfriend but after a few months we split up, then I found out he's got a new girlfriend and she's pregnant. What is wrong with me?

My opinion of these articles and personal problems are very possitive. I agree with the idea of asking people to write in there problems to the magazines because it gives people ways in which they can relieve all there stress and plus it helps to talk a someone. I also agree because it helps people who are too shy to reveal there problems and showing viewers and

Figure 7.4 Kelly, fourteen, expresses enthusiasm for teenage magazines as sources of information about sex.

the more pleasurable engagements with the media that young people then described in interviews.

Glenn (sixteen) offered a variation on the 'school' voice, constructing well observed cameos of family viewing, in which he spoke as a researcher or anthropologist:

> Sitting in the living room watching Bad Girls with my mum, little brother and sister. There are two sex scenes ... when that comes on, the two siblings look away and start doing something else, one asking me a question involving music and the other playing with his phone.

A similar scenario was offered by a twelve-year-old girl, who described going to a local newsagents and seeing a group of young boys gathered round the 'top shelf' magazines and laughing. Both accounts showed the potential for positioning young people as researchers, and they anticipated our own interview questions, some of which revolved around the contexts of media consumption in the family or the social functions of sexual media. They also rewarded closer textual analysis. When Glenn discussed what seems to be pornography (and was in fact the 'documentary' TV programme *Club Reps*), for example, he wrote:

> Clips of nudity. I am watching it with my brother upstairs in my bedroom and he [dad] walks in and catches you watching it ... and teases you for the rest of the week ... I blame my brother and when dad tells the two little siblings that he caught him watching porn, they tease him and I join in.

The uncomfortable shifts between 'you' and 'I' have the effect of partially disavowing his own involvement, defending himself against both his family's teasing and the moral judgments made on the consumers of pornography, and thereby demonstrate the ambivalence attached to such consumption (see Figure 7.5).

At other times, young people used a 'fan' voice – for instance, Tania (ten), wrote on the cover of her notebook '*the media is heavy phat cool wicked fab brill!*'. Some voices were 'participative' in media culture rather than distanced and reflective, commenting emotively on celebrities ('Britney, who's gorgeous...'). Such voices are relatively unlikely to be heard in the context of the school, which 'disapproves' of such responses. Indeed, in some cases the scrapbooks appeared to be a 'return of the repressed', with young people gleefully using pages of topless models from tabloid newspapers such as *The Sun* as if aware that they were taboo in school. Others drew on media formats to play with identities; for instance, they would introduce themselves through the magazine interview format, listing favourite activities, music, ambitions and so on, as if they were a celebrity being quizzed. Krystal (fourteen) drew on the conventions of teenage magazines, constructing a layout of short 'soundbites' (often raising questions rather than providing answers: 'Why are girls mainly the softer sex?')

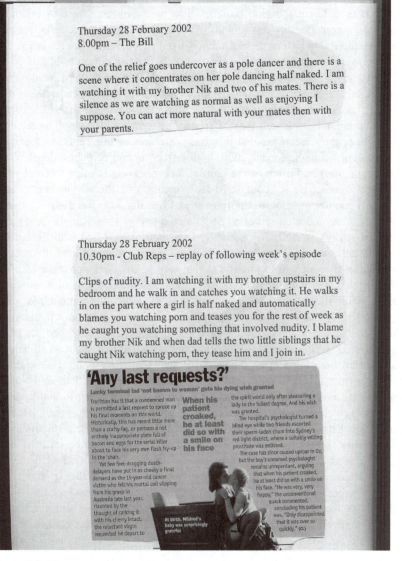

Thursday 28 February 2002
8.00pm – The Bill

One of the relief goes undercover as a pole dancer and there is a
scene where it concentrates on her pole dancing half naked. I am
watching it with my brother Nik and two of his mates. There is a
silence as we are watching as normal as well as enjoying I
suppose. You can act more natural with your mates then with
your parents.

Thursday 28 February 2002
10.30pm - Club Reps – replay of following week's episode

Clips of nudity. I am watching it with my brother upstairs in my
bedroom and he walk in and catches you watching it. He walks
in on the part where a girl is half naked and automatically
blames you watching porn and teases you for the rest of week as
he caught you watching something that involved nudity. I blame
my brother Nik and when dad tells the two little siblings that he
caught Nik watching porn, they tease him and I join in.

Figure 7.5 Glenn, sixteen, the anthropologist of family media consumption.

interspersed with icons of hearts and flowers and doodles, using colour to highlight key statements and a conversational, informal tone to capture 'how we
really talk'.

By engaging her friends in writing contributions, Krystal also demonstrated how
media texts can be used in group interactions, in social rather than solitary ways.

This 'youth magazine' style may have enabled her to explore a range of contradictory feelings and views without enforcing closure. Such media genres gave young people rather different speaking positions than the scholastic 'voice of critique', voices that were noticeably less moralistic and more self-conscious, reflective and open; they thereby helped us understand how the media act as a resource in identity construction and in thinking about issues such as the conduct of personal life.

We also identified 'child' and 'adult' voices, which were dialogic, responding to imagined interlocutors. Young people showed an acute awareness of the public debate about their relationship to sexual media, which shaped the narratives and presentations of self they offered in the scrapbooks (as well as in interviews). Since they are aware that they are positioned as innocent, as especially vulnerable, or as media-incompetent, both in the domain of public debate (and media regulation) and often in the family, their response is often to emphasise their knowingness, be it about sex or the media, and thereby to construct a (powerful) counter-position to the (powerless) one that is marked out for them. Thus they presented themselves as both 'media-savvy' (MacKeogh, 2001) and often 'sex-savvy' as well. For example, Lysa (ten) anticipated adult responses when she cut out a problem page to include in her scrapbook and announced emphatically 'I want you to know that the page below does not make me feel uncomfortable in any way, it's excellent!'. Others wrote in a tone of disgust and rejection about the sexual images around them, a 'childhood' approach to sexuality that Kehily has suggested might provide a refuge from more threatening 'adult' approaches (Kehily, 2002, p. 120). Ten-year-old Will merged the child and adult voice when he included in his scrapbook an article about an advertisement for Carlsberg lager using the model Helena Christenson, headlined 'Probably the sexiest advert in the world'. He wrote underneath it, 'I think I should know about it but not right now because I think I am too young to understand'. His reflective self-awareness, in which he comments on his own youth, but in a mature and distanced way, offered insights into young people's dilemmas in contemporary society. It suggests that the media may indeed be creating new ways of being a child – not that they are corrupting them, as critics argue, but that they are confronting young people with choices about whether to 'remain' a child or whether and when to enter into the 'adult' world of sexual media.

When, at the start of the project, we sought parental consent for young people's involvement, we were contacted by one parent who was concerned that there would be 'too much' emphasis on issues such as homosexuality. Whilst this was something we did want to explore, there were clearly sensitivities to be negotiated. It was therefore interesting to see not only how often lesbian and gay issues were raised by young people themselves, but also that many participants expressed avowedly 'liberal' positions – for instance, being critical of 'compulsory heterosexuality' in the media, vocally asserting support for gay rights, and enthusing about the liberal treatments of gay relationships in some drama and comedy. When even one of the younger participants, Tania (aged ten), included in her scrapbook a newspaper image showing two women lovers, and remarked approvingly of it that 'I think these two women who are lovers are OK to be in a newspaper because they are happy and if they're happy they're happy', she helped point us towards what could be seen as a genuine shift in codes of ethics, away from predetermined moral teachings to questions of self-determination, honesty, happiness and personal freedom.

The method therefore provided us with thought-provoking material on problematic issues, yet it was led by our contributors rather than by us.

Dilemmas in using scrapbooks in research

Although we would emphasise the potential richness of the scrapbook approach, it would be naïve to assume that young people simply used them (or indeed any visual media) as a means of self-expression or a way of 'making their voices heard'. They are not a neutral tool, but highly contingent. As our analysis makes clear, young people came to the task of making them with a history – of academic and media experience, of familiarity with different cultural forms and conventions – and different degrees of awareness of the institutional context of the research or of the audience for which they were writing. All these factors meant they produced recognisable 'genres' of response, rather than transparent or unmediated presentations of their viewpoints or experiences. (This is of course also true of interviews, where what participants say cannot be taken at face value as evidence of what they 'really' think or feel).

We have already discussed the influence of the school context on the shape many scrapbooks took. Describing the scrapbook as a 'diary' might also have had implications for how boys and girls responded to it. 'Diary' writing is a genre that has its own specific conventions; to the extent that the realm of feelings and the 'personal' mode of diary writing is coded as feminine, boys may have been more resistant to adopting it. Indeed, the girls' notebooks were on average longer in terms of page length than the boys, and more discursive. There may also have been a gender bias in access to media that lent themselves to the task, as boys were less likely to refer to magazines that contain the images and advertisements that proved such a rich resource for young women. We would argue that it is the nature of a research task, and how it is defined and presented, that has a significant bearing on outcomes, rather than those outcomes being the product of 'inherent' gender differences.

Additionally, qualitative research often claims an inherent moral dimension to its interest in subjectivity and personal narrative, in contrast to quantitative methods, which are seen to objectify by rendering the rich tapestry of human life as statistics. As we have seen, research with young people often claims also to 'empower' them by 'giving them a voice', as if this resolves difficult questions about the power relationships between researchers and researched. However, a more sceptical interpretation might focus on researchers' own 'will to truth' in seeking access to more private areas of young people's experience. Our own qualitative approaches might be seen as reproducing a trend that has been identified as taking place in the media and in neo-liberal societies. Anita Harris has remarked that the media 'regulate interiority', inviting the display of the self and experiences (Harris, 2004). Nikolas Rose and others have argued that under neo-liberalism, individuals are required to invent themselves as self-regulating and responsible individuals (Dean, 1999; Rose, 1999). To some extent, inviting our participants to produce a scrapbook might be read as disciplining them into current requirements for contemporary citizenship, regulating their interiority, with the scrapbook method as a technology serving to position young people as reflexive and 'opinionated' individuals, rather than enabling critique of such practices.

Finally, we were of course following our agenda rather than that of our participants. To some extent the project may have been self-selecting, in that young people who had no burning concerns about processes of sexualisation in the media may have opted not to be involved for that reason. And even amongst those who did participate, there were some who had to explain, in answer to our questions about their feelings in relation to sexual images, that they were not really that interested in 'stuff like that'. And in interpretation, it is again our concerns (and those of our funders) that shaped at least some of the focus points of our analysis and thus the versions of young people's 'voices' we present.

Scrapbooks in the context of teaching

A follow-on project to the research, 'Media Relate', worked with the English and Media Centre in London to produce teaching materials about the media, sex and relationships for use in schools with twelve- to fifteen-year-olds (see www.mediarelate.org), encouraging teachers to use media education approaches within teaching about Citizenship, and Sex and Relationship Education (Bragg, 2006). This project was mainly funded by the European Commission, so we also worked with partners in the Netherlands and Spain, although this aspect will not be discussed here. The teaching materials cover four modules about sex and relationships in different media forms: Research, Magazines, TV Drama, and Advertising. The modules were piloted as they were being developed, in a range of schools, mostly with Year 8 students aged twelve to thirteen.

The first unit, Research, draws on the idea of the scrapbook about their views on media images. Students are given instructions similar to those we had used in the research – that is, to explore the media they normally consumed for its depiction of love, sex and relationships, mostly as homework. The scrapbooks here, however, are much more explicit about positioning students as 'researchers', asking them to adopt an investigative approach. Media education has often had a particular awareness of identity in the classroom, which partly accounts for this mode of address (Buckingham, 2003). However, this also brings the practice closer to other 'students as researcher' projects, in which young people themselves have carried out research (Fielding & Bragg, 2003).

The dilemmas in using scrapbooks in this educational context are rather different from those that arose in the research project. Rather than seeking a snapshot of children's views, the pedagogic aim is to move them on, to enable different understandings of their existing positions, and to develop new perspectives and insights. Thus the task is accompanied by extension activities, in which students are asked to read each others' work and then use it as the basis of a fictional radio debate about teens and sex in the media. Thinking about their peers' work, hearing the views of an 'audience' on what they themselves had produced, and articulating both in different contexts, aims to 'decentre' their own thinking and help them view it critically and reflectively.

There were a number of reasons for using the scrapbooks again. The idea echoed what young people in the research had told us about their preferred self-image and learning mode. Participants had consistently presented themselves as autonomous, self-regulating and in control of their own quest for knowledge, in relation both to sex and sexual media material. They wanted to make judgments about what they did or didn't 'need to know', and often resisted or rejected parents' attempts to decide on their behalf. The media were preferred, as a source for learning about love, sex and relationships, above school sex education or parents, partly because they could fit this model of learning, partly because they often addressed them as knowledgable, mature and 'savvy', without predetermining outcomes or preaching to them. The challenge of our teaching approach was to address young people in the same way as do 'their' media texts, to extend and challenge rather than pre-judge or belittle students' existing knowledge of the media and of relationships.

In other words, we were also interested in good classroom control and relations, and the scrapbooks offered a more student-centred approach to learning. It did appear that the scrapbooks were popular – demonstrated not least by how willing students were to do the work outside class time – perhaps because they allowed children to take control of what they wrote about and how. Students commented, for instance, that they liked 'expressing their views' or that '[the scrapbooks are] really good because we get to write down our thoughts ... we can write about practically anything we want that's to do with love sex and relationships' (girl, twelve). Similarly, they were able to draw on the discourse of 'savvy': for instance, one girl aged twelve described her scrapbook as showing 'how much more we know about love, sex and relationships', presumably in contrast to ignorant earlier generations.

Equally important, from our point of view, was the response from teachers, who were 'pleasantly surprised' and even 'amazed' at the work students put into the scrapbooks, relating how diverse and challenging their ideas had been. They saw them as motivating for students, but from our point of view it was equally significant that they seemed to have helped teachers to understand more about the world their students inhabit outside school. It seems that many teachers, like adults generally, underestimate young people's existing critical faculties and their ability to highlight contradictions and inconsistencies in the media's treatment of sex: the scrapbooks may help to develop different kinds of classroom dialogue about such issues.

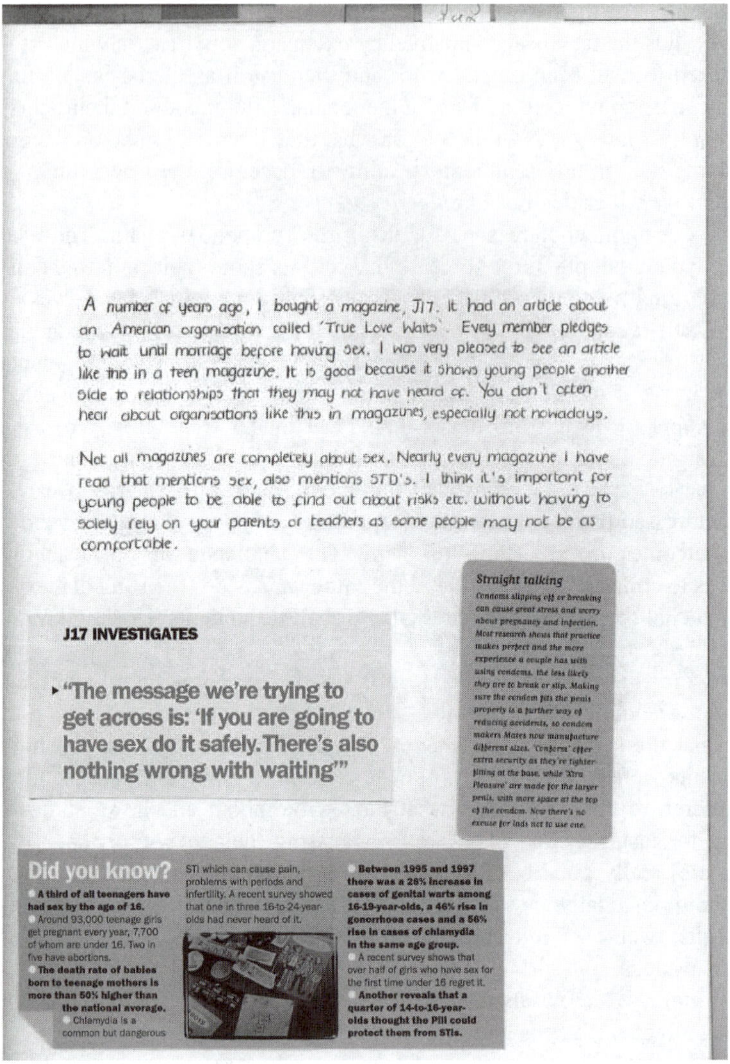

A number of years ago, I bought a magazine, J17. It had an article about an American organisation called 'True Love Waits'. Every member pledges to wait until marriage before having sex. I was very pleased to see an article like this in a teen magazine. It is good because it shows young people another side to relationships that they may not have heard of. You don't often hear about organisations like this in magazines, especially not nowadays.

Not all magazines are completely about sex. Nearly every magazine I have read that mentions sex, also mentions STD's. I think it's important for young people to be able to find out about risks etc. without having to solely rely on your parents or teachers as some people may not be as comfortable.

J17 INVESTIGATES

Straight talking

Condoms slipping off or breaking can cause great stress and worry about pregnancy and infection. Most research shows that practice makes perfect and the more experience a couple has with using condoms, the less likely they are to break or slip. Making sure the condom fits the penis properly is a further way of reducing accidents, so condom makers Mates now manufacture different sizes. 'Condoms' offer extra security as they're tighter-fitting at the base, while 'Xtra Pleasure' are made for the larger penis, with more space at the top of the condom. Now there's no excuse for lads not to use one.

▸ **"The message we're trying to get across is: 'If you are going to have sex do it safely. There's also nothing wrong with waiting'"**

Did you know?

● A third of all teenagers have had sex by the age of 16.
● Around 93,000 teenage girls get pregnant every year, 7,700 of whom are under 16. Two in five have abortions.
● The death rate of babies born to teenage mothers is more than 50% higher than the national average.
● Chlamydia is a common but dangerous STI which can cause pain, problems with periods and infertility. A recent survey showed that one in three 16-to-24-year-olds had never heard of it.

● Between 1995 and 1997 there was a 26% increase in cases of genital warts among 16-19-year-olds, a 46% rise in gonorrhoea cases and a 56% rise in cases of chlamydia in the same age group.
● A recent survey shows that over half of girls who have sex for the first time under 16 regret it. Another reveals that a quarter of 14-to-16-year-olds thought the Pill could protect them from STIs.

Figure 7.6 Lissa, sixteen, from a religious family background, emphasises teenage magazines' morality.

Conclusion

The scrapbooks gave us access to young people's perspectives in ways that other methods might not, and provided insights into how young people use and interpret the media that are often ignored or oversimplified in other research; they therefore helped us understand young people's relationship with the media more sympathetically as well as to respond to the public debates about these issues. However, we should avoid being naïve or sentimental about how far they do this. No data speak for themselves; we are never absolved of our responsibility to interpret, and we did so in dialogue with more analytical work that has suggested avenues for how we might read and understand the significance of the data we generated.

References

Banks, M. (2001). *Visual methods in social research*. London: Sage Publications.
Bragg, S. (2006). 'Having a real debate': using media as a resource in sex education. *Sex Education, 6*(4), 317–331.
Bragg, S., & Buckingham, D. (2002). *Young people and sexual content on television*. London: Broadcasting Standards Commission.
Buckingham, D. (1993). *Children talking television: the making of television literacy*. London: Falmer Press.
Buckingham, D. (2003). *Media education: literacy, learning and contemporary culture*. Cambridge: Polity Press.
Buckingham, D., & Bragg, S. (2003). *Children, media and personal relationships*, London: Advertising Standards Authority, British Board of Film Classification, BBC, Broadcasting Standards Commission, Independent Television Commission. Available online at www.mediarelate.org.
Buckingham, D., & Bragg, S. (2004). *Young people, sex and the media: the facts of life?* Basingstoke: Palgrave Macmillan.
Buckingham, D., & Sefton-Green, J. (1994). *Cultural studies goes to school*. London: Taylor and Francis Ltd.
de Block, L., & Buckingham, D. (2007). *Global children, global media: Migration, Media and Childhood*. Basingstoke: Palgrave.
Dean, M. (1999). *Governmentality: power and rule in modern society*. London: Sage Publications.
Fielding, M., & Bragg, S. (2003). *Students as researchers. Making a difference*. Cambridge: Pearson Publishing.
Harris, A. (2004). *Future girl. Young women in the twenty-first century*. London: Routledge.
Kehily, M.J. (2002). *Sexuality, gender and schooling. Shifting agendas in social learning*. London: Routledge Falmer.
MacKeogh, C. (2001). 'Taking account of the macro in the micro-politics of family viewing – generational strategies' *Sociological Research Online, 6*(1), U109-U126.
Pink, S. (2001). *Doing visual ethnography. Images, media and representation in Research*. London: Sage Publications.
Richards, C. (1998). *Teen spirits: music and identity in media education*. London: UCL Press.
Rose, G. (2006). *Visual methodologies. An introduction to the interpretation of visual materials* (2nd edn). London: Sage Publications.
Rose, N. (1999). *Governing the soul. The shaping of the private self* (2nd edn). London: Free Association Books.

Chapter 8

Using video diaries to investigate learner trajectories

Researching the 'unknown unknowns'

Andrew Noyes

This chapter focuses on the use of video diaries as part of research into the learning of mathematics. The researcher Andy Noyes, like Kaye Johnson in the second chapter, makes very explicit the processes he used in order to set up a video diary room. And, like Clark-Ibáñez in Chapter 6, he shows how this visual research method afforded access to children's experiences and opinions in ways that more conventional methods did not.

Introduction

Reports that say that something hasn't happened are always interesting to me, because as we know, there are known knowns; there are things we know we know. We also know there are known unknowns; that is to say we know there are some things we do not know. But there are also unknown unknowns – the ones we don't know we don't know.

(Donald Rumsfeld, February 2003)

This chapter explores the use of video diaries in my research. This technique, which I approached in a rather experimental way in the early stages of my doctoral fieldwork, proved to be highly influential in my investigation of the complexities of learning (mathematics) at the primary–secondary school interface. The reasons for its success were twofold. First, through its evocation of the ubiquitous visual diaries of reality television the children engaged enthusiastically with the process. Second, their self-presentation went beyond their well-established school behaviours and they spoke with disarming candour about school, friendship and families. So I was confronted by, and was then able subsequently to explore, previously 'unknown unknowns'. These unknown unknowns might be best understood as important findings (and leads) that could not have been inferred or guessed at from previous fieldwork. In hindsight such 'unknowns' appear less surprising, but at the time they opened up new areas of investigation. The diary approach engaged my sociological imagination in quite a different way from the other ethnographic methods that I was using in the case-study research. No doubt the visual nature of the recordings was central to this, although what I used most in the analyses were the audio transcripts from the entries. My research, which made use of Pierre Bourdieu's sociological tools (e.g. Bourdieu, 1977), was particularly focused upon understanding how children's dispositions, acquired largely in their families, were translated into school and classroom practices, so steering their academic trajectories (Noyes, 2006).

Research focusing only on classrooms has limited capacity to explore and explain why various groups of young people might respond differently to a subject like mathematics. I wanted to understand the mathematical learning trajectories of children moving from upper primary education into secondary schooling. From the outset of the study it was apparent that many of the data I wanted were not readily available in the classroom, or at least not in a clearly observable form. Moreover, semi-structured interviews with the young people were limited by the power differential between me and them. As a result of this research dilemma the idea of experimenting with video diaries was considered and implemented, although admittedly the power issues remained in some way. This was not a pre-planned strand of the empirical work but was a rather spontaneous development that turned out to have considerable impact on the research. The implications of this can be seen in the way the method developed over the period and in the ethical complexities of such methods, which have stirred considerable debate when this work has been presented in conferences. There is little discussion in the literature of this technique, and so it was very experimental, particularly in the diary-room form that I adopted (cf. Bloustein, 1998; Watling, 2001). Visual research methods have been the poor relation in social science research (Holliday, 2000; Prosser, 1998), and within that area video diaries make only a minor contribution.

Studies of school transfer indicate that mathematics is in the top two of 'least looked forward to' aspects of the move to the secondary school for all groups except high-attaining boys (Galton, Comber, & Pell, 2002). Despite this consistently negative view of the subject there is a huge range of attainment in the subject, and so the express aim of the research was to understand the structuring of these attainment and attitudinal differences. What was surprising about the use of video diaries was the way in which they began to surface what for me were these 'unknown unknowns' in these learners' lives and learning experiences. Some of these unknowns were evidenced in very small comments and short stories that the children would present to camera. These often unexpected moments helped to open up new avenues of further exploration that enriched the data collection and analysis. Such data were invaluable in the final analyses of learning trajectories.

In order to describe this video-diarying process further, I will make use of the case study data of one of the participants: Stacey. In the context of this volume the focus remains upon the methodology, and so I will reflect upon the affordances and constraints of this approach, the latter of which necessarily involved some discussion of the ethical peculiarities of this approach. But before presenting and discussing Stacey and her use of the video diary, I will briefly outline the process.

Getting started

There is increasing international interest in using video technology in education research; the Trends in International Maths and Science Study (TIMSS) video survey being one example. In many of these studies, video recordings of classroom interactions are used to enhance an existing methodology – namely observation. The possibilities for participant observation are expanded by the opportunity to record and replay learning contexts. As a result, analyses can be more extensive and complex; they can make use of video-capable qualitative data analysis software; they allow for collaborative analyses by many 'observers' and this can even occur on the internet.

Video diaries are a significantly different application of the technology (Noyes, 2004). They do not attempt to improve traditional observation techniques by increasing the possibility for more realistic and apparently reliable quantitative and qualitative data analyses. Due to their usage in 'reality' television, video diaries are very much a cultural phenomenon. However, despite their real appearance we are actually witnessing the interplay between actor and imaginary audience, and we do not really know the identity of either. Moreover, programme editors offer us, the viewer, a digest of the whole. So, despite the allure of reality, such diaries are an edited collage of improvisations which may bear little or no relation to anything real. Alternatively, they might present a fairly realistic account; the point is that we, the viewers, do not know. Those reality diaries are therefore, much more a Baudrillardian (2004) simulacrum. They offer some semblance or image of reality or truth, but we can have little confidence in the realities they offer. Similar questions regarding my use of video diaries have arisen, but there are some notable differences. As the editor, I have a privileged view and see the whole interplay between child and camera/audience. Furthermore, when the video diary data is compared with complementary ethnographic data the simulations of the diary room can be analysed as dispositional improvisations within my theoretical framework.

In an attempt to make use of this television parallel, my diary research utilised now outdated and bulky analogue recording equipment rather than the commonplace digital video cameras. That way I could have a large camera set-up in a dedicated 'diary room'. The six children with whom I was already working were very excited about this new development in the research, and immediately associated it with examples from popular TV programmes. The camera and tripod were initially set up in front of a large teacher's chair in an unused room. Over the course of the diary-making, the chair became a large bean bag in front of a large brightly coloured PE mat.

The diary room was available on one day of each week for a couple of months. The children were allowed to leave their classroom to make their entries at whatever time was appropriate. We had an agreed set of rules for using the camera, which had been discussed at the outset of this phase of the research. In this meeting we sat in the diary room together, in front of the camera, to discuss what we were going to do. First we explored the question 'what is a video diary?' In their responses it was immediately apparent that the six children had very clear but differing preconceptions of what this process might be about and how they intended using it:

TOBY: Well it's like when you talk to the camera and it's like your own diary.

EDWARD: It's like *Big Brother* cause that was like ... er ... they sort of always had a camera on you to see what you're doing and they're like taping your actions and stuff.

SONYA: It's like telling your diary to the cameras.

MARIE: It tells you about the people.

STACEY: Same as Marie but when you don't want to tell anyone else you can talk to the diary.

EDWARD: Like your own private video.

TOBY: That [*Big Brother*] isn't private though 'cause millions of people are watching on TV.

MATT: It's kind of a place where you can share your feelings.

The children agreed it could be used in two ways, either for the diarists to record something for themselves, or as a means for others to gain an understanding of the lives/situations of others. Either way, it should be used primarily for the individual to talk about him/herself rather than as a forum for talking about others, unless of course one needed to talk about others in order to describe one's own experiences, e.g. breakdown of friendships. It had the potential to be either very private or very public. The issue of recording privacy was seen as very important. The children wanted to know that the diary room was going to be located away from where they could be heard, then they could really say what they wanted. Although the chosen room was private, noise could be heard from adjacent classrooms and the children would often stop to explain to the camera what was going on next door.

Leading on from that initial question, I asked them what kinds of things they might say to a video diary. They agreed that their diary entries might include feelings, descriptions of what they had been doing, points of view and thoughts about other people. There appeared to be some initial disparity concerning audience, which is linked to their various notions of the public/private nature of the diary. During their work I also attempted to make my own diary, but found it very challenging. Despite knowing that the only person that was going to have access to my recording was me, I was acutely aware of feeling nervous and visible before the camera's gaze; I was being watched. The children were told that, as with the taped interviews, I would ensure that no-one that they knew would see the video but that I would watch them, sometimes with colleagues. They gave their consent to this but the extent to which this was truly 'informed' is debatable (Lindsay, 2000).

We proceeded to discuss what extra things they might, if they so chose, include in their diary to describe their experiences of learning and doing mathematics over the coming weeks. Apart from the groans of disappointment, there were some constructive suggestions which in themselves revealed very different kinds of understandings of mathematics. They agreed that they might include thoughts about having used mathematics out of school as well as in school. They also suggested that they could include their feelings about the mathematics that they were doing, or a test result that they had received. As they were keen to get started, we set up the room and they proceeded to make their first entries. In encouraging them to talk about mathematics I had in some sense directed their contributions, but they also talked about all kinds of things of which I had no prior knowledge. So it turned out to be a constraint or framework that offered the freedom for *entering* other data.

Analysing the diaries

There is a variety of approaches that have been employed for analysing video data. Some have used a grounded theory approach, where ideas for analysis are inspired by watching the video tapes themselves (Pirie, 1996). The analysis is only carried out from the videotapes; there is no transference to audio or transcriptions due to the significant data loss. I chose to construct logs of the diaries, with notes of what was taking place interspersed with verbatim sections at 'critical moments'. This was a time-intensive process, and there was a lot of seemingly superfluous material to work through. However, the 'pearls' that can be found scattered through material were well worth looking for. For some of the children the entries were very rich, with critical moments appearing densely throughout the video. For others there were periods of awkward silence, where my observations focus more on the body language and the nature of the comments immediately following these thinking spaces.

My own approach centred initially on what I considered to be the critical moments in each diary entry. One might call them 'critical incidents', and although the context in which I was using this phrase was somewhat different from that of Tripp (1993), the same process can be applied. Whilst my analysis was not primarily concerned with classroom learning, there existed lots of critical moments which, as in Tripp's writing, provided significant insights to the object of my enquiry. For him it was classroom learning; for me it was the analysis of learner's dispositions.

Following viewings of the videotape I made a note of critical moments in the entry. These critical incidents often followed a pause, when the child was not really sure what to say next. On some occasions, the children later informed me, they went into the diary room with pre-planned things to say, sometimes in response to the pre-agreed content/questions for the diary. It was after these contributions had been exhausted that some of the most interesting material was recorded.

When the two-month period was complete, the diary entries were edited and a single tape produced for each of the participants. I then watched each of these with the particular child. We agreed that in this reviewing process either of us would be allowed to stop the tape to make comments or to clarify/question. Perhaps unexpectedly, it was me that stopped the tape more often. The reviewing was one of the most useful aspects of the whole process, but it was time consuming and meant that the participants missed some lesson time.

Stacey

Now let me turn to Stacey. What I cannot do here is isolate the video diary data from the whole dataset, but the following should serve to exemplify some of the affordances of the process. There is a great deal that could be written about Stacey, and so I will focus here on data that arose directly from the video-diary process and how this contributed to the broader understanding of her learning trajectory. What there is not space to do here is to offer more detailed analyses or theorisation of the data. Rather, I want to demonstrate what is added by the method.

Stacey's mathematical attainment was amongst the lowest in the group but, in contrast to her relative academic ability, she proved to be very capable of reflecting upon her personal and social circumstances, being able to articulate her thoughts and feelings clearly, although sometimes with muddled speech. Her style of speech, being unsophisticated in comparison to the other children, regularly contained spoken errors and a relatively low level of linguistic capital. At one point she tells her diary 'I don't know if I'm saying this right' and later explains:

> well people come up to me and say like erm 'could you say that again' cause I always come up with jumbled up words … I don't know what I'm saying at the time really.

Stacey lived at home with her mum and older sister, not far from the school in a small semi-detached house. She often spoke in her diary of her relationship to her older sister, usually in negative terms, describing what Laura had said or done to her. The impact on her mathematical development and developing attitudes to school and learning can be seen in a number of places. In her first video diary entry Stacey made it clear what she thought about, or what she wanted me to think she thought about, mathematics:

STACEY'S DIARY: Maths … I hate it! I hate it! I hate it! Three things about maths … boring, boring, boring!
[Follow-up interview]
ANDY: Would you like to explain a bit about that?
STACEY: I don't like maths cause it's hard.
ANDY: Could you be more specific?
STACEY: Well I can't really time that well … my sister calls me a dumb-ass. Excuse me.

ANDY: Is your sister good at maths?
STACEY: I don't know, she doesn't go to school ever.
ANDY: How old is she?
STACEY: Sixteen.
ANDY: What year is she in?
STACEY: Er ... year 10 or 11.
ANDY: So she just doesn't go to school?
STACEY: Well she does sometimes ... it depends whether my mum makes her.
ANDY: What does she do when she doesn't go to school?
STACEY: She hangs around with her friends.
ANDY: Who are they?
STACEY: Tammy Watson, but they ran away twice so they are not allowed to make contact with each other so Laura's getting mardy and she pretends to be ill.

The move to talking about her sister effectively shifted my attention away from mathematics through her admission that her sister calls her a 'dumb-ass'. Stacey was generally not comfortable talking about her mathematics learning, partly due to what mathematics made her feel like. Here again, the influence of the older sister is apparent:

STACEY'S DIARY: The thing that makes maths hard for me is that I don't think I'm really good at it ... erm ... I have to say this prufully, I mean trufully ... erm ... I know what everyone's thinking, that ... I'm the dumbest kid in the class, and, me and Sonya really need desperate help. I'm not saying that she's bad or anything but me and Sonya need really desperate help.
[Follow-up interview]
ANDY: Do you really think that everybody thinks you're 'the dumbest kid in the class'? *(Stacey nods)* How do you know that?
STACEY: Because every time I put my hand up I normally like, roughly get it wrong.
ANDY: But you do get some things right don't you? [Stacey shrugs] Do you still think that Mrs Clarkson doesn't like you?
STACEY: She didn't like my sister as well. She kept on shouting at my sister and everything.
ANDY: She doesn't shout at you though does she?
STACEY: Well not roughly. She kind of like shouts a bit then after I've done my spelling test she goes [*in teacher voice*] 'I just want the best for you'.
ANDY: Do you think that she does want the best for you?
STACEY: No.
ANDY: What do you think that she does want then?
STACEY: Erm to be like Matt cause everyone thinks that like Matt's the teacher's pet. [*pause*] My sister says that I might have to go to a school that helps people that like need help but I'm scared of that. Don't know why I'm telling you that.

ANDY: I would think that you are scared of that. Did she say where you would go?

STACEY: No she said like this school where all the dumb kids have to go and you never see your mum or dad again.

Stacey's video entries are full of pathos, and colleagues have found her accounts deeply moving. She did often 'roughly get it wrong' in lessons that I observed, and although she didn't appear to mind much in the classroom, it was a cause of anxiety, confirming her self-designation as 'the dumbest kid in the class'. Here Stacey is subject to her own and others' classifying work, and there is a certain amount of emotional violence to this process. She evidently felt that she would not be able to please the teacher if she could not become like Matt, and her mocking use of the teacher's voice adds further weight to her feeling that her best was not good enough. Stacey's profound understanding of how teacher rhetoric can disguise subtle forms of favouritism reveals her sense of how the school system is unjust. She knows that schools value highly and reward children like Matt, and she also knows that despite her best efforts she cannot be like him. Even in the normal interactions of the Year 6 classroom, the teacher's subtle messages give children a clear idea of their relative position in the group. So Stacey reveals how the teacher uses language to strengthen the children's intellectual, and therefore cultural and social positions, within the group.

Stacey not only talks about her sister in the diary entries, but also offers plenty of insights into how her family works:

STACEY'S DIARY: I haven't been getting on with my family very well. My Mum's divorced from my Dad. I see him every Sunday. My Mum is getting remarried. She's engaged now...

And on another occasion she explains how she deals with being a ten-year-old 'home alone':

STACEY'S DIARY: Last night when my mum was at work, my sister had gone out to the shops. About five minutes and the insurance man came and he said 'Can I speak to your mum please?' I thought 'Oh no! What am I going to do?', so I just said, well, my mum told me to say, 'She's in the bath'. He came back half an hour later and said 'Is your mum out of the bath?' and I said 'I'm sorry. I'm sorry my Mum's still at work lah di dah di dah' and I'm thinking 'Where has my sister gone?' and then she phoned up after he came saying 'I'm at Sophie's' – her friend – and then he came back again saying is your Mum not back yet. She finished work at 5 and she actually came home at 10 past 6.

Understanding how parental roles impact upon classroom learning is important, as some modes of help are more supportive of the young person's progress in school. What is noteworthy here is that these kinds of stories of everyday class lives seem to surface far more freely in this kind of medium than through interview conversations. Other descriptions of her relationship with her mother reveal something of the kind of support she gets with her schoolwork (which is not a great deal) and help to explain the general feeling of isolation and vulnerability that she expresses.

STACEY'S DIARY: my friends ... my friends at school ... I do have problems making them ... I roughly in the whole school have two friends ... Francesca and Sophie but she does hurt me sometimes.

All of this would help to explain why she repeatedly apologises to the camera with phrases like, 'I don't know why I'm telling you this', and 'I bet I'm boring you'. But who is this 'you' that she is addressing? In Stacey's case it is the researcher, i.e. me, the person taking a very real interest in her, that had become the person 'behind the camera'. At times, such a 'behind the scenes' understanding was quite literally what she envisaged. On one occasion I had to enter the diary room to call time on her (she had started to produce long meandering entries, as she knew that she could miss more lesson time), and on viewing the videotape I saw her apparent confusion:

STACEY'S DIARY: [*I leave the room. Stacey pauses and turns to the camera*]. How come you can be in two places? If you're watching that ... and you just came in there ... ugh ... whoa.

This suggests that at that time she thought the camera was being watched live. This view was not repeated amongst the other participants. Later I questioned Stacey about this episode, and her unconvincing explanation was that she was merely joking. Her view of the camera was not consistent; sometimes she is very definitely talking to me, on other occasions she is addressing a third person ('why am I talking to this camera? It's going to be shown to Mr Noyes'), and at other times she appears to have a non-personal audience. Later in the project she described how the camera was like a friend to her, 'the only one I can talk to'. The camera had become for her a listening ear, a counsellor, a confessional that she could come to and speak candidly about her emotions, relationships and so on. Her diary entries are extremely rich data sources, partly as a result of her high level of self-awareness and reflection. They include data that I could not have accessed through interviews, and in addition layer visual images on top of these narratives. Often her throw-away remarks triggered lengthy unstructured interview sections that explored her own attitudes and dispositions and the very real ways in which they related to her experiences amongst her peer group and in the family.

Working with the video diary data

So the audio data are interesting by themselves, as the diary process produces data that probably would not be available to the researcher in other ways. The surfacing of these *unknown unknowns* was the main contribution made by the diarying process to the wider study that included data triangulation from interviews and observational field work. The diary data are rich, and could be analysed and interpreted in a range of ways and using various theoretical frameworks. Whilst watching the diaries with the children, many of their concerns were about image, style and mannerism rather than about their speech content. They were able to see themselves as others could see them. Although I too made use of such visual data, in the same way that teachers in the secondary school would do when they arrived (Noyes, 2003), these data were already available through other fieldwork. However, their reactions to seeing their diaries indicated something of their sense of self, which was useful.

In the video diaries the children initially adopted something akin to a television personality which reflected how they wanted to be seen on 'film'. In the same way that they might position themselves for photographs, these children adopted postures, mannerisms and language that communicate to the viewer something about status, self-belief, and so on. For example, Stacey (see entry above) befriended the camera, whereas Matt responded quite differently:

MATT'S DIARY: [*approx. 2 minutes into interview*] ... as it is my first day of the diary I find it really good today ... [*pause for effect*] ... to get to know ... YOU [*points, stares and grins proudly at the camera*] ... because ... first time I've been in front of a camera ... don't feel bad ... [*grins*] ... feel good ... feel famous. [*satisfied giggle*]

Whether one can draw any conclusions from the varied types of child–camera relationships or not, the point that needs to be borne in mind is the way in which the child's conscious or subconscious choice of relationship establishes a unique filtering, transforming effect upon their entries. One might try to categorise the children's camera identities (e.g. audience, confidant, counsellor, friend, researcher, etc.), but in doing so it must be acknowledged that such interpretations are not fixed but may change, not only from entry to entry but within single sessions. There is a sense in which these children feel free to move between camera roles without contradiction, but their predominant choices are not arbitrary and so form part of the analysis.

Over the first few weeks the child–camera dynamic settled down so that they presented themselves in ways more typical of their behaviours elsewhere. This does not render this early evidence useless, but rather provides a range of data. For example, the contrast between Matt and Stacey is very much related to their feelings of self-worth and academic success. Initially the new context allows the freedom to improvise and so alternative dispositions might be 'seen' more clearly than later in the diary, or in the more structured classroom environment.

Careful consideration of potentially distorting effects of the early tendency towards performance is necessary. However, there remains coherence in each child's diverse performances, and the range (of simulations) tells a better story.

The video-diary approach allows researchers to hand over some of the responsibility for data collection to research participants. This need not necessarily be in the kinds of static diary rooms seen on reality TV shows, although such a format does have clear practical advantages. In contrast to some video-diary formats in popular culture there was no interactivity in my diary room, and on occasions I was asked by the children to provide some prompts to help structure entries. However, they really only needed such prompts to get them started, and it was the following improvised and individually initiated content that made the method unusual and appealing.

Bloustein (1998) used video diaries with teenage girls in Australia; a number of important effects are paralleled in the two studies, and are worth mentioning at this stage. One of these relates to the diverse ways in which children assumed, and then developed, their relationship with the camera, and how this framed their diary accounts. For some the camera was like a best friend or confidant, whereas for others it was a very public window to a watching world. What was less clear was how the researcher was included in this complex of imagined, simulated and/or actual relationships, and a good example of this is seen in Stacey's entries. A second parallel in the two studies is the way in which improvised entries generate spontaneous and pre-reflective insights into life contexts ('unknown unknowns'). Often the children in my research began their diary entries with a short, pre-prepared speech. This covered the things they wanted and/or thought they ought to say, and then, often after an awkward pause, they would simply blurt out the things that were on their minds; concerns worries, stories from their families and friendships, etc. It was these entries that offered the most intriguing insights into their current life experience. Many of these diary entries referred to aspects of their day-to-day lives that I had no way of knowing about, and so to which I had no easy means of access.

Ethical issues

My own experience of the video-diary process was as part of my doctoral study, and although I had considered some of the ethical implications there are still some grey areas. As a researcher interested in the methodology, one of the most useful means of talking about the process has been to use the data in conferences presentations. These presented diary accounts, which have become more like the reality TV simulations, enable the children to speak for themselves, although this is mediated by my editing power as the controlling researcher. We did not get to the stage of the children compiling their own diary accounts for public viewing, so issues of ownership and informed consent are problematic. Although such informed consent was given, Lindsay (2000) has pointed out that such a concept is questionable. How should these ten-year-olds make sense of my request to present their video diary material to the assembled international mathematics educators at a conference half-way around the world? Of course they were all quite happy to consent, and they had been informed, but understanding the implications of this is not straightforward. And then, what should the 'shelf life' of this data be? Published textual accounts of research that include anonymised data of young people are permanently in the public domain, but are visual images different? Do such data age more quickly? In order to address some of these ethical concerns, all video data were retained and not made publicly available for re-use. All of the research was conducted within the British Educational Research Association ethical guidelines, but that document does not deal with some of the issues of visual methodologies very well.

Final comments

At the outset of this chapter I highlighted two aspects of this approach that contribute to its success: the echoing of reality TV formats, which helps to motivate and engage participants, and the surfacing of 'unknown unknowns' which can subsequently be explored. Despite the visualising potential of the video-diary process, the main purpose was to offer an environment in which children could initiate data collection. I have not made extensive use of the visual dimension of the diaries, and arguably such analysis was unnecessary in the context of the wider study.

Video research is a poor relation in the social science arena, and there is little agreement on accepted qualitative analysis techniques (Pirie, 1996). Prosser laments this state of affairs, writing that:

> The general message, perhaps unwittingly, is that: films, videos and photographs are acceptable only as a means to record data or as illustration and subservient to that of the central narrative: they are an unacceptable way of 'knowing' because they distort that which they claim to illuminate; and images being socially created and mediated are skewed by the socio-context of 'making', 'talking' and 'reading'; and summatively images are so complex that analysis is untenable.
>
> (Prosser, 1998, p. 98)

I am in full agreement with him here; the argument that the analysis of such data is 'untenable' is significantly flawed. Admittedly, extensive analysis of the diaries is non-trivial and time-intensive, but they do help to surface these 'unknowns unknowns'. The data are only complex in that they offer a fuller representation of experience and in some ways are more in the hands of the participant than the researcher. With this increased complexity in the data, so the challenge of recording, analysis and interpretation are magnified. My broader aim of understanding the social structuring of the individual's learning dispositions and trajectories makes use of the looks, facial expressions, body language, body shape, clothing, and so on. The diary entries have much to offer here, and although it could be argued that such data could be gathered during normal classroom observation, the diaries enable the researcher to look in a very focused way at one individual. In Stacey's case, for example, she was incessantly fiddling with her jumper sleeve, and when asked about it she explained:

STACEY: . . . it's because its like ten years old.
ANDY: Was it your sister's as well?
STACEY: Yeah. My sister was so fat when she was younger but now she's dead skinny.

Stacey says a lot about her body and image.

The video entries are representations, as what the children say and do is unique to that particular occasion. Only limited information can pass across the camera interface, and there is some kind of translation that takes place as the data are recorded and subsequently interpreted. Reflexivity is essential concerning 'how the camera and the video footage become an element of the play between themselves and informants, and how these are interwoven into discourses and practices in the research context' (Pink, 2001, p. 80). It is these very concerns that I have discussed in part, when considering how the children related to the camera, how that was interpreted by me, the researcher, and subsequently how that affected the way that I dealt with them and developed the project.

> Images are no more 'transparent' than written accounts and while film, video and photography do stand in an indexical relationship to that which they represent they are still representations of reality, not a direct encoding of it. As representations they are therefore subject to the influences of their social, cultural and historical contexts of production and consumption.
>
> (Banks, 2001, p. 2)

Consideration of these influences within this research is essential. For example, the children's notions of the purposes and processes of video diaries in reality television would give them some framework with which to approach their own diary-making. These prior understandings ensured that initially the children approached the project with some excitement, seeming to adopt an air of celebrity; they were the special ones, selected for this privileged role of taking part in their very own reality TV setting. And they came with the same largely naïve, uncritical perspectives with which many people view similar 'realities' on television. This was their stage; their game. Then, once within this familiar unreality, they opened up previously unconsidered areas of investigation, what I term the 'unknown unknowns'.

References

Banks, M. (2001). *Visual Research methods*. Social Research Update. Accessed 2001, from www.soc.surrey.ac.uk/sru/SRU11/SRU11.html.

Baudrillard, J. (1994). *Simulacra and simulation* translated by Sheila Faria Glaser. Ann Arbor: University of Michigan Press.

Bloustein, G. (1998). 'It's different to a mirror 'cos it talks to you': teenage girls, video cameras and identity. In S. Howard (Ed.), *Wired-up: young people and the electronic media* (pp. 115–134). London: UCL Press.

Bourdieu, P. (1977). *Outline of a theory of practice*. Cambridge: Cambridge University Press.

Bourdieu, P., & Passeron, C. (1977). *Reproduction in education, society and culture*. London: Sage Publications.

Galton, M., Comber, C., & Pell, T. (2002). The consequences of transfer for pupils: attitudes and attainment. In L. Hargreaves & M. Galton (Eds.), *Transfer from the primary classroom: 20 years on* (pp. 131–158). London: Routledge Falmer.

Holliday, R. (2000). We've been framed: visualising methodology. *The Sociological Review, 48*(4), 503–521.

Lindsay, G. (2000). Researching children's perspectives: ethical issues. In A. Lewis & G. Lyndsey (Eds.), *Researching children's perspectives*. Buckingham: Open University Press.

Noyes, A. (2003). Moving schools and social relocation. *International Studies in Sociology of Education, 13*(3), 261–280.

Noyes, A. (2004). Video diary: a method for exploring learning dispositions. *Cambridge Journal of Education, 34*(2), 193–209.

Noyes, A. (2006). School transfer and the diffraction of learning trajectories. *Research Papers in Education, 21*(1), 43–62.

Pink, S. (2001). *Visual ethnography*. London: Sage Publications.

Pirie, S. E. B. (1996). *Classroom video recording: when, why and how does it offer a valuable data source for qualitative research?* Paper presented at the 18th Annual Meeting of the North American Chapter of the International Group for the Psychology of Mathematics Education, Panama City, Florida.

Prosser, J. (1998). *Image-based research*. London: Falmer Press.

Rumsfeld, D. (2003). http://news.bbc.co.uk/1/hi/world/americas/3254852.stm.

Tripp, D. (1993). *Critical incidents in teaching*. London: Routledge.

Watling, R. (2001). Keeping hold and hanging on: video diaries with stroke patients. In B. Warren (Ed.), *Creating a theatre in and beyond your classroom*. Ontario: Captus.

Chapter 9

Dialogues with artists

Analysing children's self-portraits

Pat Thomson and Christine Hall

> Like Andy Noyes in the previous chapter, researchers Pat Thomson and Chris Hall also focus on unknowns – the difficulties of interpretation of children's visual artifacts, in this case paintings. They show that the apparently obvious solution, asking the children what they mean, is not as easily accomplished as it may sound.

Our three-year research project, into the creative arts and inclusive pedagogies at Holly Tree Primary school, began because we heard the headteacher talking about a self-portrait project that Year 5 children had done. We were interested in the idea of self-portraits because they seemed to afford children interesting opportunities to explore questions of identity. In this chapter, we tell the story of what we learnt about working with, on and around these self-portraits.

We present findings from our pilot project as a chronological narrative to represent the ways in which we learnt about what we were doing, and how we changed our views about the processes we were using. We have chosen to write in this way because messy 'research stories' are often not made public, and this can lead readers to think that research is not only neat, straightforward and logical, but also goes without any hitches. Our kind of retelling makes explicit the 'following your nose' quality of ethnographic research, and also reveals our fallibilities as researchers.

We begin by discussing the children's self-portraits and go onto describe what happened when we talked to the children in focus groups and then individually. However, before we start, we need to introduce the school and our research project.

Holly Tree Primary school

Situated in a large English Midlands city, Holly Tree Primary has 300-plus children on roll and sixty-plus in the nursery. Half the children live in local authority housing on the two council estates close to the school. A higher than average percentage of children qualifies for free school meals (24 per cent). The school is known as successful, and has inspection reports[1] which deem it 'outstanding'. As a result, there is a small number of pupils who come from nearby suburbs on the basis of the school's reputation: their parents are professionals with firm ideas about what constitutes a good education.

The school is situated to one side of the Holly Tree estate, which was built in the late 1960s on a non-linear plan. Modest white-stuccoed semi-detached homes line winding streets intended by urban planners to create small communities. There are a few open and green spaces – Holly Tree Primary is one, and its cul de sac is cut off from a major arterial road by a long landscaped mound. The single-storey red-brick school is open-plan and subdivided by furniture and colourful curtains into usable spaces, giving an impression of openness and flow while maintaining barriers between activities, and some protection from noise. Every available area of wall is covered in carefully mounted and well-organised displays.

The school is a founding member of a school-based primary teacher training consortium, and works with a local FE college to train teaching assistants. With a strong and long-standing commitment to the arts, and partly through funding made available through Creative Partnerships (a national funding scheme intended to promote creativity and whole-school change), the school has recently expanded its commitment to creative teaching and learning, with generally positive effects (Hall & Thomson, 2005, 2007; Hall, Thomson, & Russell, 2007; Thomson, Hall, & Russell, 2006, 2007). The headteacher, Miriam, started the school in the early 1970s, and was until mid-2005 one of the longest serving heads in England. The remainder of the staff is a mix of very experienced, relatively experienced and early career teachers. Four teachers and one of the teaching assistants have been in the school for more than fifteen years. The staff is also overwhelmingly female, with only two male teachers.

Miriam is a well-known figure in the Midlands city, where she has spent all of her professional life. She was a leader in the primary heads' network in the local authority, and it was in this context that we heard her speaking, with great excitement and pride, about the self-portraits that Year 5 children in her school had done. The school had paid an artist, Dorothy, to work with an entire year group of children over a whole year, and the culmination of the programme had been the production of self-portraits. The school had shown them at a public exhibition in a major book chain gallery, and since then the portraits had been on loan to a range of local agencies. Curious about these art works, we arranged to see a selection that was on display close to our university campus.

The portraits lived up to Miriam's description. Each featured a child's head, and sometimes torso or entire body, against a backdrop of lively depictions of family, favourite objects, pets, sporting activities and/or locations. Mounted and framed in bright colours, the portraits had a vitality and exuberance that intrigued us.

Our interest in the self-portraits

Our curiosity about the self-portraits related to questions of identity and inclusion.

Schools are places where children and young people are continually engaged in identity formation, but where formal opportunities to play with, represent and find an answer to the 'Who am I'? question are not routinely provided within the classroom. Philip Wexler and his colleagues (Wexler, Crichlow, Kern, & Martusewicz, 1992) describe the quest to find a legitimate identity in school as 'becoming somebody', and they argue that children actively shape identity/ies either through or against the practices of the school. Resistance to schooling produces particular kinds of identities – other, drop-out, failure (see Eckert, 1989; Reay & Wiliam, 1999; Smyth & Hattam, 2004; Willis, 1977; Youdell, 2006). Researchers (such as Derrington & Kendall, 2004; Gillbourn & Youdell, 2000; Miron & Lauria, 1995; Yon, 2000) have shown that many children are inscribed – through setting and testing, patterns of interaction and through the production of classroom texts – with particular 'student' identities (e.g. good, bad, bright, slow, talkative, class clown). When the approved identities available in the classroom are highly limited, the narrow range of options excludes many children. In choosing not to take up legitimate ways of 'being student and doing school', children form oppositional identities. In contrast, inclusive schooling provides resources and opportunities through which children not only learn what is required, but can also manufacture affirming identities (Dyson, 1997; Hill, Comber, Louden, Reid, & Rivalland, 1998; Janks, 2000).

Identity is a difficult and contested issue in academic literature. We do not have space to go into the debates here (see Du Gay, Evans, & Redman, 2000; Mansfield, 2000; Miller, 1993 for overviews), but our story will not make sense if we do not outline our basic premises here and now. We see identity as being:

- *social*. While identity is a story we tell ourselves about who we are, why we are the way we are, and how we got to be this way (Bruner, 1986), none of this happens in isolation. Identities are formed in the company of others and through culturally inflected ways of thinking, speaking and acting – they are, in other words, discursive (see S. Hall, 1997 for discussion). Furthermore, the social circumstances in which we find ourselves change the ways in which we think about ourselves, act and speak (Gutmann, 2003; Holstein & Gubrium, 2000). And aspects of identity are not just about us as individuals, but also about the constellation of social relations (class, race, gender, ethnicity and so on) in which we are enmeshed (S. Hall, 1996). Location can be important too – while both of us are white middle-class academics, we come from different parts of the world, and our different geographical locations are significant aspects of the ways in which we act as well as think and talk about ourselves (see Corbett, 2007; Kenway, Kraack, & Hickey-Moody, 2006; McDowell, 1999). Our various circumstances, contexts and life trajectories also allow us to understand things in particular ways. So the notion that identity is just 'in the head' is profoundly misleading.

- *in formation.* Identity is not fixed. It changes over time and in response to events and the people with whom we mix and where we find ourselves. It is not determined, however. We are able to exercise some agency over our identities – a phenomenon that therapists rely on and use when they attempt to help people reframe their lives and their futures (Epston & White, 1994). One of the characteristics of our consumer society is an increased focus on the outward manifestations of identity through clothing, hairstyle, personal accessories, choice of music, etc. Changing appearance can signify a change of the 'tribe' you belong to (Maffesoli, 1995), that is, what identity you are assuming. Pop icon Madonna is often seen as the epitome of someone who shifts her identity through continuous physical makeovers. Today, adolescence is a time when young people typically experiment with a range of consumption-based identities (see Bettis & Adams, 2005; Kenway & Bullen, 2001), and finding a 'self' can be a struggle for many of them (J. Hall, 2001; McDonald, 1999).

- *multiple.* Because the ways in which we think about ourselves, act and speak change depending on the social circumstances in which we find ourselves, we actually have multiple identities. An individual can simultaneously be a competent professional in one situation, and a complete novice in another. This is the kind of identity work, for example, that sits behind the struggle that many teachers have in coming to postgraduate study (see Kamler & Thomson, 2006). The dominant identity available to doctoral candidates is novice, and only in some contexts is this inclusive of professional experience. Doctoral researchers can therefore feel almost schizophrenic about who they are, and feel like very different people depending on whether they are at work or engaged in study. The institutional context powerfully frames what identities are possible (see Alvesson & Willmott, 2002; Du Gay, 1996 for other examples).

We suspected that the arts afforded more occasions for children to actively experiment with questions of identity/ies – as individual/social, ongoing and multiple. We brought these understandings, and an interest in finding out more, to our viewing of the self-portraits.

The self-portrait pilot project

Our preliminary investigation suggested that the self-portrait project seemed to be remarkably inclusive. All children had produced them, all were on display, and none particularly stood out as being 'better' than any others. It seemed as if the activity had allowed all children to be successful and to put on display a positive identity. Furthermore, as a collective entity, the portraits represented the diversity of race, gender and class that constituted their Year 5 group.

On this basis we focused on what opportunities the self-portraits afforded children to represent their identity/ies, what pedagogies the artist used to produce these affordances, and whether these were, as we suspected, inclusive of all of the children. These intellectual puzzles had to be translated into a research design that would provide us with some of the answers.

The major difficulty was that the self-portrait project had concluded, and we could not observe any art lessons. The best we could do was to interview the children, the artist and the class teachers about the portraits and the process of their production, knowing that they would invoke their memories of what had happened. While we could put all of the accounts against each other and produce some kind of general picture, the accounts would always be retrospective. Such remembrances after the event may well have been heavily influenced by the official school 'public relations' story about the project.

We resolved these issues by deciding that we would conduct a pilot for a bigger study[2] through which we could observe the process from beginning to end. The data we could produce in the pilot would not answer all of our questions, but would help us find out some things and also allow us to try out approaches to 'reading' the children's art works. Our first step was to gather together a photographic record of the self-portraits and to interview the children, now in Year 6, in small focus groups of four to five. While we were waiting for the ethical permission notes to come back from parents, we took a preliminary look at the photos and the originals.

Our first impression was that there were very few portraits which we could not interpret. We also had the catalogue of the exhibition, where each child had named their art work and written a few sentences about it. So when we looked at a portrait where a boy was standing in an ice arena, hands spread out in a triumphant finale position, with a packed house behind him, it seemed clear to us that this was probably an aspirational portrait from someone who saw himself as a possible professional skater, or at least a gifted amateur (see Figure 9.1).

When we saw another boy posed as Robin Hood, that too was easily interpreted as a boy's own adventure fantasy. The siren with the red dress outside the department store was clearly painted by someone heavily into girlie shopping ... and so on.

When we had all of our consent forms back, we embarked on the first round of children's interviews in focus groups.

Talking to children about art

The focus groups were held in the head's office off the small staff room.[3] This was not quite as imposing as it sounds: Miriam was generally out and about all day so her office was used by all of the staff, and it was not unusual for children to come into the staffroom and the office. The questions we asked were around the self-portrait project and the arts: we asked children to tell us what they did

Figure 9.1 Britain's next Christopher Dean?

and why, and we also asked them some speculative questions which invited them to create metaphors about their experiences – for example, if the self-portrait project was a picture, what would be in it? If someone was going to write a story about the self-portrait project, how would it go?

In focus groups, the children were generally very talkative. They impressed us with their enthusiasm about the project. A number of them volunteered that they hadn't liked art before and now did, and that they were surprised by what they had achieved. They told us that there weren't mistakes in art, unlike other subjects, and they used an impressive array of art-specific language, such as abstract, collage, surrealism and pointillism, and talked in some detail about how to mix colours to get specific shades. In these conversations, a few children made reference to their specific portrait and sometimes to those of other children.

In discussion, we noted that the children referred both to the artistic decisions they made, and those that they made with the artist-in-residence:

> Before Dorothy came I would use a paintbrush and really press down to get the paint out but now she's come we do it slowly and you can't paint it all over the place, you paint it all in one way.

Children assumed some agency in relation to their portraits, but also attributed influence and the benefits of direct instruction to the artist, Dorothy.

> …when we draw the picture you can just draw your family, you can draw anything you want and you get to colour it in and do the painting of it. I

drew my picture, when I had plaits, I had like 3 plaits on my picture I did of myself and it was good and I did a garden and I was sitting in it.

Things that we couldn't draw, we cut out of a magazine.

But if you wanted to put a picture of somebody on it, you'd go into a magazine and stick it on, Dorothy would sometimes go, 'Well we don't want everything to do with a magazine, you have to cut the head off and do it yourself.'

(Focus group 9)

This conversation is typical of the ways in which children saw themselves as having some decision-making power, while also being students at the same time. They mimic Dorothy's didactic mode – telling them what to do – and her use of the collective 'we' to create a sense of agreement about the direction she is telling them to follow. The children noted that, despite having some restrictions and some clear instructions, the degree of autonomy Dorothy allowed was much greater than in other lessons, when there was pressure to complete tasks in limited timeframes. 'If you're in Maths and you go wrong, you feel really stressed but if you're in art, you just say it doesn't matter I can go over it' (Group 9). When asked to describe the project as a picture and as a story, the artist was writ large.

Well the hero would probably be Dorothy.

The happy ending would be kind of like the finished thing with where we had all our portraits in the gallery – that would be like kind of great.

And like the teachers crying, 'Oh that's fantastic'.

(Group 4)

The children attributed much of the success of the portrait project to the artist and her skills in imparting art practice/knowledge. Their understanding that the project was a success was not simply derived from their own enjoyment and sense of achievement, but was also constructed by the experience of public exhibition and the experience of seeing themselves through the eyes of an appreciative audience – opportunities they attributed to Dorothy and the teaching assistant who worked with her.

While we learnt some things about the process of the project through these focus-group interviews, we decided we still needed to know more. We decided to interview each child individually.

Talking to children about their identity work

We knew the focus groups had exerted a regulatory effect on what could and couldn't be said, because we had observed a kind of 'group think' emerging in several of the conversations. We also knew that we would be unlikely to consistently get data about specific identity issues in a group setting.

We therefore embarked on interviews with twenty-two individual children. We selected a range of children from different socio-economic circumstances, including the few Afro-Caribbean children in the school, and a balance of boys and girls. We also checked the self-portraits for interesting, puzzling and diverse items, and included the children who had painted them, and read our interview notes to see which children had been talkative and lively. We deliberately included two pupils who had been less positive about the self-portrait experience.

We were very aware of the views of other researchers about the problems with individual interviews with individual children. Jean Rudduck and Julia Flutter (2004), for example, point to the very considerable power imbalances between children and adult researchers, and the potential for coercion and second-guessing that this creates. Bronwyn Davies (1982) and Jan Nespor (1997) both suggest that individual interviews produce referential, segmentable and presupposing forms of response compared to groups which present 'rich verbal forms suppressed by individual interview' (Nespor, 1997, p. 233). Nevertheless, we had been in the school a fair bit, had already talked with the children and we thought that we had enough skills to work through these issues.

But we did not think that we ought to interview the children alone. We were mindful of current child protection practices in English schools which suggest that no single adult should be alone with a child, and thus we decided that, in order to interview single children, both of us should be present. Our ethical consent forms had been worded so as to allow this possibility, and we decided to ask each child individually if they agreed to an interview, making clear that they could say no, before we actually began. With some residual misgivings about the real potential for coercion, we proceeded.

Our first individual interviews with children bore out all of the warnings given in the literatures. Children who had been animated and confident in the focus group became reticent and monosyllabic when faced with two researchers and our recorder. Of course, we *should* have known better than to ignore all of those messages about power relations between children and adults; we even taught about this in our research methods classes.

After three such interchanges, one of us, without discussion with the other, rearranged the room (see researcher notebook, Figure 9.2). We moved away from the table. One researcher sat on the floor with the child on a chair, both looking at the self-portrait and with their backs to the other researcher and the recorder. The researcher on the floor began the conversation by pointing at the portrait and asking specific questions about the content and techniques of the picture.

This shift produced more than a change of material positioning. Not only were the interviews now much more animated, but the children were also much more authoritative when talking about their work. After the event, we remembered that this was precisely what Labov (1969) did in his seminal research on Afro-American children's speech. Monosyllabic and apparently 'non verbal' children were shown to be talkative, playful and expressive when

Figure 9.2 Researcher notebook.

the researcher brought potato chips to share, reduced the height imbalance by sitting on the floor, and introduced taboo words and topics into the conversation (p. 148).

However, we think more was going on in our interview than a change in height and mode of address. By putting the children in the situation where they were the experts on the painting placed in front of them, and ourselves in the position of 'learners' who needed to have the painting explained to them, we constructed the children as artists. We spoke to them as artists, and they answered in this vein.

When we looked at the transcripts of the conversations, what became immediately obvious was that, when describing their portraits, the children referred to their decisions first of all, rather than to the project per se.

[N]ot long before we started doing the pictures I went to a park that I'd never been to before and it had, like, a pond where we could feed the fish. And we sat under a tree, near the pond. It gave me the idea to, like, do a picture of that park. So I did the pond and did the tree. I think it helped because I had actually been to that park and I knew what I was aiming for. It was a lot easier than if I had just thought of something else to draw about that I'd never seen before. So that's why I picked it. And when I was there I just enjoyed it so much – because we were playing football and we stayed there ages so that's why I decided to … My favourite part of doing it was the tree trunks. I just love mixing all the different colours and adding the textures.

(J1)

Here, J has an 'idea', and an 'aim'. The vision that motivated the portrait was his – he 'picked it'. He referred to Dorothy as helping rather than teaching. '[A]nother thing I like best is the colour on the yellow jumper. I like that. That was Dorothy's idea' (J1). Sometimes J's assumption of agency extended to leaving Dorothy out altogether. In this next exchange our questioning focuses on the child-artist's actions, and in response J describes the process of building up the portrait layer by layer.

R: … You're using the whole picture, aren't you? If you compare it with others you've got a big image there, haven't you?
J: Because, as I say, I wanted mainly a portrait of me…. Because I actually put the background in first before I put my portrait of me on.
R: Oh, right. So then you put yourself over the top of the background. That's interesting. So you thought of the background and put yourself in it.

(J1)

In reality, we knew that this process – getting the background filled in before beginning the actual portrait – was one of the things that Dorothy had taught the children and that she had insisted on. But here, J has either forgotten this or it has receded into the background, as he represented himself to us as the painter in control of the progress of his portrait.

While we have presented a single example here, that of J, this transaction was similar to those that occurred in every one of the interviews where we assumed this spatial arrangement and a line of questioning that focused on the background to and meanings in the picture and the production process. Of our twenty-two individual interviews, we had three that were almost useless and eighteen that were rich with information. The difference in the interviews was one that we had made.

As we suggested earlier in this chapter, people do not have fixed identities. Identities are produced in specific social relations, and people often have several of them, all related, but nevertheless somewhat different from each other. Here, we suggest, the change in spatial relations and questions produced an artist identity, rather than a student identity. When we had the children in focus groups, and sitting as an individual with us, they spoke as students and in relation to adults who were from a university and 'experts' in education. When we shifted the furniture, we positioned ourselves as learners, and the child as knowledgable and as the creator of the artistic work under discussion. They knew things we did not about the portrait's creation, and they could choose to tell us as much or as little as they liked about it – and them.

The artist identity was also a position from which the children were able to tell us more about what their picture meant.

Making meaning of the portraits

As explained, our key interest in the self-portraits was around questions of identity and what the arts afforded by way of resources for identity work. Accordingly, we decided to ask the children in individual interviews a set of questions about identity and representation (see Figure 9.3).

We had been relatively confident that we had a fair idea of what was going on in the self-portraits. There were a few puzzles which we wanted to pursue, but we did not expect major surprises. All of the children were very clear about the choices that they made in representing themselves and family in their pictures. Some told us that they wanted to show their favourite people and things; some wanted their pictures to stand out in the crowd; while others thought that the picture should be happy, because sad pictures were inappropriate for a public viewing. But surprises were not long in coming.

One boy chose to represent himself as Robin Hood. We assumed that it was because, like other little English boys in the Midlands, he sometimes dreamt of being the daring archer with redistributive politics (see Figure 9.4). This was not the case, it seemed. He told us that Robin Hood was from his hometown, and his picture should be integral to any local exhibition. When he looked at the pictures being painted by the children in his class and saw that there was no Robin Hood, and that it was possible that a public exhibition of children's art would have no local hero, he felt duty bound to rectify the situation. We do not assume that this explanation was necessarily 'the truth', but nevertheless we were not expecting our interview to produce such an explicit representation of and reference to the cultural significance of iconography.

One girl produced a picture of herself at the beach (Figure 9.5). In interview

---

Identity

- What does this picture say about you?
- What else did you think you might want your picture to say about you?
- Were there other yous who could have been shown in the portrait? E.g.?
- Why did you choose to say the things you did say about yourself?
- Why didn't you choose the other yous to show in the picture?

Representation

- How does your picture say those things about you?
- What else did you think about putting in the picture to represent you?
- What is the feeling and mood in this picture and how did you try to create that feeling and mood?

Figure 9.3 Interview schedule.

Figure 9.4 'Robin Hood'.

she told us a story we would not have imagined, although once hearing it, it is hard to see this painting in any other way.

Here we were faced with a story arising from a life-world where children routinely wear hand-me-down clothes.

T: I've got this friend called A and I got the swimming suit off her and she left the badges on. But she's the swimmer.

R: Do you like swimming?

T: Not much.

R: You look like you might have been sunbathing there don't you? The colour of your skin – is that what you were trying to show?

T: Yes. I like sunbathing.

Figure 9.5 'Life's a beach'.

We did not pursue the circumstances of hand-me-downs in the interview and we later were told T's story, which was indeed a sad one and the expression in the portrait is indeed reflective of her experiences. Our interview, however, was not the place to pry into painful life events. But in another painting which portrayed a rich boy and a poor boy, where we had assumed a story of poverty, the artist told us in no uncertain terms that this was merely a picture. He was neither rich nor poor, he said, but enjoyed the fantasy of being suddenly put in another's shoes (as in many popular films) and the two-sided painting represented this transposition. Questions of poverty, then, were both there and not-there in the children's portraits, and we needed the artists' help to understand this.

Another boy told us that doing his picture had been cathartic. He had been fighting all year with his little brother, and had felt that his mother had taken his little brother's side against him. When he had the opportunity to paint his family he decided that he would portray his father as a superhero who would protect him against his mother and brother (Figure 9.6). The painter is the biggest character in the painting and has a somewhat gleefully cross expression, while his little brother is the tiny figure in the corner. Dad is holding a sword. Here we had a brief insight into another function of the arts – that of imaginative play – and something of the difficulties of living in a family. Not all families are happy places for children, even if they are 'good' ones.

The rather mature girl whose picture we had dubbed The Shopping Queen (Figure 9.7) also surprised us.

Our interview began as we had predicted

> Well it's about me going shopping and then you've got like some shops at the back and then it's just like little clues to what I like. So as you can see

Figure 9.6 'My ideal family'.

I've got some fashion shops, a handbag, some nice earrings, I like gold, I like dresses.... So I've done a woman's shop with a woman designing some clothes and an outfit next to her and then I've done River Island with a man and an outfit next to him.

But then the interview took a different turn. While the conversation remained focused on consumption, S outlined for us that the painting was not a simple representation of her 'self', nor ought we to get totally enamoured of any explanation she might offer of her intentions.

R: So how is she feeling?

S: She looks shocked 'cos she's spent all her money so she's quite shocked but she looks quite happy because she's been shopping, she's got lots of jewelry on, she looks like she feels special because she's got lots of jewelry on and handbags.

R: And how does her red dress make her feel?

S: I don't know because I'm not her but she probably feels quite nice because that dress looks very nice, it looks like, because as you can see underneath, we're just looking at different colours and we did a spotted one, it had blue and red spots on and then I decided I didn't like that so I painted over it and painted over it a dark red so you probably wouldn't be able to see it as much.

R: I'm really interested that you just said that wasn't you.

S: It is me but I just – I can't tell how she feels in that dress.

R: So it's not a dress that you've got?

S: No. Yeah I have got a dress kind of like that but it goes all weird at the

Figure 9.7 'The shopping queen'.

bottom but when I painted it and what I thought of was her feeling very special, feeling very special and just going out, lots of jewelry, handbag, earrings, necklace, a nice red dress, spending all her money, she must feel quite happy.

R: So she's not going off to meet her boyfriend?

S: No, I didn't think of that when I painted it but when people look at pictures, you can think like different things.

S simply explained to us that paintings had multiple readings and hers was no exception. The movement in her conversation – from describing the me/not me who is 'she' the portrait's subject, to the artist who works on getting just the right colour for the dress, the right accessories to symbolise feeling 'nice' and an expression that hints at being shocked at spending so much money – is indicative of the work of representation. In this case it is both self-conscious and unconscious, uncritical of consumption, yet distantiated enough to consider other possible readings.

Through these and other examples we found that our 'identities' questions produced more subtle and sophisticated data than we had anticipated. It seemed that we had allowed children to express/represent some ideas about change-able and public/private selves, just as the portraits themselves had.

We were also helped to understand (again) something about the limitations of reading visual texts. When we interviewed children about the pedagogies of the arts activities, we had already made a reading of their paintings. It was not until we asked the children themselves about their portraits that we were confronted with our mis-readings. In some cases our versions were quite different from what the children reported they intended, while in others they were almost identical. In saying this, we are not suggesting that these texts were not available for multiple readings – indeed, S reminded us powerfully about that – nor that what the children told us was 'authentic'. They produced a particular reading of their portrait for us at a particular time and place.

We are claiming, however, that adults can read visual texts in ways that are perhaps not very enlightening. In particular cases, such as that of Robin Hood, the children's representations were startlingly at odds with our readings. Bringing the painting/text into the interview and making it the focus of conversation produced much more interesting data. Rather than keeping the text as a separate set of data available for analysis by discrete 'methods' in sequestered 'analytic moments', we had brought the two together and the result provided much food for thought. While there was still much we could not know of the children's life worlds, by virtue of who we were (white, middle-class and middle-aged academics), with their help we had moved a little beyond simplistic and naïve interpretations of their artistic texts.

Lessons learned

Our Holly Tree pilot project reinforced two important lessons for our bigger project.

The first was that children are not 'unified subjects'. As researchers, we are in a position to construct them as more or less expert in their own experiences, narratives and opinions. When we materially and semiotically positioned children as artists, we got qualitatively different data than when we had unthinkingly reproduced the more common school relations of power. Our second lesson, which followed from the first, was that child artists could disrupt simplistic interpretations of the visual representations they produced. While their conversations could open tiny glimpses into some children's life-worlds, they could also startle us through reminding us of the dangers of glib readings and easy assumptions.

This is not to suggest that there was *no* value in our readings of the paintings. Because children's pictures (re)produce stereotypical social relations and practices (Weber & Mitchell, 1995), their art ought to be seen in the same way as any other research data – open for researcher interpretation and deconstruction. We could write, for example, an entire chapter about the tangle of commercial activities and children's out-of-school activities based on the number and kinds of images in the paintings. Yet even though such a discursive reading of pictures could stand alone, this too would be enriched by the conversations we had with the artists.

So, in sum, we suggest that speaking with the artists, while not about producing an essential 'truth', is certainly generative, and ought not to be omitted from research which uses children's artistic artefacts. And in so doing, researchers must consider the ways in which the physical and social elements of conversation can construct specific kinds of responses.

Notes

1 We cannot cite the actual reports because this would reveal the identity of the school; we have also blurred some other key identifiers.
2 The following larger ethnographic study was funded by the ESRC (RES-000–22–0834, *Promoting social and educational inclusion through the creative arts*) and also included co-researcher Lisa Russell.
3 We could understand all of these interviews as strongly classified, but with problems around the appropriate framing for individual interviews (see Walford, 2007)

References

Alvesson, M., & Willmott, H. (2002). Identity regulation as organisational control: producing the appropriate individual. *Journal of Management Studies, 39*(5), 619–644.
Bettis, P., & Adams, N. (Eds.). (2005). *Geographies of girlhood. Identities in-between.* Mahwah, NJ: Lawrence Erlbaum Associates.
Bruner, J. (1986). Life as narrative. *Social Research, 54*(1), 11–32.
Corbett, M. (2007). *Learning to leave. The irony of schooling in a coastal community.* Halifax: Fernwood Publishing.

Davies, B. (1982). *Shards of glass. Children reading and writing beyond gendered identities*. Cresskill, NJ: Hampton Press.

Derrington, C., & Kendall, S. (2004). *Gypsy traveller students in secondary schools. Culture, identity and achievement*. Stoke on Trent: Trentham.

Du Gay, P. (1996). *Consumption and identity at work*. London: Sage Publications.

Du Gay, P., Evans, J., & Redman, P. (Eds.). (2000). *Identity. A reader*. London: Sage Publications.

Dyson, A. H. (1997). *Writing superheroes. Contemporary childhood, popular culture, and classroom literacy*. New York, NY: Teachers' College Press.

Eckert, P. (1989). *Jocks and burnouts. Social categories and identity in the high school*. New York, NY: Teachers College Press.

Epston, D., & White, M. (1994). *Experience, contradiction, narrative and imagination. Selected papers 1989–1991*. Adelaide: Dulwich Centre Publications.

Gillbourn, D., & Youdell, D. (2000). *Rationing education. Policy, practice, reform and equity*. Buckingham: Open University Press.

Gutmann, A. (2003). *Identity in democracy*. Princeton, NJ: Princeton University Press.

Hall, C., & Thomson, P. (2005). Creative tensions. *English in Education, 39*(3), 5–18.

Hall, C., & Thomson, P. (2007). Creative partnerships? Cultural policy and inclusive arts practices in one primary school. *British Educational Research Journal, 33*(3), 315–329.

Hall, C., Thomson, P., & Russell, L. (2007). Teaching like an artist: the pedagogic identities and practices of artists in schools. *British Journal of Sociology of Education, 28*(5), 605–619.

Hall, J. (2001). *Canal town youth: community organisation and the development of adolescent identity*. Albany, NY: State University of New York Press.

Hall, S. (1996). Who needs 'identity'? In S. Hall & P. du Gay (Eds.), *Questions of cultural identity*. London: Sage Publications.

Hall, S. (Ed.). (1997). *Representation. Cultural representations and signifying practices*. London: Sage Publications.

Hill, S., Comber, B., Louden, B., Reid, J., & Rivalland, J. (1998). *100 Children go to school: connections and disconnections in the literacy experience prior to school and in the first year of school*, Vols 1–3. Canberra: Department of Education, Employment, Training and Youth Affairs.

Holstein, J., & Gubrium, J. (2000). *The self we live by. Narrative identity in a postmodern world*. New York, NY: Oxford University Press.

Janks, H. (2000). Domination, access, diversity and design. *Educational Review, 52*(2), 175–186.

Kamler, B., & Thomson, P. (2006). *Helping doctoral students write: pedagogies for supervision*. London: Routledge.

Kenway, J., & Bullen, E. (2001). *Consuming children. Entertainment, advertising and education*. Buckingham: Open University Press.

Kenway, J., Kraack, A., & Hickey-Moody, A. (2006). *Masculinity beyond the metropolis*. London: Palgrave.

Labov, W. (1969). The logic of non-standard English. *Georgetown Monographs on Language and Linguistics, 22*, 143–161. Washington, DC: Georgetown University Press.

Maffesoli, M. (1995). *The time of the tribes: the decline of individualism in mass societies* (trans. D. Smith). London: Sage Publications.

Mansfield, N. (2000). *Subjectivity. Theories of the self from Freud to Haraway.* Sydney: Allen & Unwin.

McDonald, K. (1999). *Struggles for subjectivity. Identity, action and youth experience.* Cambridge: Cambridge University Press.

McDowell, L. (1999). *Gender, identity and place. Understanding feminist geographies.* Minneapolis, MN: University of Minnesota Press.

Miller, T. (1993). *The well tempered self. Citizenship, culture and the postmodern subject.* Baltimore, MA: Johns Hopkins University Press.

Miron, L., & Lauria, M. (1995). Identity politics and student resistance to inner-city public schooling. *Youth and Society, 27*(1), 29–54.

Nespor, J. (1997). *Tangled up in school. Politics, space, bodies, and signs in the educational process.* Mahwah, NJ: Lawrence Erlbaum.

Reay, D., & Wiliam, D. (1999). 'I'll be a nothing': structure, agency and the construction of identity through assessment. *British Educational Research Journal, 25*(3), 343–354.

Rudduck, J., & Flutter, J. (2004). *Consulting pupils? What's in it for schools?* London: Routledge Falmer.

Smyth, J., & Hattam, R. (2004). *Dropping out, drifting off, being excluded: becoming somebody without school.* New York, NY: Peter Lang.

Thomson, P., Hall, C., & Russell, L. (2006). An arts project failed, censored or...? A critical incident approach to artist-school partnerships. *Changing English, 13*(1), 29–44.

Thomson, P., Hall, C., & Russell, L. (2007). If these walls could speak: reading displays of primary children's work. *Ethnography and Education, 2*(3), 381–400.

Walford, G. (2007). Classification and framing of interviews in ethnographic interviewing. *Ethnography and Education, 2*(2), 145–158.

Weber, S., & Mitchell, C. (1995). *That's funny, you don't look like a teacher.* London: Falmer.

Wexler, P., Crichlow, W., Kern, J., & Martusewicz, R. (1992). *Becoming somebody. Toward a social psychology of school.* London: Falmer.

Willis, P. (1977). *Learning to labour. How working class kids get working class jobs.* London: Saxon House.

Yon, D. (2000). *Elusive culture. Schooling, race and identity in global times.* New York, NY: State University of New York Press.

Youdell, D. (2006). *Impossible bodies, impossible selves: exclusions and student subjectivities.* Dordrecht: Springer.

Chapter 10

Seeing beyond violence

Visual research applied to policy and practice

Rob Walker, Barbara Schratz and Peter Egg

Through a discussion of a four-country project which aimed to have children visually represent their understanding of the opposite of violence, the researchers, Rob Walker, Barbara Schratz and Peter Egg, raise important questions about the nature of participatory research and the particular ethical dilemmas that are raised when visual research methods are used. They identify key elements of a new approach to research ethics.

'Seeing Beyond Violence' is a project initiated by SOS Children's Villages in which children in four countries engaged in research to investigate the question 'What is the opposite of violence?' Digital photography was a key method used by children in the project.

Visual research in the world of policy and practice

While it is easy to see the appeal of visual methods for academic research and to appreciate the excitement with which researchers grapple with the technical problems that visual methods involve, the world of policy and practice tends to be more cautious in its response. For those working at the forefront of difficult social issues, the priority is for research that is high in credibility and appears, at least, to provide clear directions for policy and practice. Pictures are often located within organisations in public relations sections and seen as lacking the authority and credibility accorded to 'facts and figures'.

'Facts and figures' might provoke social researchers to engage in deconstruction and critique but, providing they are reasonably robust, they provide a sense of security for those in care organisations who face the need to persuade managers and sponsors. Highly condensed and selective statistics of a kind that are treated by researchers with professional scepticism are often taken by administrators and policy people to represent an undeniable truth. It is not always easy to see why this is so, but perhaps it represents a carry-over from the financial figures that tend to rule organisations. Qualitative research, on the other hand, is frequently mistrusted because it seems to take the user back into the selective perception and value bias from which figures provide an escape. Images (especially photographs and video) appear even more prone to partiality, seen as the obvious victim of unsystematic sampling, subjectivity and the singular point of view.

Researchers often encounter this response, but do not always realise that within organisations the discussions around research may be more contentious than they seem from outside. In some organisations, when the 'frontline service' feels very distant from management, qualitative methods may appeal because they convey the reality of fieldwork to those who might be seen to be distant from it. And, in the case we describe here, in organisations undergoing significant policy change, research itself can become a point for negotiating new meanings and new policy directions or perhaps a means of unsettling an existing set of power relations.

This is not to say that people who might be sceptical about visual research do not appreciate the power of the image, and are very ready to use it, in promotional activities, in training presentations and even in reporting research (though usually restricted to the role of illustration, or to the front cover of the report). Recent examples of the use of images in educational policy include the advertising campaigns in the UK to attract graduates into teaching, the extensive use of illustration in reports (a good example is the *DfES Bulletin*, 2002, 'Schools for the Future') and the campaigns by almost all non-governmental organisations (NGOs) to promote their work in alleviating world poverty.

SOS-Kinderdorf

SOS-Kinderdorf is no exception. A well-established charity providing long-term care for children who have been orphaned or abandoned in countries around the world, SOS has as its main priorities fund-raising and providing care where it is most needed (see www.sos-childrensvillages.org/). Like many comparable organisations, SOS has had to manage a significant policy shift in recent years as the dominant discourse in the field has shifted from 'needs-based' to 'rights-based' provision (a shift enshrined in the UN Convention on The Rights of the Child). This is not an easy transition for an NGO established by a charismatic individual (Hermann Gmeiner), whose influence on the organisation remains strong some years after his death. Nevertheless, SOS has responded to a range of criticisms, while holding to its central values. It has, for instance, established new forms of support for children and families outside its core investment in 'children's villages', providing help for single mothers, for youth and for unaccompanied young refugees as well as communities. Yet the defining image for the organisation remains the idea of the 'Children's Village', with its associated ideas of the SOS family and the key role played by the SOS mother.

Until recently research has been a low priority for SOS, which, because it is a devolved organisation, does not have a central database beyond knowing how many villages and other projects are supported and how many children are in their care. Until a few years ago policy was relatively undeveloped, and it is only as the organisation has needed better information in order to implement quality assurance procedures, training for those in key roles and to address a range of human resources issues (including education, child safety and protection), as well as addressing questions about efficiency and effectiveness, that research has become visible within the organisation. Research in SOS is therefore not neutral, but integral to the policy process and to the changing policy focus of the organisation.

SOS and CARE

In the Centre for Applied Research in Education at the University of East Anglia (CARE), we have a long history of working with a range of organisations (government and non-government) on research projects. Almost always these projects have been action-oriented, often including involvement in programme evaluation, in training and in policy change. A key issue in such research is always around the independence of the research and the researcher (MacDonald, 1974), and in practice we have often retained independence by confining our involvement to working on commissioned projects – the work closely defined in scope, extent and duration by a proposal, a contract and committee.

In recent years, a growing concern in evaluation and applied research has been the way that organisations (especially government agencies and departments) have imposed conditions on applied research that exert greater control, reduce impact and lead to an effective loss of independence for the researcher. Increasingly, the policy model has become that of external consultancy focused on closely defined and limited tasks, rather than of sponsored (and independent) research. The impact of critique, the fostering of dialogue and discussion, and support for high-risk innovative practice have all been constrained and minimised.

In the work CARE has been doing with SOS, we are trying to develop an alternative model for applied research based on collaboration rather than commissioning. The project we describe here is a first attempt to bring together shared interest in the use of visual methods in a collaborative project. For SOS, the project aims to develop trust in the organisation's capacity to do useful and credible research in association with a university, and for the university it is about finding new forms of working relationship between researchers and practitioners other than those predicated on the notion of the 'outside expert'. Visual methods provide fruitful ground in this respect, because this is an area in which we are all to some degree de-skilled and need to develop expertise together.

Origins of 'Seeing Beyond Violence' and project design

The project originated with a request from the United Nations[1] to NGOs and other agencies to provide research data on 'violence against children', which were to be collated prior to a large campaign. When the request was received by

SOS, staff realised that while they had extensive experience of the consequences of violence, this information was dispersed through the organisation and did not exist in forms that were readily accessible, or in a form that could be made available to the wider aid community. SOS felt that it knew a lot, but was not able to present what it knew in a form that those in the UN wanted. It felt unable to present convincing research findings to the wider world and, to some degree, anxious about the credibility of its own knowledge outside the organisation.

Furthermore, when SOS staff started to think about ways in which relevant information could be collected and collated, a new set of issues arose. For example, to treat SOS children as 'research subjects' and to ask them about their experiences of violence seemed both to contradict the UN Convention and could also be seen as a further act of symbolic or methodological violence in that it would necessarily position the child as victim. Standard ethical procedures did not appear to address the problem – for the very act of securing informed consent could be seen as interventive and compounding the problem. What was needed, it was argued, was a form of research that was participatory, did not exploit the child but provided opportunities for creativity of expression. The problem became, was it possible to do research on children and violence that respected the rights codified in the UN Convention, and especially those rights requiring participation?

Authority of method or authority of phenomena?

What seemed at the time in SOS to be a local problem is in fact widespread in science and social science. Researchers rely on standard methodological templates to conceptualise and operationalise research designs, but they need always to be aware that proceeding in this way will always be interventive and inflict a degree of methodological violence on the phenomena. On the other hand, the phenomena alone cannot speak for themselves; some degree of intervention is necessary to make them available for interpretation. The process of research design has always had to manage this difficult balance by finding degrees of intervention that create the basis for understanding yet do not completely change the world they are looking at. At one extreme might lie vivisection, experimental-treatment designs and the totally immersed observer, and at the other end of the scale, methods that lie more lightly on the phenomena. But it needs to be noted that it is how intervention is perceived by the subject that is important (not how it is seen by the researcher), thus even the questionnaire is not entirely inert, and the open-ended interview can represent a considerable intervention into people's lives. There are few truly non-obtrusive measures.

The way we normally resolve the issue is by negotiating the scope of the study, how and where it will be reported, and by negotiating procedures through ethics committees. Less often do we try to start from the phenomena and look to devise methods that are appropriate and sympathetic at the local level.

Because 'Seeing Beyond Violence' was necessarily sensitive to this issue, we worked hard to find methods that, while we recognised that they were interventive, were interventive in ways that were engaging and creative, and maximised the control that participants had over them.

The research design

Barbara Schratz from SOS assembled a team of people that intentionally mixed disciplines and professions. Barbara trained as a sociologist and has worked with visual images, especially in the context of memory-work. Gerhild Trubwasser came with a background in psychotherapy, an interest in adolescent development and extensive experience in training. Peter Egg works with children and young people in a range of participatory projects, often using visual methods, and Rob Walker is a university-based educational researcher. English was the working language of the project, but Gerhild also speaks Spanish and used it in the Latin American sites.

As always, operationalising the research questions involved locating the work in available times and spaces, and this in turn inevitably meant a degree of compromise in the research design. The study had to be completed quickly to meet the UN deadline for submissions, the budget meant that we could each of us stay in one site for no more than two weeks, and the locations available depended on the willingness of Regional Directors and Village Directors to give access.

In the event, three of us were involved in the fieldwork; Peter Egg in Thailand, Gerhild Trubwasser in Colombia and Nicaragua, and Rob Walker in India. We were each allocated a local person to act as research assistant, translator and organiser, though this role was very differently interpreted at each site. We elected to work with a group of fifteen to twenty children between ten and thirteen years old at times they might be available (depending on school and other commitments). We each had three digital cameras and a printer, plus whatever other equipment we chose to take. A month after completing the fieldwork, we met for three days to write and assemble a draft of the Report.

Our first task in the Villages was to explain to the Village Director, staff and the SOS mothers what the project was about, how children would be involved and what we hoped to achieve. We said we would be letting the children take photos but that we would give people the chance to edit these later, we said too that we would hold an exhibition in the village before we left. These practical considerations were easy to explain, though doing so did not lessen the impulse of some adults to intervene when they saw children with one of 'our' cameras. Much more difficult was explaining the idea of this being an exploration of 'the opposite of violence'. This was an idea which left most people puzzled, perhaps because it was not entirely clear to us either, since we saw it more as a way to start a process than a question with a clear answer.

The children, though, were less hesitant. The conceptual question did not seem to trouble them as they rushed to use the cameras. However carefully we tried to introduce the project, the process took on a life and dynamic of its own.

Very quickly the children moved on from taking posed pictures of themselves to posing others. Their first thought was to photograph families and homes – mothers cooking, small children being put to bed, older sisters coming to visit, as well as the (relatively few) material objects around the house, such as posters on the wall, prizes won at school and rows of lunch bags ready for the next day (see Figure 10.1). They wanted to show us places that were special to them (a place in the woods where mushrooms grow, a special tree, a plant one child had grown, a place for bonfires, a pond and a lake where ducks came after the monsoon).

Where the conceptual work naturally began was in looking at the photos rather than in taking them. At each site local circumstances meant that we each worked differently – for instance Peter Egg produced large numbers of prints, whereas Rob Walker gave children the use of a laptop – but in both cases we were amazed at just how much time children would spend, mostly in small groups, looking over and over again at the pictures. And in this process some emerged as 'favourites'. Pictures were not chosen against criteria but for more personal reasons – initially pictures taken by an individual and identified with the photographer and pictures of people or places that they particularly liked. It

Figure 10.1 This photograph represents a common theme. Children valued the routines of what they saw as normal life. What was in some ways a shocking image to select from the perspective of Western feminists was seen by the children as one of the small things that make up settled family life.

Figure 10.2 Of the several hundred images from Thailand, this was the one that the village voted as best representing the opposite of violence. Interestingly, from a Western perspective, it lacks either the smiling faces or the extreme desperation that are often used to promote the work of charities and NGOs.

was out of these conversations and discussions around the pictures that we were often able to ask them about pictures that represented 'the opposite of violence' (Figure 10.2). But it is important to note that we had first to establish a context, including a bank of selected images, within which this question could be asked. To have done otherwise would have run against the grain of the children's sense of group authorship and ownership.

In terms of participation, we learnt the importance of children being deeply involved in the process of interpretation and analysis. Being involved in data collection was important in this project, but what gave the children a sense of ownership of the images and an understanding of the context in which they were taken was the control they had over the process of selection and interpretation. The process of digital photography was clearly critical. The feedback was rapid (sometimes instant) and positive (there were few totally unreadable images). The darkroom process – which often leads to a focus on the quality of the image itself – was bypassed, and attention was much more on content (both literal and symbolic) than form.

We learnt to take some degree of risk and trust the process to manage itself. For instance, one weekend the Village Director in India offered us the school bus to go anywhere we wanted to go. He mentioned a large fun park, and the children leapt on this as an opportunity. I was not sure how this fitted with the research question, but it turned out that I was wrong to be hesitant. Taking the children into an environment that was unfamiliar to them revealed vulnerabilities that were not visible when they were in familiar surroundings. It also revealed the strength they had as a group and in friendships within the group. The Fun Park photos provided a good source of discussion around the idea that fear and fun can be closely allied; that they are not at ends of a continuum as we sometimes assume, but more like two faces of the same experience (Figure 10.3).

Rethinking fieldwork ethics

One aspect of the process that quickly emerged concerned the ethics of photography in the context of applied research. There are many photography projects that make no claims to be research (examples include the influential studies, 'Baghdad Stories' and 'Born in Brothels'). But in research there are different sensitivities, assumptions about ownership and practical procedures to be negoti-

Figure 10.3 The girls who were crying and gripped by fear one minute could not wait to get back on the same ride a few minutes later.

ated. In particular, we have learnt to be very careful with images of children, and aware of the ways in which these can be misused. This helps explain why some organisations have re-categorised studies of the kind we report here to take them out of the research arena (in health, for example, the notion of 'audit' can include studies of this kind but does not require clearance by an ethics committee).

Part of the problem is that research ethics committees require a close specification of the process. They want to know the extent of children's involvement, what the images will be and how they will be used. The contrary notion, which it was important to establish in this project, that children's participation needs to be more than token, raises issues about intellectual property rights, which are different in kind. How these different perspectives fit with one another is not at all clear, and often results in studies like the one we have described being rejected by ethics committees because they lack specificity in describing conditions and outcomes in advance of fieldwork.

On the other hand, we do not want to give up on the claim that this work can count as research just on the grounds that practical procedures are too difficult to negotiate. The claim is important, we believe, because it then requires other researchers to provide critique of studies of this kind. They cannot be easily dismissed, but have to be set alongside more conventional studies.

More generally, standard ethical procedures do not work in many contemporary projects, especially those that use digital photography, that cross cultures, invite participation or concern children; issues which together cover some of the areas of greatest current interest for visual research. This is partly a consequence of the fact that in many projects the time-scales of conventional ethical procedure collapse. A child can take a photograph, view it, show it (to the subject and others), rethink the purpose and the content of the image, improvise a response, view it and show it again, negotiate a new set of framing assumptions, take another image – all in the space of seconds. In a digital environment, the rational plans of conventional research that separate researcher from subject, plans from practice, involvement from consent, collection from publication, shrink, often to vanishing point. But the collapse of relevance of procedures is also a consequence of the changing relationships between research and practice, of awareness of the growing demand for participation by human subjects and the capacity of technology to respond reflexively.

Does this mean that some kinds of research have outgrown the capacity of their institutions and need to be recast in other moulds: as action or appreciative enquiry, perhaps? Or can we rebuild ethical procedures to extend their capacity to contain new and emerging forms of enquiry?

What is needed, we argue, is an approach to ethics that steps back from procedures and returns to principles, then reconnects principles to methodologies. This has significant consequences for researchers, because it returns the basis of trust to the area of professional judgment and to the actions of the researcher-in-action. Researchers need to be accountable in different ways, we suggest, through more direct reporting to those involved and implicated in research studies as well as to their peers, their institutions and those who commission their studies.

Sketch for new ethics for participatory research

We have suggested that in digital environments, and particularly in the context of participatory research projects, conventional procedures for securing research ethics do not work particularly well and may be at the point of collapse. What can we suggest as an alternative?

At the heart of the problem lies not the technology but the need to rethink the role of the 'subject'. In participatory and action research there are no subjects, as the role is conventionally understood in social research, for to be included or involved is to have an interest (or at least the right to an interest) in participation in the research process. Participation in this context includes the right to have a voice in terms of research ethics.

Given our experience, what would we need to take into account in rethinking the need for an ethics of participation?

The potential misuse of images

We have to recognise that we cannot provide guarantees about the ways in which images might be used (and misused). What we can do is to make judgments about where we should restrict access. For example, we can screen out images that for one reason or another embarrass people or expose them in a way that creates discomfort.

But to do this flies in the face of the methodological instincts of the conventional researcher and of the working ethics of the documentary or news photographer, who both tend to assume that once 'taken', the images/data are 'theirs'. At first sight, to exercise editorial judgment of the kind we are suggesting looks like tampering with the data, but in research of the kind we have described, the purpose is different from both conventional research and investigative journalism and we need to recognise this difference. The decision about what to publish is not for the researcher alone, but needs to involve all participants.

On the other hand, there is often extensive discussion and debate inside a project about such issues. What we should reveal is the source and focus of these discussions. This shifts the emphasis of reporting back to the need to provide extensive accounts of the research process.

Time-scales

There is a tendency in conventional research to see the negotiation of ethical procedures as a preliminary to research, but we have suggested here that it needs to be a more continuous process. It is also an educational process, since it involves getting all those concerned to think about the consequences of what they are doing and how they report their work. This in turn makes it difficult to plan. The shift here is from reliance on public accountability in terms of conforming to required and agreed procedures to a reliance on personal integrity and professional judgment. The first sounds less prone to individual fallibility and malpractice, but the second is increasingly unworkable in fast-moving circumstances.

Intellectual property issues

The offer of (or requirement for) anonymity for participants and institutions becomes problematic in participatory projects. In 'Seeing Beyond Violence' we used fictitious names for the children, but in doing so we were aware that we were taking away from them some ownership of the images and the research. This is a difficult balance. We claimed to be acting in their interest by disguising their identities (and, acting in the role of parent, the Village Directors asked that we did so) but did this diminish recognition of their participation and their intellectual property rights in the images?

Note

1 The United Nations Secretary General's Study on Violence Against Children (available online at www.violencestudy.org/r25).

References

'Baghdad Stories', www.worldphotoproject.com/.
'Born into Brothels', www.kids-with-cameras.org/bornintobrothels/.
Department for Education and Skills (DfES) (2002) *Schools for the Future. Designs for learning communities. Building Bulletin 95*, Stationery Office, London.
MacDonald, B. (1974). Evaluation and the control of education. In B. MacDonald & R. Walker (Eds.), *Innovation, evaluation, research and the problem of control.* Norwich: CARE, UEA. Later reprinted in various other publications.
'Seeing beyond violence' Children from Colombia, India, Nicaragua, Thailand with Peter Egg, Barbara Schratz Hadwich, Gerhild Trubwasser and Rob Walker, SOS Kinderdorf 2004. The report can be downloaded from the CARE website at www.uea.ac.uk/care/people/RW_recent_writing/Recent_Writing.html.

Chapter 11

Being 'seen' being 'heard'

Engaging with students on the margins of education through participatory photography

Ian Kaplan

> Many researchers become interested in the potential for students' use of images to bring critical issues to light. However, as Ian Kaplan points out in this narrative about a project conducted with students diagnosed by their school as having 'special needs', this needs to be carefully negotiated. Even then, as this chapter shows, the realpolitik of the institution may mean that what the students want to say in pictures is too confronting.

This chapter will consider one of a series of five linked student voice projects done with groups of students on the margins of education in northern England. The projects engaged students in using photography to explore and share their perspectives of schooling with the aim of addressing the outcomes of the *Every Child Matters* policy. Ultimately these projects were intended to move beyond consultation to actively involve the students in the processes of improving their experiences of education, and the potential for and challenges in doing so will be discussed.

Accessing the perspectives and insights of students with learning difficulties/disabilities and emotional and behavioural difficulties presents methodological challenges, and such students typically have little if any control of where, how and to what ends their perspectives are represented. The students I worked with took and used their own photographs and commentary in school as a means of considering and representing issues of importance to them about their experiences of schooling. I focus my discussion in this chapter on one particular project, which engaged students with learning difficulties in a mainstream secondary school. I will share several of the students' images and commentary to address some of the methodological and ethical issues which may arise in doing such participatory work.

A policy background

The emerging recognition of the importance of the perspectives of children and young people has been heralded and encouraged by the UK becoming a signatory to the United Nations Convention on the Rights of the Child (UNCRC)

(UN, 1990), and is reinforced through current UK government policy such as *Every Child Matters* (DfES, 2003) which legislates for the involvement of children and young people in the provision of services (such as schooling) which affect their lives. The introduction of *Every Child Matters* represented a major shift in UK policy in that it linked what had been separate service provisions for children's health, education and welfare in an attempt to create a more integrated and holistic approach to dealing with children and young people. Another key feature of *Every Child Matters* is the emphasis it places on the importance of children's rights and parental responsibilities.

Although a social policy which links formerly disconnected services and explicitly forefronts children's rights is of great potential benefit to children and young people, *Every Child Matters* is not without its problems. The scheme can be seen as evidence of the advance of the 'social investment state', which primarily values children in terms of their future economic potential. This is manifested, as Williams explains, in

> the investment of the child as citizen-worker-of-the-future, achieved through anti-poverty and education measures in which a notion of partnership of the state with parents, business and the voluntary sector, is central. The overall aim is to maintain competitiveness in the global economy.
>
> (Williams, 2004, p. 408)

On the surface, *Every Child Matters* and related policy initiatives are encouraging in terms of their potential to promote greater social inclusion in the UK by directly involving children and young people in the provision of social services they receive. However, the nature of this direct involvement warrants close and critical scrutiny as it is often predicated on unproblematised notions of 'voice' and 'participation' which seem to be addressed independently of important considerations about power, equity and social justice that impact upon them.

In this chapter I will use the process and outcomes of a student participatory photography project to consider some of the potentials for and tensions around the concepts of children's 'voices' and 'participation' in regards to their schooling.

Participatory photography as a method for working with disadvantaged students

> Many of the students I worked with had trouble writing; they would labour painfully over a sentence or two. But when they worked from a photograph that had something to do with their own lives, especially a picture they had taken themselves, they were able to write more – and what they wrote about was their own experiences.
>
> (Ewald and Lightfoot, 2001, p. 12)

In her work with children in schools, Wendy Ewald recognised that students' own photographs often stimulated their reflective writing. This *elicitative* potential of the photographic image, explored also in the work of John Collier and Douglas Harper (Collier & Collier, 1986; Harper, 2002), suggests that photography is a medium which can be well suited for working with children and young people, particularly those who have difficulty writing. Accordingly, photographic and other image-based methods have been credited with offering a means for children and young people to represent their lived experiences whilst at the same time providing adults with access to these youth perspectives (Wagner, 1999; Prosser & Burke, 2007).

On the surface, such activities are not necessarily overtly political acts; however, when participatory photography is practised as a public form of expression it becomes enmeshed in the wider politics of power and representation. Indeed, participatory photography as practised in various forms today traces at least some of its origins back to the community photography movement in Britain and the US in the 1960s to 1980s, a movement, particularly in Britain, with an explicitly socialist political agenda, concerned as much with the democratisation of art as with the politics of representation (De Cuyper, 1997–1998). During this heady period of support for community arts, participatory photography flourished, funded in part by increased government spending on arts and social programmes.

Participatory photography practised as a method of community empowerment was underpinned by feminist and Marxist theory and influenced by notions of the empowerment of 'oppressed' communities, as outlined in the work of the philosopher and educator, Paulo Freire (Wang & Burris, 1994). The popular growth of photography practised as a form of self-representation and social commentary done by (and with) instead of on members of the community was inspired and advocated by photographer/activists such as Jo Spence (Spence, 1995), Wendy Ewald (Ewald & Lightfoot, 2001) and Jim Hubbard (Hubbard, 1991), Ewald and Hubbard doing much of their work with children and young people. Developing in parallel, although not without cross-over, participatory photography also existed as a facet of social science research over the same mid- to late twentieth century period (with the inevitable blurring of distinctions between community arts and the social sciences).

The notion that visual media such as drawings and photographs are easy to access, particularly in comparison with other textual forms, has contributed to their popularity as methods of choice for conducting social science research with children and young people, but the power of such visual methods to represent 'pure' perspective is often overstated. Discussing her participatory drawing work with children in the Philippines, Mitchell cautions that the construction of visual methods as offering unproblematic and unmediated windows into children's worlds is '...tied to both adult-ist and North American centric assumptions about drawings and about children' (Mitchell, 2006, p. 62). With this note of caution in mind, I will consider the powerful, if problematic, method of children's and young people's engagement with (and through) participatory photography.

The project in context – 'Learning from Learners'

An informal group of local authority learning support staff in the northwest of England, 'Learning from Learners', has been interested in developing methods of engagement with the children and young people they support, many of whom have learning difficulties/disabilities, are at risk of exclusion for behavioural problems, or are otherwise struggling in mainstream education. As such, these young learners are least likely amongst their peers to have their perspectives on their experiences of education taken account of by adults or other students. Also, their marginalised status means they rarely have access to the traditional mechanisms of student participation, such as school councils.

The 'Learning from Learners' group became interested in participatory photography's potential to give the learners who the members support an accessible opportunity to consider and share their perspectives within (and beyond) their school communities. Crucially, 'Learning from Learners' anticipated that the sharing of these students' perspectives might lead to actual changes in schools.

Over a nine-month period I worked with members of the 'Learning from Learners' group within mainstream and special schools in five local authorities in the northwest of England. In each case, I organised a participatory photography project working with a small group of disadvantaged students, their teachers and a member of learning support staff from the respective local authority, the common linking theme being that each group of students engaged in the overall project was considered to be excluded from or under-represented in other student voice/student participation initiatives. Because of their circumstances, behaviour and difficulties/disabilities, these students were considered to be disaffected and particularly challenging to engage. With regard to expressing their perspectives about their educational experience, they were effectively unseen and unheard.

The context within which such participatory project work is done engenders a complex web of roles, relationships and responsibilities. As a university researcher working with students on participatory projects in schools, at the behest of the local authority, I felt at times that I was positioned awkwardly with regard to whose interests I represented and what my role within the projects should be. Conflicts in relation to participants' roles and positioning within a project are not always apparent if that project seems to be running smoothly, and can be difficult to pinpoint even when tensions arise. In order to ground this discussion in practice, I will look at one particular project, done in Redfield School, in which it took very specific tensions over several of the students' photographs and accompanying commentary to really bring out some of the unacknowledged contradictions underpinning my involvement in the project.

Participatory photography in Redfield School

Redfield is a large, mainstream secondary school in the northwest of England, serving a primarily white, working-class community. The area surrounding the school was described to me by the school's deputy head teacher as being socially deprived, with 30 per cent of Redfield's students receiving free school meals (a common indicator of poverty).

I worked in the school alongside a member of learning support staff from the local authority as well the teacher in the school with responsibility for students with special educational needs (SEN), both of whom provided invaluable support.

We worked with a group of younger students who had learning difficulties (such as dyslexia) and were seen as struggling to make the transition from primary to secondary schooling. These students had been placed in a 'nurture group'[1] within the school, a group intended to provide learning support and help better integrate the students into the mainstream of the school. 'Nurture groups' can offer a great deal of emotional as well as practical support for students who are, for whatever reason, not adjusting well or 'fitting in' to mainstream secondary schooling. However, in terms of student voice initiatives, nurture groups can actually obstruct or at least distract from the fostering of politically situated and active forms of student participation, in that they seek to modify students in order to integrate them into existing structures rather than challenging the structures which, arguably, marginalise the students in the first place. To apply a Freirien critique, 'nurture groups' constitute one of the softer forms of oppression by which 'marginals' (in this case students) are ' "incorporated" into the healthy society that they have "forsaken" ' (Freire, 1970, p. 55). Nurture-group students I worked with in Redfield were not unaware of the irony of their positioning within their school, and I think this speaks in some way for the feelings of disaffection several of them displayed and articulated during the project.

Seven Redfield students were chosen by their learning support teacher to participate in the project on the basis that they were considered to have learning and behavioural difficulties in school, low confidence and low self-esteem, and might gain something from involvement in the project. The students were given a choice as to whether or not they wanted to participate in the project, which was explained to them as being an opportunity to take photographs in school as a way of sharing their views. I was initially unsure as to whether the students really believed they had a choice about participating in the project. In the event, all seven students participated throughout much of the project, but several of them 'voted with their feet' by not attending certain project sessions which conflicted with classes or activities they enjoyed or felt were too important to miss.

Negotiating consent

(School) (a)dministrators see in visual aids not only valuable educational tools but also implements for the cultivation of better public relations. Here is an effective way of 'selling' the school, or ever increasing budgets, to the taxpayers.

(Kinder, 1942)

Recognition of the potential value of a school's use of visual imagery to positively influence public perception is certainly not a recent development as indicated by Kinder's comment on the use of visual aids in American schools in the 1940s. Kinder even notes (albeit uncritically) the mercantile relationship between a school and its public, a relationship which, arguably, has changed little in the intervening six decades.

Although visual imagery can help to foster positive perceptions, it can also have the opposite effect. Images can engender or reinforce negative public perceptions of a school, particularly within its own community, possibly affecting the numbers of students it attracts and consequently the school's overall funding. Put simply, negative perceptions can put schools at risk.

Researchers interested in pursuing visual research in schools need to be aware of the potential for visual imagery to impact negatively on a school. Schools which have experienced periods of difficulty and been subject to negative public perceptions may be especially wary about how they are perceived by outsiders, and protective of their reputations. I've found it useful to foreground these issues in my initial discussions with a school, before beginning a participatory photography project, and return to them at various points during the project.

It was explained to me, before I began work in Redfield School, that in the previous few years the school had struggled with leadership changes and a poor reputation in the community. During my first meeting in the school, the school management told me that although Redfield had managed to overcome these challenges and become a popular and, in fact, oversubscribed local school, they were concerned that any seemingly negative photographs taken by their students might be viewed outside the school and could damage their newly improved image in the community. The deputy head of the school explained

I am very happy for our children to tell me what they know ... what's right and what's wrong here. I'm not happy about dirty linen being washed in public. And that's the line that I want to draw really.

At the time, my local authority colleague and I were pleased that the school management had themselves raised these concerns, and our ensuing discussion helped us develop the parameters for working with photographs and commentary generated by the students during the project. However, we had our own concerns that the school might dismiss, or censor, any images and commentary they felt were negative or in some way critical of the school. Ultimately, we negotiated an agreement under which the senior management of the school, including the head and deputy head teacher, would view, take seriously and address all images and commentary from the students. Any images and commentary in which the school could be identified would first have to be approved by the management before being used outside of the school, thus giving them censorial control.

This seemed a reasonable balance, as we were primarily concerned that issues raised by the students were dealt with within the school. Our agreement with the school seemed straightforward, but it was to prove more complex once the students began to take and comment on their photographs.

The project structure

Much of the project work took place during seven half-day sessions over the course of six months. This process involved a variety of activities, outlined as follows:

- Initial and subsequent meetings with senior staff
- Working with the students to translate the five *Every Child Matters* outcomes into accessible language
- A workshop on 'reading'/interpreting photographs, and discussing issues about ethics and consent
- Instruction in using the cameras, and basic photographic technique
- Initial photography with digital cameras in groups
- Individual and group work to consider the photographs and their possible meanings
- Project work – putting the photos and commentary into PowerPoint presentations
- Giving the PowerPoint presentations in school
- Preparing modified PowerPoint projects and presenting them outside the school.

Every Child Matters

We used the five *Every Child Matters* outcomes (DfES, 2003) as a way of orienting the students to the project:

1   Be healthy
2   Stay safe
3   Enjoy and achieve
4   Make a positive contribution
5   Achieve economic well-being.

As these outcomes underpinned this work I wanted to be explicit about them with the students, and so we spent time deconstructing them together during our first project session. Although the outcomes seem relatively straightforward at first glance, they are not as clear or unambiguous as they might appear. The concepts are quite broad, and the language vague in places and open to different interpretations. This lack of clarity extends beyond the outcomes and is also evident in other places within the *Every Child Matters* documentation (Williams, 2004). For example, within the Redfield School project, several of the students interpreted 'making a positive contribution' in the financial sense of giving money to charities.

Some of the more explicit aspirations in the outcomes do provide a good basis for participatory photography work. The students were able to use them, particularly the first three outcomes, as a starting point for their photographic enquiry in school, and many of their images relate in some way to issues of health, safety and enjoyment (or lack of enjoyment) in school.

Initially we spent some time looking at and discussing photographs taken by other students in similar projects, with the intention of opening up the potential for different interpretations of the same images. We considered photographs with and without additional captioning/commentary in thinking about the ways in which commentary affects interpretation. Specific photographic examples were also useful in discussing some of the ethical issues around photography and consent. These discussions emphasised the importance of negotiating consent, particularly in regard to people who might be visible in photographs.

Before taking their photographs, student participants were encouraged to draw and map where and what they might like to photograph in school (see Figure 11.1). These plans helped give structure to their subsequent photographic activities.

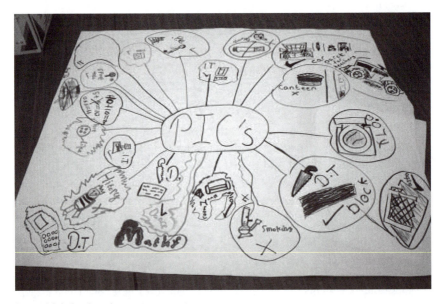

Figure 11.1 Students' mapping exercise.

The seven student participants (four boys and three girls) were initially divided into three mixed-sex groups, but as the project evolved they realigned themselves into two single-sex groups. These groups proceeded to take digital photographs, select the ones they felt were most important and organise these into PowerPoint presentations.

Project facilitation

One of the main forms of facilitation in the project involved organising discussions with the students about their images. Initially, I printed the students' photographs and returned them to the groups in order for them to select and organise the images they wanted to use for their projects. Concerned that the students' learning difficulties made handwriting difficult, we developed a style of working in which conversations with the students about their photographs were tape-recorded, transcribed and then fed back to the groups. The students selected commentary from electronic versions of their transcripts, which they then cut and pasted (and sometimes modified further), to accompany specific photographs in creating PowerPoint slides. Most of the student participants were adept (often more so than the adults) at negotiating the technology of PowerPoint, and were able to type and modify their commentary on laptop computers with an ease and confidence they did not display in their writing.

Several of the students we worked with during the project were understandably wary about sharing their more critical comments about the school with us. They expressed concern that they might be ignored or even get into trouble if they were candid. As project facilitators, we spent a lot of time assuring the students they would be taken seriously; that we wanted to know about and act on their concerns; and that they would not get into any trouble as a result of sharing their views. As it turned out, we were somewhat over-optimistic about the school's readiness to engage with the students' more critical perspectives.

Tensions over perspective

The development of PowerPoint presentations in the Redfield project went through several stages, the first of which involved a basic slide presentation of the students' initial choices of photographs and commentary. We had planned that the students would revisit these initial photos and comments during the next stage of the project, before they actually presented them in school. This was intended to allow the students time to consider and discuss their work, test certain assumptions, challenge each others' interpretations, edit as necessary and agree on a more finalised set of images and commentary. Unfortunately, this second stage in the process was to some extent pre-empted by the schools' deputy head who, between sessions and unbeknownst to my local authority colleague and I, viewed the initial, rough version of the students' PowerPoint slides.

When we returned to the school for our second stage meeting with the students we were ushered unprepared into an emergency meeting with the deputy head, before having a chance to discuss what had happened with the teacher or to meet with the students. During this meeting (the students were not present) the deputy head expressed his serious concern that some of the students' images and commentary were 'untrue' or 'unfair' to the school and, in the case of certain images/comments, offensive to him personally.

Photographs and commentary

Many of the students' images and comments were intended to be positive reflections of their school experience and, unsurprisingly, these were relatively uncontested by the school management, who in fact encouraged the student participants to share these both in and outside of the school. I make a rather crude division here between positive and negative images – considered more carefully, much of this work was far more nuanced and less polarised than the positive/negative dichotomy suggests. However, I think such a distinction here is useful, as it reflects the way in which the students' images were understood within the context of the school community. Students' positive images and commentary, which in many ways celebrate aspects of schooling, make a worthy subject of discussion, but are less interesting than their negative counterparts in terms of illuminating some of the contradictions and issues of power and control which are sometimes unacknowledged in accounts of student voice work. Consequently, the following examples fall more within the 'negative' category, but are not meant to be wholly representative of the larger project.

The following selected images and text are presented together as they appeared in slide form in the students' PowerPoint presentations. The captions are the students' commentary on the accompanying image.

Figure 11.2 depicts a girls' toilet without a seat. The girls who created the slide were unhappy with the condition of the schools' toilets and chose to document this photographically, addressing it as a health/safety aspect of their project. Negative images and commentary about school toilets are typical in participatory photography projects done by students (Schratz & Steiner-Löffler, 1998; Kaplan, Lewis, & Mumba, 2007) as, unsurprisingly, school toilets are often crowded, dirty and unpleasant places. Also, as Lodge (2005, p. 143) points out, toilets represent one of several 'comfort' issues that students are likely to be encouraged to address (as opposed to issues about teaching and learning) in student voice initiatives.

The image and commentary in the slide are provocative (a sense which is enhanced by their juxtaposition) and sparked an immediate reaction from both the school's learning support teacher and the deputy head. The deputy head's initial response was to dismiss the students' comments, and he was at pains to explain that although the toilet was visible in the photo without a seat which had indeed been broken (it would have been difficult to claim otherwise), it had been

Figure 11.2 'In the changing rooms people take their trainers off and they stink. They're disgusting. Some of us don't even use the toilets they smell that bad, or we use them only if we really need to. The toilets never get washed out. There's two toilets and like 300 girls. One of the toilets is locked'.

promptly repaired and should not be indicative of the general condition of toilets in the school. Despite his initial reactions, both he and the learning support teacher were concerned enough about the students' emphatically negative critique of the school toilets that they felt the matter deserved more careful consideration. The learning support teacher was later able to use the students' toilet photo and comments to discuss the issue with them more thoroughly.

Figure 11.3 is a modified version of the students' original toilet slide, produced after the photographers discussed their concerns with the learning support teacher and then, together with the teacher, revisited the school toilets. Although it would be an overstatement to suggest that the issues underlying the students' dissatisfaction with toilets were fully resolved, the students' concerns were eventually taken more seriously. This modified slide was used in a presentation in the school which led to a school-wide review of toilets and a cleanliness drive in which the student photographers participated.

Photographing teaching and learning

The medium of photography allows for both literal and more figurative or metaphorical representations (and these can of course occur together in the same image). Participatory photography need not be a rigidly stepped activity in the

Figure 11.3 'In the main toilets they are clean, there's lots of toilet roll. The PE toilet doesn't have a seat on. There's two toilets and like 150 girls. One of the toilets is sometimes blocked'.

sense that participants must decide first on what to photograph, take their photographs, and only then discuss the resulting images. Also, the process of image-taking need not be conceived as a means of representing objective reality (a concept which is problematic in any case). Spontaneity can be an important part of the process, and some of the most interesting photographs for the purposes of a project may be accidental or even constructed to be deliberately symbolic.

Although the physical environment lends itself to being represented fairly easily (if selectively) in photographs, concepts and relationships can be more challenging to depict photographically. At first, it was easier for the Redfield students to focus on relatively concrete issues of health and safety in their projects as opposed to more abstract concepts about teaching and learning. Although the students would often make comments such as 'I like art' or 'This teacher is boring', it was difficult for them to articulate or discuss the feelings, experiences and reasoning underlying these statements.

During one of our project sessions, I was talking with a group about their favourite school subjects when the conversation shifted unexpectedly into a discussion about how some of the students felt as if teachers in the school didn't really know them. This seemed an important issue for them, and one which needed further unpacking. I encouraged the students to consider creatively how they might construct a photograph to represent this issue (see Figure 11.4).

In further discussion with the students, they clarified that it was actually supply (temporary) teachers whom they felt did not know them in school. Their

Figure 11.4 'Most of the supply teachers don't know anything about us. They make us do loads and loads of writing and the same things over and over again. They don't know what we've done and what we've not done. It's boring to do the same things over and over and over again. You could look at different days and we've done the same work'.

visual depiction of this in Figure 11.4 involves an image of three whiteboards with very similar drawings of a house, dated as if they were done on three consecutive days.

Schools with staffing shortages often have few options but to employ temporary teachers, potentially disrupting the continuity of learning for any students but causing particular difficulties for students with learning difficulties, who often benefit most from teachers who know them well and are able to accommodate their teaching to fit the students' individual learning styles.

Figure 11.4 was one of the slides most strongly objected to by the deputy head during our emergency meeting to discuss the project. He wanted the slide taken out of the project altogether, did not want to discuss it with the students and did not even want the head teacher to see it. Although I could certainly understand why he might not want this slide displayed outside of the school, not to discuss it internally seemed to directly contradict our original agreement that the school would take seriously and address with the students any issues which were brought up during the project.

The students' comments about their relationships with supply teachers were not something any school wants to hear from its students. However, they did seem to reflect the experiences of some of the students in the nurture group and their marginal status within the school.

As the students' commentary was serious and specific, we did go back to them to discuss the issues and specific slide in more detail (as we had planned to do in any case with all of the slides). The students were adamant that this was their experience and only altered the wording on the slide slightly, changing 'most of the supply teachers' to 'some teachers' and removing an 'over' from 'over and over and over' again. Regardless of the changes to the commentary and the students' insistence that this was what they wanted to say, the slide with its image and commentary were vetoed by the deputy head teacher and stripped from the slide presentation. With the photo of the whiteboards, it seemed we had reached the limit of critical student voice in Redfield School.

It can be difficult as an outside researcher to know how to react in such situations. In the case of Figure 11.4, I felt there were clearly some serious underlying issues behind the students' commentary, even if these were more to do with a general feeling of being unknown or unappreciated in the school than actually about specific temporary teachers. My local authority colleague and I together tried to pursue these issues, first in the emergency meeting with the deputy head teacher and then again in another meeting with both the head and deputy head teacher, but without any real engagement on their part. Although we tried to shift the discussion beyond the literal 'truth' of the photograph of the whiteboards, the fact that the image had been staged was enough to justify the management's dismissal of the concepts it was intended to represent.

Tensions around the interpretation of the most contentious of the students' slides left me with a sense that the school's senior management was unwilling or unable to acknowledge that students' perspectives which challenged existing structures of teaching and learning might have veracity and be of value in stimulating reflection and even change within the school.

Conclusion

Despite (if not in some sense because of) the tensions over the project, the student participants were able to build confidence in presenting and defending their views, and were subsequently able to present some of their work in the school to the senior management team and outside at several local conferences.

Although the school failed to address all of the students' concerns, they began a process of dialogue with the nurture-group students which may in future develop to a point where issues of teaching and learning are more open for discussion. My colleague from the local authority continues to work with the learning support teacher towards this end. As a direct result of the project, the nurture group asked for and currently has a representative who feeds into the school council. Small steps perhaps, but creating a culture in which a school can really engage with the perspectives of its most marginalised students is a long-term process.

As my experiences with Redfield School have shown, it can be difficult to speculate in advance about the possible impact of images in or outside of a school, particularly before any images have actually been generated. Still, before embarking upon a participatory photography project in a school it is challenging but necessary to discuss the potential for photographs/commentary to create or exacerbate tensions within a school. To better ground these discussions and make the issues less abstract, it can be helpful to use examples of existing photographic images. I often use examples from previous projects (such as students' photos of vandalised toilets) which were in some way contentious in their original contexts, but it is also possible to use images taken from the Internet, newspapers, or magazines ... photographs that are potentially provocative and can be 'read' in different ways. It is my experience that tensions around perception, control (of images) and meaning are never settled, but manifest themselves in different ways throughout the life of a project and beyond. In working with schools, the value of frequent and ongoing dialogue between researchers and school staff cannot be overstated. This necessitates the development of a longitudinal relationship between researchers and participants. Short-term or one-off participatory image-making projects offer the least opportunity for depth and increase the potential for misinterpretations and misuse of data on all sides.

I have argued elsewhere (Kaplan *et al.*, 2007) that too literal an interpretation of students' photographs (by the photographers themselves as well as other audiences) can be unhelpful in that it closes down possibilities for different interpretations and the dialogues these might create. A positivist notion that photographs necessarily tell simple truths fails to take account both of the variegations of context (of image creation and image consumption) and a process of meaning-making which allows for multiple interpretations and re-interpretations (Barthes, 1981; McQuire, 1998). It can be a source of enjoyment for students to challenge their own and each other's photographic interpretations and come up with alternate meanings, and this is indicative of the type of deep engagement and creative potential that participatory photography offers. Meanings may shift for the photographers over time, and this again is where a longitudinal approach can be helpful if it can provide time and space for students' perspectives to change and develop.

Researchers should encourage participants to challenge literalism and absolutism in regard to photographic representation and meaning, but this needs to be handled carefully. Too strict an interpretivist line runs counter to the ethos of student voice work and does the student photographer a disservice, because it suggests that his or her photograph is so open to interpretation that it is effectively meaningless. Essentially, this approach can devalue photographers' intentions behind taking a photograph and diminish their confidence and trust. When considering students' photographs and commentary, it is easy to flippantly push truisms such as 'everyone is entitled to their own opinion' without really engaging with the power differentials that determine which and whose opinions are dominant. Relativism in this sense can be practised as an obfuscating and equivocal form of control in that it purposefully seeks to confuse meanings and elide students' perspectives. It is crucial that student photographers are given space and encouragement to consider and articulate the meanings and intentions behind their photographs before these are too aggressively challenged. Given time, and approached sensitively, with gentle encouragement, students will themselves often challenge their own initial interpretations of their images.

Over the course of the project with the nurture group in Redfield School, the ways in which we as adult facilitators approached the students' consideration of their images over time affected the process and content of their discussions. When we encouraged the students to look through their original images and commentary at their leisure, and with a degree of openness and gentle questioning on our part, they often took their commentary in new directions and sometimes challenged their original interpretations. When, feeling the pressure of the school management, we chose specific slides for the students to re-consider, they picked up on our tension and discomfort and questioned us as to why they needed to change their images/commentary (even when we didn't ask them explicitly to make changes). These more forced re-considerations understandably engendered feelings of mistrust from the students and reinforced the conviction that adults were not going to take them seriously. In a very real sense the students felt we had asked for their 'voices', not liked some of what we'd heard and were now asking them to change what they had to say.

Student voice initiatives are sometimes treated and discussed as if they were conducted in a vacuum; however, such work is always done in highly politicised contexts. Young learners themselves are rarely privy to the wider political discussions about student voice, and often find themselves on the receiving end of even the most well-intentioned student voice initiatives. Being seen and being heard can be an empowering and confidence-building experience, especially for young learners on the margins of educational systems, but comes with the risk that adults will disagree or not even engage with what they have to show and say. Researchers and others who advocate for and support young learners to share their perspectives and participate in the politics of education need also to work towards ensuring that there are real and legitimate spaces in and outside of schools where these perspectives can be engaged with.

Note

1 Nurture groups, first established in London schools in the 1980s, have since become fairly common within the UK school system (O'Connor & Colwell, 2002). The groups, which often have their own classroom base, work as support structures and resource centres within primary and secondary schools for students with emotional, behavioural and learning difficulties. These groups tend to be small (usually no more than ten students), are generally overseen by staff with specialist training and are conceived as 'safe' spaces where students can be emotionally and pedagogically supported and helped to integrate into mainstream school life.

References

Barthes, R. (1981). *Camera lucida.* Farrar, Strauss and Giroux.
Collier, J., & Collier, M. (1986). *Visual anthropology. Photography as a research method.* New Mexico: New Mexico University Press.

De Cuyper, S. (1997–1998). On the future of photographic representation in anthropology: lessons from the practice of community photography in Britain. *Visual Anthropology Review, 13*(2), 2–18.

Department for Education and Skills (2003). *Every Child Matters.* Green Paper, Cm. 5860. London: The Stationery Office (TSO).

Ewald, W., & Lightfoot, A. (2001). *I wanna take me a picture. Teaching photography and writing to children.* Boston, MA: Beacon Press.

Freire, P. (1970). *Pedagogy of the oppressed.* London: Continuum Publishing.

Harper, D. (2002). Talking about pictures: a case for photo elicitation. *Visual Studies, 17*(1), 13–26.

Hubbard, J. (1991). *Shooting back. A photographic view of life by homeless children.* San Francisco, CA: Chronicle Books.

Kaplan, I., Lewis, I., & Mumba, P. (2007). Picturing global educational inclusion? Looking and thinking across students' photographs from the UK, Zambia and Indonesia. *Journal of Research in Special Educational Needs, 7*(1), 23–35.

Kinder, J. S. (1942). Visual aids in education. *Review of Educational Research, 12*(3), 336–344.

Lodge, C. (2005). From hearing voices to engaging in dialogue. Problematising student participation in school improvement. *Journal of Educational Change, 6,* 125–146.

McQuire, S. (1998). *Visions of modernity.* London: Sage Publications.

Mitchell, L.M. (2006). Child-centered? Thinking critically about children's drawings as a visual research method. *Visual Anthropology Review, 22*(1), 60–73.

O'Connor, T., & Colwell, J. (2002). The effectiveness and rationale of the 'nurture group' approach to helping children with emotional and behavioural difficulties remain within mainstream education. *British Journal of Special Education, 29*(2), 96–100.

Prosser, J., & Burke, C. (2007). Childlike perspectives through image-based educational research. In J.G. Knowles and A.L. Cole (Eds.), *Handbook of the arts in qualitative research. Perspectives, methodologies, examples and issues.* Thousand Oaks, CA: Sage Publications.

Schratz, M., & Steiner-Löffler, U. (1998). Pupils using photographs in school self evaluation. In J. Prosser (Ed.), *Image-based research. A sourcebook for qualitative researchers* (pp, 235–251). London: Routledge Falmer.

Spence, J. (1995). *Cultural sniping. The art of transgression.* London: Routledge.

United Nations (1990). Conventions of the Rights of the Child. Geneva: UN.

Wagner, J. (1999). Visual studies and seeing kid's worlds. *Visual Sociology, 14,* 3–6.

Wang, C., & Burris, M. (1994). Empowerment through photo novella: portraits of participation. *Health Education Quarterly, 21*(2), 171–186.

Williams, F. (2004). 'What matters is who works. Why Every Child Matters to New Labour. Commentary on the DfES Green Paper Every Child Matters' *Critical Social Policy, 24*(3), 406–427.

Chapter 12

'Voice' and video

Seen, heard and listened to?

Kaye Haw

In this chapter the researcher, Kaye Haw, draws attention to three kinds of 'voice' that were elicited during a participatory video project designed to inform a school about the views of some excluded students. Like Kaplan in Chapter 11, her discussion about the outcomes of the project raises questions about the contexts in which such work can be said to achieve all of its aims.

Introduction

This chapter discusses one approach to the articulation of 'voice' within the participatory research process, and has two aims. The first is to help increase awareness of the methodological problems and possibilities of working with video and voice. The discussion highlights the power of the medium to influence the change process, while drawing attention to its equivalent potential to obstruct this process, through reference to one research project funded by the Joseph Rowntree Foundation involving young people excluded from school. The second aim is to problematise the use of video within the participatory research process. The chapter does this by looking critically at the notion of 'voice' and participation, and issues about who is listened to and what is listened to, through a discussion of what happened at the end of the project.

It is claimed that participatory research is an alternative philosophy of social research because it makes a commitment to be responsive to the needs of ordinary people and makes no claim to neutrality or to serving the needs of the wealthy and the powerful (McTaggart, 1997; Park, Brydon-Miller, Hall, & Jackson, 1993). The role of 'ordinary people' throughout the process can take different forms, from those who are trained and supported to become researchers themselves, to those who work as co-researchers and have an equality of input to the whole design process, to those who are little more than engaged participants. The need to develop the participation of 'ordinary people', whatever their role, creates key methodological challenges to do with the representation of different epistemological standpoints, and issues of equity, power and dynamic models of identity. Such challenges necessitate an innovative and varied approach to data collection that increasingly has come to involve the use of video.

Video is seen as a useful medium for helping 'ordinary people' participate in research because it can help them articulate a voice through a visual rather than written text, and one which can attract a wider audience. The increased use of video across the social sciences is well documented (Banks, 1995, 2001; Pink, 2001; Prosser, 1992, 1998; Rose, 2001; Voithofer, 2005). It is also considered to be a powerful dissemination medium for a range of projects concerned with young people. For these reasons there has been a massive expansion in the use of video with young people by a range of professionals and campaign organisations trying to ensure that their 'voice' is heard within local decision-making. The National Youth Agency and British Film Institute estimated in 2005 that there were 17,000 young people being given video training with thousands more involved in video projects with no training. Video production has become a popular approach as it is seen as a means of increasing young people's participation within civic life and education, particularly those deemed alienated or disaffected (Johnson, 2001; Kincade & Macy, 2003; Tolman & Pittman, 2001).

My own work with video has been developed over previous research projects working with teams of academic and community researchers and marginalised groups and communities on a range of sensitive topics, from issues around racism through to domestic violence and perceptions of strip-search procedures in prisons. In each research project video was used slightly differently, depending on the objectives of the research and the type of users it aimed to engage in the work from its inception to its dissemination. Each of these pieces of research had a common aim: to legitimate a range of 'voices' through creating a series of spaces for critical dialogue and action using video as a professional development and community consultation tool, and combining this with Melucci's (1989, 1996) work as a means to explore group self-representation, and collective and individual identity (see Hadfield & Haw, 1997a, 1997b; 2000, 2002; Haw, 2006).

There are four methodological issues generated by working with video and 'voice' in this way: the relational, the technical, the creative, and the potential for bringing about change. In discussing these issues, the chapter begins by highlighting the different types of voice articulated in the 'Seen but not Heard' Project through an exploration of the relationships between the participants and organisations involved in the research and the tensions this created. The technical and creative aspects of working with video are discussed in the context of these developing relationships. The chapter ends by bringing together a very brief theoretical discussion of the concept of 'voice' highlighting the methodological challenges generated by working with 'voice' and video in the participatory research process with the potential of video to create change by looking at how the video was received by the school.

Listening to critical 'voices': the 'Seen But Not Heard' project

The research was wholly funded by the Joseph Rowntree Foundation as part of an initiative aimed at raising the 'voice' of young people in preventive work with families, and involved a team of researchers from University of Nottingham working in partnership with community youth workers. Throughout the project the researchers kept research journals. The following discussion concerning the relational, technical, creative and change challenges presented by the research draws on these journal entries.

The project began by looking for a partnership with an organisation that was already working with a group of young people. Several organisations in the inner-city area of Nottingham were considered before the 'Time Out' programme, run by a local community group called 'The Edge', concerned with young people and drugs, was chosen. The Time Out programme worked with a group of young people who were excluded or at risk of being excluded from school, and had several important features. The Edge, in partnership with the school, had established the programme as a way of positively engaging with these young people and so had credibility with the school and the young people living in the area. The youth workers from The Edge working on the Time Out programme told us that through this programme the young men were familiar with discussing sensitive issues and working in small groups. The group was all male, and indicative of the disproportionate number of young men excluded from school in this locality.

The group met at a local house, used by The Edge as a drop-in centre, every Wednesday morning. The research began by identifying and raising the issues surrounding exclusion as seen by them. The outcome from this first phase was a group statement, part of which said: 'The school system is unfair ... You skive and you get excluded. Teachers don't listen to you ... In school you don't get to talk about important things'. Exploring the validity of this statement, and collecting the views of those involved in the exclusion process, formed the basis for the making of the video. Together with the Time Out team, we encouraged them to take on the responsibility for organising themselves and making decisions about the content of their video and the direction of the research.

They were adamant from the outset that they wanted to make a video about the unfairness of the school system, the ways in which they had been singled out for attention and how they were frequently denied any real say in their treatment. The production of their video meant the young men became involved in group and individual work as they organised and conducted interviews with a range of adults, such as teachers and educational welfare officers as well as people living in the area, and dramatised an exclusion panel meeting.

Initially the group planned to screen the video to four key audiences, staff at their school, local head teachers, governors, and the Chief Education Officer of the Local Education Authority. Their intentions were twofold, to have their 'voice' heard clearly in a debate about these issues and to encourage teachers and officials to be more sensitive to the needs of young people when tackling the joint problems of exclusion and non-attendance. They wanted to provide a critical 'voice' that would challenge the perceptions of professionals about excluded pupils.

Different relationships, different agendas, different 'voices'

Relationship building and maintenance is a key part of any participatory research process because in different relationships different voices are articulated, prioritised and privileged. We had several research relationships to maintain, between the school and ourselves, between the Time Out team and ourselves, and between the Time Out team and the school. At the same time we also needed to establish a relationship with the young men that would not harm the existing relationship that they had with the Time Out workers, and we did this partly by attending social events with the group throughout the lifetime of the project.

The therapeutic 'voice' of the Time Out team

The Time Out team was part of The Edge whose brief was to counsel drug users through a therapeutic approach aimed at the development of self-esteem. To maintain our relationship with the Time Out team we agreed that we would have regular de-briefing sessions, especially as they were actively involved in the research and had particular insights into the experiences, circumstances and relationships within the group of young men. Sometimes these de-briefing sessions concentrated on practical issues, such as transport, administration or the location of activities, and sometimes they were more concerned with group dynamics, the strengths and weaknesses of the research, or on links between the team and the school. In addition to finding out more information about the young men in the programme, we also touched on aspects of the team's work with schools. The first tension we experienced was in making the most of these sessions, especially in the critical early stages of the research when we had to rely on their 'insider' knowledge of the young men. We all had other demands on our time, and working with the group, either by encouraging them or by managing their heated discussions and 'walk outs', was exhausting for both the Time Out team and ourselves.

This team was committed to supporting these young men to talk about themselves in ways that would promote key therapeutic outcomes for them, such as improving their self-esteem and awareness. Trying to support these young men in this way at times cut across our attempts to develop their more critical 'voice' directed at the school. Additionally, from the beginning the Time Out team expressed a desire to be more flexibly integrated into a range of school activities. They hoped we would facilitate this through the research, but we knew from our discussions with the school that the activities of the Time Out team did not always meet with approval at the school, mainly because of the therapeutic nature of their work. Some staff felt that pupils' attendance at the programme was effectively a 'reward for bad behaviour', and that it consisted of too many 'outings' and not enough 'work'. One teacher was pleasantly surprised when we described the detail and depth of the activities that the group engaged in as part of the programme in general, and of the research project. Similarly, youth workers at The Edge were not always aware of the ways in which the school perceived them.

Dealing with these differences in perceptions and agendas between partner organisations was the basis of a series of tensions that had to be managed by us as 'go-betweens' as we crossed these professional boundaries. This was time consuming in a short and tightly budgeted research project which was committed to developing the critical 'voice' of the young people, and inevitably affected both the video production process and its content as different 'key players' (most notably in the school) started to feel more and more uncomfortable about some of the things they 'heard' the young people wanted to do.

The dominant 'authoritative voice' of OFSTED

Implicit in the design of the project was an intention to work with the school on issues identified by the young men, but we always knew that this was going to be a difficult task. The school had a history of falling rolls and underperformance, and had been subject to a range of external interventions. It had not done well in its a recent OFSTED inspection, and was attempting to tackle a number of 'serious weaknesses' identified by the inspectors. All this, in our opinion, made the school important to work with and support. In particular, it seemed like a good time for us to work with them as they were forced through their own change process. We believed they would welcome the opportunity to listen to the voices of some of their excluded pupils as part of the change they were hoping to achieve through their new action plan.

At the beginning of the project, the acting head teacher and the head of Year 11 both agreed to be interviewed and to respond to the research statement. It was also encouraging when the drama teacher that the young people considered 'safe' was given permission to be involved in the project. As the research progressed, working with the school became fraught with difficulties, even though the 'safe' teacher was involved in the discussions about content and gave advice on the best way to present potentially contentious sequences. The sheer pressures of years of inspection and re-inspection, of being subjected to 'special measures', of declining staff morale and a bruised reputation, made the school increasingly inaccessible, and key members of the management team were increasingly difficult to contact and meet with.

As an organisation overwhelmed with externally imposed change, it became less able to cope with internally generated change from its own pupils and staff. It became more apparent that this was probably one of its underlying problems. By the time the video was finished the school had been placed in 'special measures', and the 'voice' of OFSTED began to silence more marginalised perspectives of the young people.

Developing the critical 'voice' of the young men

In our work with the young men, possibly the single biggest challenge we faced was how we dealt with the existing beliefs the group had about itself. Over their time on the programme the young men had developed a 'group think', a number of perspectives that had become self-supporting and crucial to maintaining their resistance to what was happening to them at school. At the start of the project, their 'voice' was a more naïve and critical 'voice' that came from an intuitive reaction to what was happening to them. School played a dominant and in many senses a secure part of their lives.

> Learning new things makes you aware of what you don't know, and these young people don't think they know a lot. I expect they've been told that before now, and they tell each other often enough.
>
> (Journal entry 22.6.98)

A key dilemma for us was how to deal with this 'group think'. Adopting too critical a stance too early might have jeopardised our relationships with them and amongst the group itself. Initially, we tended to 'buy into' this group solidarity rather than critique it. For very different reasons, the workers on the Time Out programme were also uncomfortable in challenging certain aspects of this 'group think' because of the importance they placed on the therapeutic aspects of their role. They felt this perspective required them to adopt a very accepting stance towards the group. Here we were faced with a tension between two approaches that were trying to develop very different types of 'voice', therapeutic and critical.

These young people knew what they wanted to say but despite their external bravura, they lacked self-confidence and were easily intimidated when placed in situations in which they perceived they had no control, such as interviewing their senior teachers (see Figure 12.1). When talking to them about showing their final video they expressed a desire to run into the room, start the film and run out again, because they felt they would not be able to deal adequately with the resulting discussion. We used several strategies to overcome this. One of these was to get them to present the ongoing work to a group of academics at a conference on social exclusion. This was extremely well received. As the filming and editing progressed, their 'voice' became more sophisticated. They became particularly concerned that pupils following them would not have to face similar experiences, and hoped their video would help. As our relationship

Figure 12.1 Setting up an interview with a senior teacher.

with them developed it became 'good enough' to challenge their group perspective, but we often found ourselves being drawn away to deal with other issues. Most notably, these were the political aspects of the project concerned with managing diverse relationships and different voices.

As we tried to mediate between different agendas, relationships and voices, our priority was listening to the critical 'voice' of the young people. This created a series of tensions with the Time Out team, as we asked them to step back from their therapeutic approach and encouraged them to use their knowledge of the group to develop their criticality, and with a school that was already being critiqued by OFSTED. In our management of these tensions we remained true to our own agenda: that of developing the critical 'voice' of the young men and producing a video that they could be proud of. This is where the technical and creative aspects of the approach became important.

The technical aspects of the process

At the beginning of the research, introducing the video-based process and the technical aspects of video production dominated discussions with the group.

> Why use video? This for me is an important question in that we have them speaking to each other, them asking people questions, lots of talking but no

'voice'. So what then is the advantage of using video that is different in this context from using other research tools? What should video be able to do and have we really talked to the group about this? What are we going to come out with, one video, two videos, who are we going to show them to and how? I just have the feeling at the moment that the technology has closed down rather than opened things up which I think the model is all about.

(Journal entry, 21.3.98)

The video, both as a technical and a creative process, shaped our own thinking and placed additional demands on how we managed our work with the group. There was also the lag between introducing video and the technical aspects of filming, story-boarding and editing, and us feeling comfortable with its ability to prompt self-reflection through these technical processes.

Matching what these young people were 'saying' and what they brought with them, to what we were implicitly demanding of them is an ongoing process that we should have managed better than we did. We were not reflective enough about our own processes and demands ... too instrumental in applying a video production process to our research and thinking.

(Journal entry, 18.6.98)

Possibly the most problematic issue was that the 'natural' rhythm of demands that video production placed on the group did not match with the development of our relationship with them and their own internal dynamic as a group.

They say, 'We are: swearing, smoking, go-carting, skating, eating free stuff, getting more free stuff out of people, doing and seeing new things, playing with equipment, talking when we feel like it, making people listen to us, do first think later, just do and see what happens, getting a reaction for the sake of it and pushing people's buttons once you've found them. If any one of those things gets boring we'll jump to another one.' That's what the young people came to us with. That's what they left us with. We said to them: 'We need: order, processes, listening, thinking, reflecting, long-term-stuff, overview and democratic decision making. We'll help you to give us this stuff, but its up to you, because this is yours and it's about you.' Some of our demands connected with those at school and others had little connection with their lives at all. The last, democratic decision making was very useful in getting the job done, but from Gary's point of view it was, 'Take it or leave it'.

(Journal entry, 17.6.98)

The creative aspect of the process

The creative aspects of video production interacted continuously with the technical. There were two particular hurdles: the first was concerned with increasing the group's confidence with different forms of filming so that they moved away from the 'talking heads' interviews they associated with the documentaries they saw on popular television; the second was getting them to realise that their final product would not be the 'slick' production that they constantly watched on television. We also had to be very inventive in supporting them to cope with editing the large amount of film they collected. This was time consuming and emotionally charged.

While the majority of the group enjoyed going out and filming and often messing about with the camera, it was only a minority that could be persuaded to take part in the laborious process of reviewing and then editing this material. Making a group decision about the overall structure for the video, what stayed in and what went, was the cause of heated discussions, some of which escalated out of control and seriously affected relationships within the group. In the end we mitigated this by giving smaller groups responsibility for the editing of individual sections, and at the very end only worked with one or two volunteers to edit the final video (see Figure 12.2).

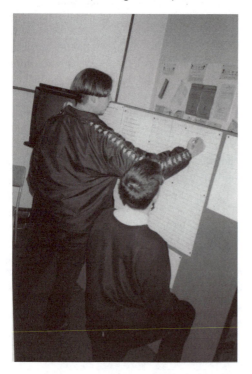

Figure 12.2 Brainstorming ideas for editing the video.

Managing the technical and the creative processes

Several of the researchers had successfully used this video method before, but this was the first time that we had worked in such an in-depth way with a group that had come together because of how they been treated and categorised by others. This, and the instability of their lives, amplified a number of tensions within a process that required them to have both creative and technical control over what was happening.

The work began well and enthusiastically. The list of people they wanted to interview and film included senior education welfare officers, head teachers, the head of Year 11, school governors, and representatives from large local employers. The model of video production we were working with focused on making a video that was both critical and reflective, and not just about teaching them the technicalities of the process. In this respect they came up with some excellent ideas for places and events to film, such as key meeting points out of school (see Figure 12.3).

We worked with them to get them to think about the process of change within an organisation such as a school, and what kind of material could initiate change. The group was quite specific about the audience that they wanted to reach, turning down suggestions that it might be a good idea to show their video to their families or the local community. They made it clear that exclusion was a problem that needed to be addressed by professionals involved in education, and we therefore discussed with them what kind of balance they wanted to strike

Figure 12.3 Learning to film background shots of key meeting points.

between being critical of how they had been treated in school, and getting teachers to change how they had behaved and thought about school exclusions.

As the work progressed, the impact of the limited experiences of the young men in expressing their 'critical voice' on the creative process became clearer. It had not been encouraged in school because it was more often than not confrontational and disruptive. We needed continually to re-adjust our involvement in the creative process so as to give increasing control to the group as their expertise developed. We concentrated our inputs on encouraging them to put their 'voices' more up front in the video, and to do this in an increasing variety of forms. Their lack of self-confidence was very apparent during this process, and especially noticeable as they interviewed powerful adults. This contradicted the general 'outside' perception of them as 'mouthy' and aggressive individuals. The challenge for us as the academic researchers became one of keeping them in touch with their original ideas so they did not become swamped and immobilised by these professionals and the issues they raised during interviewing that effectively silenced them. We provided them with as much time and space as possible to reflect on the new issues their work kept uncovering, while completing other parts of the video to maintain their motivation, and we did this by working in a different environment and moving our sessions to the university.

Initially they had decided to create a video that would represent their views and be shown to four key audiences: head teachers, teachers, local authority officials, and governors. Their intentions were twofold, to have their 'voice' heard clearly in a debate about these issues, and to encourage teachers and officials to be more sensitive to the needs of young people when tackling the joint problems of exclusion and non-attendance. They wanted to provide a critical 'voice' that would challenge the perceptions of professionals about excluded pupils. By the end of the project they had narrowed this audience down to their teachers as part of a staff development event on pupils who had been excluded or who were at risk of exclusion. This was because of their lack of confidence in their own voice and a growing realisation that it would compete with others outside of the completed video as well as inside it.

The last part of this chapter therefore links together a brief theoretical discussion of the notion of voice with what happened at the end of the project.

'Voice'

'Voice', whether articulated or embedded within actions or artefacts, is a constant issue within the participatory research process. Researchers are positioned as 'outsiders' and 'insiders' as they move across various cultural, political and organisational boundaries (Haw, 1996; 1998) raising issues about who and what is heard, what is listened to and how it is listened to. Whether as a white researcher running focus groups within black communities or community activists creating professional development materials for policy-makers, the complexity and fluidity of participatory research highlights the limitations of much of the discussion of 'voice' within the UK, which tends to coalesce around issues such as the 'voice' of the reflective practitioner or notions of articulating the 'voice' of excluded groups. However, as 'voice' has become increasingly linked with the issue of participation in civic life and local decision-making, these more individualistic and passive notions have become less relevant.

Work claiming to use the 'voice' of young people is part of a general move towards social inclusion, and 'voice' is now being used in a wide variety of projects and policies ranging from advocacy to consumer rights and citizenship education. In the UK it has become an established element of central and local government rhetoric, but this popularity has increasingly opened it up to question and criticism over the issue of whether the focus of working with the 'voice' of young people should be on supporting young people in articulating their 'voice', or directed at getting adults and professionals to listen and respond. At the heart of this debate are issues relating to power and how power intersects with, and emerges through, positions of (for example) age, social class, ethnicity and gender.

To understand more about 'voice' and how it is currently constructed, a critical analysis of the concept of 'voice' as used in both research and practice and policy reveals four common themes running through much of the literature. The first theme is that 'voice' privileges experience, over theory or training, as the basis of the understanding of an individual of an issue or activity, and the meaning they give to it. This privileging of experience fundamentally relies on 'interior authenticity' that is hard to demonstrate. The second theme is that it favours excluded, silenced or subordinate 'voices' over dominant 'voices' to initiate and guide change. This raises concern over the appropriateness of existing mechanisms to facilitate the 'voice' of those already marginalised and ignored. The third theme is that 'voice' as an inclusive idea recognises the proliferation of different 'voices' and the increasingly fragmented nature of people's experiences and understanding. The validity of any 'voice' relates to who is speaking, rather than through the warrant of those who are listening. The fourth and last theme is that 'voice' is conceptually linked to issues of activism, participation and empowerment.

These four themes are linked to the issues of how 'voice' is articulated and heard, rather than to questions of whether it is being listened to, and how to get it listened and responded to. These questions about listening are very much connected to the issue of what sort of voice is being articulated and what that voice is attempting to achieve. Hadfield and Haw (2001) set out a theoretical framework arguing that there were generally three forms of 'voice' dominating current work: authoritative, critical and therapeutic (as used earlier in the chapter). While abstract typologies are necessarily simplistic, this framework is useful because it helps in the identification of the type of voice being articulated and highlights the 'voices' being silenced in any area of activity, both of which are directly linked to the issues concerned with listening and response.

The methodological difficulty is in how to honour different 'voices' along-side each other throughout the research process from the beginning right through to the end. This is where video has such promise. Its fluidity as a medium means that it can pick up different sorts of 'voices' and place them in dialogue with each other and with a range of images. However, as the research community responds to and takes advantage of a media 'savvy' generation of young people, this creates its own unique methodological problems. These problems concern the technical and creative aspects of video production in combination with the relational, as revealed graphically by this analysis of the 'Seen but not Heard' project – but also crucially the change elements that are part of the participatory research process, and are the concern of the last sections of this chapter.

The change process: what happened at the end of the project

The final video product adopted a newsreel format and incorporated a role-play where the young people researchers and the Time Out team swapped roles to debate three issues. First, 'it's not the parents fault.' In this section of the video, the young men explored their reactions to the popular view that non-attendance and bad behaviour were the fault of parents. They argued that teachers had as much responsibility for this, and needed to teach in ways that kept pupils more interested and engaged. The second issue was 'teachers want us out'. Here, the young men expressed their confusion about school policies and practices. They gave examples of teachers who openly encouraged them to skive off lessons, and described a system which (on the one hand) kept them out of school, and which (on the other hand) punished them for non-attendance. Their third and last issue was 'teachers stick together'. This final section concentrated on a major criticism voiced by these young people, that teachers regularly failed to listen to them and tended to close ranks against their opinions. They felt there were dif-ferent rules for teachers and pupils, and that they had no constructive way of expressing their grievances.

A preview copy of the final videotape as promised to the school before the research began was passed on to the acting head of the school, who viewed it together with the recently appointed new head teacher and a member of the gov-erning body. They expressed serious reservations about the tape, saying that it was undoubtedly powerful and impressive, but too one-sided and emotive. They were particularly concerned that it used the real names of the school and indi-viduals, and were adamant that this was not the representative 'voice' of the pupils at the school. They were fearful of the effect the tape might have at a time when the school was about to go into 'special measures'. They proposed several extensive, time-consuming and technically difficult changes to the tape.

The condition [to change the video produced by the young people so that it could be shown] which asks us to include a description of the young people as having special needs, of low literacy, behaviourally challenging and atypical of the school population, is clearly going to position these young people in the school. In the process of making this video useful for the school – if it is going to be used at all; and I don't think it is, though it can still affect change at the school – the school's managers will position these young people in [ways] they perceive to serve their own aims and objectives. There is no way out of this, in my view, but neither are they in control of this process.

(Journal entry, 17.6.98)

They were also changes that the young people would not agree to make. As a result, the video could not be shown to its intended audience within the school. The reaction of the young men was one of anger and frustration, and a feeling of having been discounted yet again. The Time Out workers were very much in sympathy and agreement with the young people. After some discussion a limited viewing involving those at the school who had already seen the video, together with the young men, was finally agreed.

No change there then: seen and heard but definitely not listened to

This chapter began by constructing a picture of a rapid increase in the use of video with young people in participatory research projects because video is seen as a particularly powerful dissemination medium for research concerned with influencing the behaviour of young people and professionals. The advantages of working with 'voice' and video are to do with video being a powerful tool in the recruitment of potential participants, and because it can ease access to the research process by creating a collaborative focus for joint work. It also drew attention to how a shifting and rapidly evolving media literacy amongst young people is influencing their approach to how they represent themselves and their experiences, and how they seek to influence others. However, as the production of the 'Seen but Not Heard' video progressed it became more and more obvious that although working with video had real potential, there were also several drawbacks.

The discussion of the relational, technical, creative and change potential of video while highlighting the advantages of working with 'voice' and video also revealed a number of tensions and dilemmas summed up by the following key questions. To what extent should we have pushed forward the research process before the school closed itself off completely? The danger here was that we would have effectively hijacked the research process from the young men. How should we have mediated between the young men and the school about the composition of the final video product? Through the research process the young men had become increasingly vehement about the way in which they had been treated, but the school seemed less and less able to cope with a highly critical video. If we had tried to lessen its criticality, would we have been drawn into 'cooling out' the young men? To what extent could the research team and workers from The Edge have used their influence with the school without adversely affecting their ongoing relationships with staff there? To what extent should we have helped The Edge consider the impact of the therapeutic approach to their work?

There are no right answers to these questions, only 'good enough' ones and ones which, as researchers, we felt we were better able to answer in a 'good enough' way on some days rather than on others. Video allows participants to provide accounts of their experiences in a form they may find easier than written text and can create spaces for dialogue between participants within research, and between participants and the audiences for the research. In this sense it has the potential to produce a range of research outputs that meet the needs of participants and researchers. But each of these potential benefits has associated with it a range of methodological issues, ranging from the ethical to the technical, the intensity of which varies with the form of participatory research involved. Researchers need to provide a complex mix of technical, creative and critical support to move young people from consumers to producers of media. The impact of these forms of support and how they interact with the experiences of young people as media consumers sets up methodological issues ranging from questions of ownership to the authenticity and professionalism of the product.

In this case the authenticity of their video could not be doubted. In the course of the project we were able to provide an opportunity for this group of excluded young people to consider what they wanted to say to some of the influential adults who affected their lives, and then to prepare this in a powerful and unusual way. We had also created an intrinsically worthwhile process for a group of young men who saw something through to completion. This was a new experience for many of them. They were, rightly, immensely proud of their work, even though it did not look like the programmes on television they had thought to emulate. Although angered by the reaction of the school, this strengthened their understanding of their experiences and provided a very different insight into the micro-politics of their school to the one of being excluded.

The converse of having a 'voice' is being silenced, and a key part of the discussion around 'voice' is to examine and challenge the processes 'silencing' different groups of young people. The discussion of the links between 'voice' and the methodological challenges provided by the use of video in the participatory research process as illustrated by the 'Seen but Not Heard project' provides just such an examination and challenge.

References

Banks, M. (1995). Visual research methods in social research. *Social Research Update*, 11. Guildford: University of Surrey.

Banks, M. (2001). *Visual methods in social research*. London: Sage Publications.

Hadfield, M., & Haw, K. (1997a). *Single regeneration budget impact study.* Video Products.

Hadfield, M., & Haw, K. (1997b). *Family viewing.* Video product for the European Year Against Racism. Produced by and available from Urban Programmes Research Group, School of Education, Jubilee Campus, University of Nottingham, Nottingham NG8 1BB.

Hadfield, M., & Haw, K. (2000). *The 'voice' of young people. Hearing, listening, responding.* University of Nottingham: Urban Programmes Research Group.

Hadfield, M., & Haw, K. (2001). 'Voice' young people and action research' *Education Action Research Journal, 9*(3), 483–497.

Hadfield M., & Haw, K. (2002). *Perceptions of strip search procedures.* DVD Product.

Haw, K. (2006). *Urbanfields.* DVD product. Produced by and available from Urban Programmes Research Group, School of Education, Jubilee Campus, University of Nottingham, Nottingham NG8 1BB.

Haw, K.F. (1996). Exploring the educational experiences of Muslim girls. Tales told to tourists – Should the white researcher stay at home? *British Educational Research Journal, 23*(3), 319–330.

Haw, K.F. (1998). *Educating Muslim girls. Shifting discourses.* Buckingham: Open University Press.

Johnson, L.L. (2001). *Media, education and change.* New York, NY: Peter Lang Publishing.

Kincade, S., & Macy, C. (2003). *What works in youth media. Case studies form around the world.* Takoma Park, MD: Forum for Youth investment, International Youth Federation.

McTaggart, R. (Ed.). (1997). *Participatory action research. International contexts and consequences*: Albany, NY: State University of New York Press.

Melucci, A. (1989). *Nomads of the present.* Philadelphia, PA: Temple University Press.

Melucci, A. (1996). *The playing self. Person and meaning in the planetary society.* Cambridge University Press.

Park, P., Brydon-Miller, M., Hall, B., & Jackson, T. (1993). *Voices of change. Participatory research in the United States and Canada.* Toronto: OIS.

Pink, S. (2001). *Doing visual ethnography. Images, media and representation in research.* London: Sage Publications.

Prosser, J. (1992). Personal reflection on the use of photography in an ethnographic case study. *British Educational Research Journal, 18*, 397–411.

Prosser, J. (1998). *Image based research. A sourcebook for qualitative researchers.* London: Falmer Press.

Rose, G. (2001). *Visual methodologies.* London: Sage Publications.

Tolman, J. & Pittman, K. (2001). *Youth acts, community impacts: stories of youth engagement with real results.* Community and Youth Development Series, Vol. 7. Takoma Park, MD: Forum for Youth Investment, International Youth Federation.

Voithofer, R. (2005). Designing new media education research. The materiality of data representation, and dissemination. *American Educational Researcher, 34*(9), 3–14.

Appendix
Finding out more

Pat Thomson

All the contributors to this text were asked to provide information about some resources that they find useful themselves, and those that they found helpful in supporting others to do visual research. In particular, Ian Kaplan's web resources were invaluable. I have added to the information I was sent, but not with the intention of providing a comprehensive list. Rather, this selection of texts is intended to be a set of signposts not only to issues, methods and debates, but also to finding other people who are working in the same field.

The bibliographies of the various chapters contain further references. Many individual visual researchers also have links on their pages to visual methods courses and publications. Some experimentation, googling by name and institution, will pay dividends.

Children and research

Christensen, P., & James, A. (Eds) (2000). *Research with children. Perspectives and practices*. London: Falmer Press.

Egan-Robertson, A., & Bloome, D. (Eds) (1998). *Students as researchers of culture and language in their own communities*. Cresskill, NJ: Hampton Press.

Fielding, M., & Bragg, S. (2003). *Students as researchers. Making a difference*. Cambridge: Pearson.

Fraser, S., Lewis, V., Ding, S., Kellett, M., & Robinson, C. (Eds) (2004). *Doing research with children and young people*. London: Sage Publications.

Kellett, M. (2005). *How to develop children as researchers. A step by step guide to teaching the research process*. London: Paul Chapman.

Lewis, A., & Lindsay, G. (Eds) (2000). *Researching children's perspectives*. Buckingham: Open University Press.

Lewis, V., Kellett, M., Robinson, C., Fraser, S., & Ding, S. (2004) *The reality of research with children and young people*. London: Paul Chapman.

Steinberg, S., & Kincheloe, J. (1998). *Students as researchers. Creating classrooms that matter*. London: Falmer Press

Ethics

Alderson, P., & Morrow, V. (2004). *Ethics, social research and consulting with children and young people.* London: Barnado's.

Gross, L., Katz, J.S., & Ruby, J. (Eds.) (1988). *Image ethics. The moral rights of subjects in photographs, film and television.* New York, NY: Oxford University Press.

Prosser, J. (2000). The moral maze of image ethics. In H. Simons and R. Usher (Eds.), *Situated ethics in educational research.* London: Routledge.

General research methods texts that feature visual research

Bauer, M.W., & Gaskell, G.D. (Eds.) (2000). *Qualitative researching with text, image and sound. A practical handbook for social research* Thousand Oaks, CA: Sage Publications.

Knowles, J.G., & Cole, A. (Ed.) (2007). *Handbook of the arts in qualitative research: Perspectives, methodologies, examples and issues.* Oxford: Oxford University Press.

Visual research methods

Banks, M. (2001). *Visual methods in social research.* Thousand Oaks, CA: Sage Publications.

Emmison, M., & Smith, P. (2001). *Researching the visual.* Thousand Oaks, CA: Sage Publications.

Hamilton, P. (Ed.) (2006). *Visual research methods.* London: Sage Publications.

Harper, D. (1998). On the authority of the image. Visual methods at the crossroads. In N.K. Denzin & Y.S. Lincoln (Eds.), *Collecting and interpreting qualitative materials.* London: Sage Publications.

Kress, G., & van Leeuwin, T. (1996). *Reading images. The grammar of visual design.* London: Routledge.

Pink, S. (2001). *Doing visual ethnography. Images, media and representation in research.* Thousand Oaks, CA: Sage Publications.

Piper, H., & Frankham, J. (2007). Seeing voices and hearing pictures. Image as discourse and the framing of image-based research. *Discourse, 28*(3), 373–387.

Prosser, J. (Ed.) (1998). *Image-based research. A sourcebook for qualitative researchers.* Bristol, PA: Falmer Press.

Stanczak, G. (Ed.) (2007). *Visual research methods. Image, society, and representation* Thousand Oaks, CA: Sage Publications.

Van Leeuwen, T., & Jewitt, C. (2001). *Handbook of visual analysis.* London: Sage Publications.

Walker, R. (1993). Finding a silent voice for the researcher. Using photographs in evaluation and research. In M. Schratz (Ed.), *Qualitative voices in educational research.* London: Falmer.

Visual sociology and anthropology

Banks, M. and Morphy, H. (Eds.) (1997). *Rethinking visual anthropology*. New Haven, CT: Yale University Press.
Becker, H.S. (1981). *Exploring society photographically*. Chicago, IL: University of Chicago Press.
Chaplin, E. (1994). *Sociology and visual representation*. London: Routledge.
Collier, J. (1967). Visual anthropology. Photography as a research method. In G. Spindler & L. Spindler (Eds.), *Studies in anthropological method* New York, NY: Holt, Rinehart & Winston.
El Guindi, F. (2004). *Visual anthropology*. Thousand Oaks, CA: Sage Publications.
Pink, S. (2006). *The future of visual anthropology. Engaging the senses*. London: Routledge.
Rose, G. (2007). *Visual methodologies* (2nd ed.). London: Sage Publications.

Visual research and visual studies journals

Journal of Visual Literacy, http://plato.ou.edu/~jvl/
Journal of Visual Studies, www.sagepub.com/journalsProdDesc.nav?prodId=Journal 201459
Visual Anthropology, www.wsu.edu:8080/~i9248809/visual.html
Visual Anthropology Review, http://etext.virginia.edu/VAR/
Visual Communication, www.sagepub.co.uk/journalsProdDesc.nav?prodId=Journal 201380
Visual Studies, Vol. 22 (1) – a special issue on education edited by Eric Margolis, visualsociology.org/

Visual research networks

International Visual Sociology Association (IVSA), http://visualsociology.org/

Visual research representation

Pink, S., Kurti, L., & Afonso, A.I. (Eds.) (2004). *Working images. Visual representation in ethnography*. London: Routledge.
Tufte, E.R. (1983). *The visual display of quantitative information*. Cheshire, CN: Graphics Press.
Tufte, E.R. (1990). *Envisioning information*. Cheshire, CN: Graphics Press.

Visual research web resources

ESRC funded project *Building capacity in visual research*, www.education.leeds.ac.uk/research/visual-methods/
FILTER: The Focusing Images for Learning and Teaching: an Enriched Resource in higher education, www.filter.ac.uk
Fifty crows: social change photography, www.fiftycrows.org/about/news/050706/a.php
Kids with cameras, www.kids-with-cameras.org/home/

Learn higher CETL visual research resources, http://staffcentral.brighton.ac.uk/learnhigher/ index.htm

Literacy through photography, http://cds.aas.duke.edu/ltp/

Photovoice: Social change through photography, http://www.photovoice.com/index.html

Photovoice documentary photographers, www.photovoice.org/

Sarah Pink's *Visualising Ethnography* site, www.lboro.ac.uk/departments/ss/visualising_ ethnography/index.html

Social research on line, http://sru.soc.surrey.ac.uk/

* *Social Research Update*, Issue 11: Marcus Banks 'Visual Research Methods'
* *Social Research Update*, Issue 40: Rosalind Hurworth 'Photo-interviewing for research'

The image and identity research collective, http://iirc.mcgill.ca/txp/index.php

Visual Anthropology net, www.visualanthropology.net/

Visual Sociology UK, www.visualsociology.org.uk/

Index